*World Citizen*

# *World Citizen*

## *Action for Global Justice*

**ADAM DANIEL CORSON-FINNERTY**

ORBIS BOOKS

Maryknoll, New York 10545

Second Printing, August 1982

The Catholic Foreign Mission Society of America (Maryknoll) recruits and trains people for overseas missionary service. Through Orbis Books Maryknoll aims to foster the international dialogue that is essential to mission. The books published, however, reflect the opinions of their authors and are not meant to represent the official position of the society.

Copyright © 1982 by Orbis Books, Maryknoll, NY 10545
All rights reserved
Manufactured in the United States of America

Manuscript editor: Thomas Fenton

Library of Congress Cataloging in Publication Data

Corson-Finnerty, Adam Daniel.
  World citizen.

  Bibliography: p.
  1. Civil rights. 2. Justice. 3. Social justice.
I. Title.
JC571.C672    320.9'047      81-16918
ISBN 0-88344-715-0 (pbk.)        AACR2

**For my wife,**
**Susan**

# Contents

*Acknowledgements*   *xi*

*Introduction*   *3*
  World Citizenship   4
  Why This Effort?   5

*Chapter I*
*Economic Justice I: Colonialism*   *7*
  Colonialism   9
    *The Spread of European Power*   *10*
    *Mexico*     *11*
    *Kenya*   *14*
  Underdevelopment   16

*Chapter II*
*Economic Justice II: The Post-Colonial World*   *19*
  Life in the International Marketplace   20
  Neo-colonialism   21
  The Distortions of the Present System   25
  What Can Be Done?   26

*Chapter III*
*Is There Enough?*   *28*
  How Much Is There?   28
  The Energy Factor   30
  Which Path to Choose   31
  The "Basic Needs" Strategy   33

*Chapter IV*
*The Pollution Factor*   *35*
  The Cycle of Poisoning   36
  The Nuclear Fix   38
  Environmentalism and the Third World   40
  Appropriate Technology   40
  Global Watch   43

*Chapter V*
*Arms and Militarism*   *45*
   Nuclear Madness   46
   The Deadly Triangle   47
     *The Chinese Potential*   *48*
     *The Big Two*   *50*
   The Arms Race   53
   The Third World   55

*Chapter VI*
*Social Injustice*   *61*
   Is It Our Business?   61
   Religious Discrimination   62
   Race and Caste   66
   National Minorities   71
     *Spain*   *72*
     *The Soviet Union*   *74*
   Women   76
     *Women and Socialism*   *79*
   Conclusion   81

*Chapter VII*
*The United Nations—In Weakness and in Strength*   *84*
   That Motley Assembly   85
   The Young Federal Nation   87
   Growth and Change at the UN   88
   UN Peacekeeping   89
   The Congo Debacle   90
   Nuclear Arms   92
   Decolonization   93
   Setting the Pace for the Planet   98
   Action on the Environment   100
   The New International Economic Order   101

*Chapter VIII*
*Citizen Action*   *105*
   Human Rights   106
   Amnesty International   107
   Other World Movements   109
   Our Responsibilities as U.S. Citizens   110
   Citizens' Action Groups   112
   Getting Involved   112

# RESOURCES

*Introduction to Resources    117*

*Economic Justice    121*
    For Further Reading    121
    Action and Information Groups    123

*The Global Environment    130*
    For Further Reading    130
    Action and Information Groups    133

*Peace and Disarmament    136*
    For Further Reading    136
    Action and Information Groups    138

*Social Justice    144*
    For Further Reading    144
    Action and Information Groups    146
        *General Groups    146*
        *Children    147*
        *Native Americans    148*
        *Palestinians    149*
        *Religious Freedom    149*
        *Southern Africa-South Africa    150*
        *Women    151*
        *Family Planning    153*

*Global Institution-Building 154*
    For Further Reading    154
    Action and Information Groups    156
    UN Agencies and Programs    159
        *The Secretariat    160*
        *The General Assembly    160*
        *The Economic and Social Council    161*
        *Affiliated Agencies and Programs    161*

*Human Rights    164*
    For Further Reading    164
    Action Guide    166
    Action and Information Groups    166

*Denominational and Sectarian Religious Organizations*    *172*

*Audio-Visual Resources*    *177*
   Organizations    177
   Books    178

# Acknowledgements

My special thanks go to the many researchers who helped make my task much easier. My debt to particular writers is acknowledged in the notes and in my reading lists. I owe special thanks, however, to the people who have spent hundreds and thousands of hours compiling information on groups, organizations, and relevant publications. Among them:

Michael Marien, who single-handedly began a newsletter for people who wanted to know about the latest publications in the global justice field. It began as the *Public Policy Book Forecast*, has since been adopted by the World Future Society, and is now called *Future Survey*. My annotated reading lists at the end of the book are the richer for Marien's work.

Laurie Wiseberg and Harry Scoble of the Human Rights Internet, who have dedicated themselves to pulling together the activist groups in the human rights field by making them aware of each other's activities through a first-class newsletter. Their efforts have resulted in an excellent *Human Rights Directory* (with the aid of the Members of Congress for Peace through Law Education Fund), and the Social Justice and Human Rights resource sections owe much to them.

The Gale Research Organization, whose *Encyclopedia of Organizations* is a marvel of up-to-date information on numerous activist organizations.

*The Europa Yearbook* and *The Statesman's Yearbook* for guidance to United Nations groups; and the *Yearbook of American and Canadian Churches,* for religious and denominational groups.

Thanks also to Tom Fenton for his careful editing and his challenging questions and to John Eagleson of Orbis Books for his encouragement and his patience. To the numerous resource people who took time from their busy schedules to answer my questions. To Ian Nichols and Dave Brown for help with typing.

Finally, thanks to the American Friends Service Committee, the *Friends Journal*, and the Friends Center for providing me with a home away from home, a good library, access to a copier, and an occasional chance to use the phones.

*World Citizen*

# Introduction

They brought me down Pennsylvania Avenue in a van. When we arrived in front of the White House, the crowd had already gathered. The frame on which I was to be tortured was already erect, the White House caught like a snapshot between its wooden sides.

They placed a black hood over my head, and when I emerged from the van, they tied my hands. It was a cold, rainy morning—the temperature was perhaps thirty-eight degrees—and while most people were wrapped in warm coats, I had on thin Indian pyjama bottoms, no shirt, and sandals.

Two guards led me to the frame. They chained my legs, spread far apart, to each side. Then they untied my hands and chained them above me. It made quite a picture, this hooded figure being tortured in front of the White House. Several news teams and a few tourists who had braved the cold stopped to record it all on film.

In fact I wasn't being tortured; rather I was a part of a silent "tableau" that was intended to dramatize the very real torture of prisoners in many parts of the globe. I was there as part of a week of prayer and vigil just before Easter. Passion week—the week when Christians are supposed to remember that Jesus was tortured and died—a week we had chosen to call attention to our nation's support of repressive and torture-practicing regimes around the world.

"The United States supports this kind of torture in the Philippines" read one of our signs. "Proclaim liberty to the captives" read another. Throughout the week we had made a pilgrimage through our nation's capital. Some of us had been on the steps of Congress, urging its members to block economic and military aid to repressive regimes. Others had been outside the World Bank, which, with United States approval, had recently granted loans to the Pinochet regime in Chile. We had prayed in front of the offices of United Fruit—backers of totalitarian regimes in Central America—and we had staged another "torture tableau" in front of the Washington headquarters of ITT, the company that had offered money to the CIA to bring down the government of Salvador Allende in Chile.

Now we were in front of the White House—the symbol of our nation's leadership.

I found myself thinking about the accounts of torture that we had heard and read about during that week in Washington. The beatings, the electro-shock, the suspension in the air upside down for interminable periods, the

3

plunging into filthy water until almost drowned. I thought about other victims as well—the hungry and displaced of Brazil, the shanty dwellers of Jakarta, the million or so people who sleep each night on the streets of Calcutta. And I thought about people who were cold, who didn't have enough warm clothing or a warm house.

After twenty minutes I asked them to unchain me. The chains were only loosely wrapped around my wrists and ankles, and I could see through the gauze of the black hood, but I still felt a relief when I was released.

"Are you OK, Adam?" somebody asked as I got back into the van and put on warmer clothes. I nodded my head yes, but I wasn't.

In a way I suppose I haven't been OK since Selma. Watching, on television, black people—Americans, *my* people—clubbed and abused because they wanted to walk across a bridge and vote. Then being there, feeling the hatred and tension, and at the same time the powerful love of those on the march to Montgomery. Returning north, challenged to look into the discrimination, the economic oppression of the black and poor in my own city. . . the war in Vietnam . . . the discovery that my country was involved in a labyrinth of deals and agreements with some of the most repressive and brutal dictators in the world.

The president came out of the White House while I was on the frame, and he looked across the lawn and saw us—saw me. I tried to imagine what it would feel like to be in his place, to be not an idealistic activist who had come to "speak truth to power," but a national leader with power and responsibility. Even as an idealist, how would I fare in his position? How would I respond to the pressures of those who think we are militarily weak? How would I respond to those who want the United States to support dictators in return for their oil? Or to those who feel that economic growth, at almost any price, was my chief responsibility? Perhaps, I thought, the president was the real captive that day.

The realities and the responsibilities of power. The realities—and the responsibilities—of moral outrage. Both symbolized in that brief moment when the president looked across his lawn, and we looked back.

## World Citizenship

In a very real way, all of us as U.S. citizens are caught in that moment at the White House. We live in the richest and most powerful country in the world, and we benefit from that power even as we condemn the things that are done to keep us in this favored position. We are a nation of idealists. We like to believe that we have good intentions and bear the rest of humankind no ill will. Yet we are a people whose CIA undermines governments on our supposed behalf and whose corporations seem willing to bribe, pollute, and overconsume in every corner of the globe where they are able to get away with it.

We Americans live in an age when we can no longer claim that our country can go its own way, not needing others and not affecting them. If ever there was a time when we could retreat into isolation, that time is long past. We are bound by our economy, our technology, our yearning to learn and to communicate, into a global framework that demands of us an expanded sense of citizenship.

Our sense of being U.S. citizens first and foremost—whether this causes us pride or agony—can no longer bear up under the demands of world citizenship. In speaking of world citizenship I mean this not in some starry-eyed sense of undefined identification with humankind, but in the very down-to-earth sense that we are a part of a functioning world community that is interactive and interdependent.

This book is about some of the world-sized problems we face as world citizens: pollution, nuclear armaments, economic injustice, discrimination, and denial of human rights, just to name a few.

It is a starter book. That is, a book intended for people who are concerned about these global issues, and who want to begin developing their understanding of the interrelation and the complexities of these problems. It is also a getting started book, in which the final chapters and the Resources section are designed to help people get involved in a group or a movement that is working on these themes.

I have often spoken to people who want to begin working for global justice but feel they don't know enough, or are unsure of what organization might be worth joining. The Resources section contains an annotated list of several hundred organizations that are worthy of one's attention. I have indicated the ones that I personally recommend.

For anyone who is concerned about global issues, there's one step to take: *join a group*. There are a great number of very fine organizations already in existence with members who are dedicated, sincere, and knowledgeable. These organizations are always in need of new hands, new ideas, and fresh energy. They are usually a good avenue not only for self-education but also for multiplying the impact of what their members are able to do on their own.

## Why This Effort?

In 1974 I was part of a religious gathering that drew up a lifestyle covenant which we hoped would express our sense of responsibility as world citizens, and as a people of faith. We called our covenant "The Shakertown Pledge" because we first met in a restored Shaker village in Kentucky called "Shakertown at Pleasant Hill."

Here is what we agreed on:

*Recognizing that the earth and the fullness thereof is a gift from our gracious God, and that we are called to cherish, nurture, and provide loving stewardship for the earth's resources, and recognizing that life itself is a gift, and a call to responsibility, joy, and celebration, I make the following declarations:*

1. *I declare myself to be a world citizen.*
2. *I commit myself to lead an ecologically sound life.*
3. *I commit myself to lead a life of creative simplicity and to share my personal wealth with the world's poor.*
4. *I commit myself to join with others in the reshaping of institutions in order to bring about a more just global society in which all people have full access to the needed resources for their physical, emotional, intellectual, and spiritual growth.*
5. *I commit myself to occupational accountability, and in so doing I will seek to avoid the creation of products which cause harm to others.*
6. *I affirm the gift of my body and commit myself to its proper nourishment and physical well-being.*
7. *I commit myself to examine continually my relations with others, and to attempt to relate honestly, morally, and lovingly to those around me.*
8. *I commit myself to personal renewal through prayer, meditation, and study.*
9. *I commit myself to responsible participation in a community of faith.*

For several years thereafter I was actively involved in promoting the Pledge as a tool for lifestyle assessment and personal commitment. I conducted numerous workshops on lifestyle issues, gave a number of talks to congregations and groups, and visited with like-minded people in many parts of the country.

In the course of this work I met many sincere and deeply moral people, people who cared about what was happening to our country and our planet, people who had risen above a lifestyle devoted primarily to self-satisfaction and who wanted to be of service to others. These people helped to renew my faith in the goodness of the human spirit, and to heal my own disaffection and bitterness from our war in Vietnam. They showed me that God is at work among us—healing, cajoling, inspiring, and pushing us beyond despair and despondency.

I was asked many questions that I couldn't answer. People wanted to know more about world resource consumption, more about human rights, more about the needs of the poor. Most especially they wanted to know where to turn for information and group involvement.

This book is an attempt to answer some of these questions.

# Chapter I

# Economic Justice I: Colonialism

One summer when I was twenty years old and still learning by leaps and bounds about the world in which I was to be an adult, I worked as a counselor for an inner-city day camp program, finding enjoyable things to do for ten young boys. They were a rambunctious group, always ready to run off in different directions, never seeming to have enough of racing, tagging, shouting, wrestling, swimming, and almost every other form of physical activity.

All of them, that is, except two. These boys were brothers, and were quite the opposite of the others. They were quiet, reserved, never gave me trouble; docile is perhaps the most appropriate adjective. At first I was pleased to have at least two manageable boys amid this rowdy bunch, but I soon realized that a far deeper problem was presenting itself. Simply put, these two brothers were quiet because they were hungry. Not hungry as I might be if I had missed a meal or two, but chronically, desperately hungry. Upon investigation I found that they lived with their single mother, a listless, quiet person who had so little money with which to buy food that she routinely allowed her boys to sleep late, telling them when they awoke that they had slept through breakfast—a breakfast that she had no means to provide.

We arranged for the boys to receive breakfast at the church, and lunch as well. Their school, I was told, would provide meals for them when the fall came, but the aid had probably come too late. Chronically undernourished, these boys at nine and ten years old were probably so damaged that they would never overcome the physical harm that had been done to their bodies and their brains.

Sixteen years later, while working as an administrator in an international service organization, another—similar—story came to my attention. One of our field staff had visited a rural health clinic in a poor country. A nurse on the staff told her that they often identified malnourished children who needed nutritional supplementation. The infant and childcare clinic staff would show mothers how to make up a healthful formula from soy and milk available at the clinic and would ask them to come with their children every two days in order to make up the formula for their infants. But they found that after a few days the mothers wouldn't show up. There was a small fee for the food supplements, and the mothers, unable to afford it and deeply embarrassed, would hide.

Two mothers, sixteen years and thousands of miles apart. One in a country wealthy beyond any in history; the other in a country so poor that an increase in household income of ten dollars a month might mean the difference between adequate food and an almost empty pot. Both watching their children grow up into a kind of sleepy half-life, subject to disease, unable to learn at an average rate, perhaps to die at an early age.

For many of us the call to world citizenship begins here, with these two mothers and their malnourished children. There are around the world hundreds of millions of stories just like these two, of parents who cannot provide for themselves and for their families, of people who live in cardboard shacks or on the sidewalks, of people who are prey to disease because they never drink a cup of clean water.

Their conditions can be summed up in one word: the word is not hunger, the word is *poverty*. As we shall later discuss, most countries at most times have enough food to go around—for those who can pay for it. On this planet as a whole there is more than enough to feed each and every one of us, provided the cash is available. In many countries it is not money, but land that provides the key to an adequate diet. Yet millions of rural people have no land upon which to grow their own food.

In recent years it has become common to hear of rich nations and poor nations, of a global debate between the "haves" and the "have-nots." Sometimes this debate is couched in terms that seem far away from the daily poverty of ordinary people; terms like indexing, commodity flows, agro-export, import substitutions. Residents of the industrialized nations are challenged to share their wealth with those of the developing countries. Often we in the rich nations are told that we gain unfair advantage in the international marketplace, that we have profited from the plunder of the poorer lands.

If we wish to speak of justice in the economic realm, if we wish to end poverty and hunger, then we must face up to the underlying historical and economic roots of the world's unequal system of wealth, and we must make ourselves ready to work for a world system that provides more fairly for all.

It is not enough that my church program was able to provide breakfast for those two hungry boys; what of the ones who are not fed? What of the fact that, even with enough food in childhood, they would be likely to find no avenue out of poverty when they reached adulthood?

It is not enough to send a food shipment or a foreign aid grant to a developing country; what of the natural resources that these countries daily ship to us? What of their relative powerlessness in the international marketplace, a powerlessness that so often places them on the losing end of large financial transactions?

It is not enough to admit that the world is an unfair place, and that we citizens of the West may be gathering more than is our due of the world's resources. How did this happen? What debt do *we* owe, and how do we change things?

As world citizens we must face the fact that two-thirds of humanity lives in what is called the developing world, many of them on the edge of poverty, many deep in its cruel grasp. Any global agenda for change must begin with their need for a system that brings them the basic necessities of life.

In this chapter I will try to explain certain important aspects of the global debate about our economic system. I will be content if my introduction to this topic sheds at least a little light on the "dismal" subject of economics, and helps to point the reader to the major issues that should concern us.

## Colonialism

There is a great deal that can be learned about the current debate between the industrialized North and the developing South through a consideration of the legacy of colonialism.

China, Japan, and Turkey were the *only* countries that escaped direct European colonial control in the period 1500–1945. Even these countries did not totally escape the impact of European military and economic power. In fact, the chief reason these few countries avoided becoming colonies was because of the balance of power between the colonizing contenders (especially Britain, France, Portugal, Spain) and not because of their ability to resist the superior arms of the Europeans.

China, for example, was never officially colonized by the Europeans. Yet its external commerce was totally dominated by them. After the British humiliated the Chinese Navy in the Opium Wars* of 1839–42, Britain and the other Europeans won the right to trade in certain Chinese ports, and thereafter dictated the terms of Chinese trade to the cowed and corrupt Imperial Court. Since nearby Russia and Japan were the nations most likely to try to annex Chinese territories, the more distant European powers (especially Britain, France, and Germany) joined with the United States in support of an Open Door policy in China. This policy was designed to keep any one nation from colonizing China while keeping that country "open" to exploitation by all.[1]

---

*So-called because the Chinese government tried to stop the British from selling opium to its populace. Interestingly, this was one of the few products that the Europeans could sell to the Chinese market, as most other European products were inferior to their Chinese counterparts, or not considered desirable. Since the Europeans had a great demand for Chinese products, the trade balance was decidedly in China's favor until it was discovered that opium had a ready market.

Another set of figures will illustrate the nature of European colonial expansion. In the year 1800, Europe, its colonies, and its former colonies already covered 55 percent of the world's land surface. By 1914, that figure reached an astonishing 84 percent of the land surface.[2] Given this, and the semi-colonial status of countries like China and Turkey, we see that virtually every population in the world has been influenced, challenged, and in one way or another, dominated by the Europeans. Most especially for non-whites, this domination brought with it a legacy of discrimination and humiliation that carries over into the conflicts of our present time. Resentment of European domination is, in fact, a powerful motivating force that unites the leaders and opinion-makers of many vastly different Third World cultures. Thus communists in Cuba and capitalists in Indonesia may not have a lot in common, but in their resentment of colonialism and neo-colonialism* they often stand united.

We Americans are far less aware of this colonial legacy than we ought to be. We have never thought of ourselves as a colonial power (despite our territorial expansion to the Pacific and our occupation of Cuba, the Philippines, and Puerto Rico). And during our two-hundred-year history as a nation, we have often been in the forefront of anti-colonial sentiment. Therefore, we assume that anti-colonial feelings and resentments do not apply to us.

Yet as British power and economic domination declined in the twentieth century, the United States stepped into that country's shoes—militarily and economically.** As a primarily white and European-descended population, we also inherit many of the prejudices of our white and European forebears, as well as the resentment of their former subjects. This will be discussed further in Chapter II.

*The Spread of European Power*

How did this remarkable spread of European power occur? And why were the often more ancient societies of the Middle East and Asia unable to resist it?

The historian D. K. Fieldhouse, suggests that there were two phases to the European expansion.[3] The first was led by Spain and Portugal, and began with exploration for trading purposes. In areas where the existing societies had equivalent or stronger military forces (India and East Asia), they contented themselves with establishing trading posts. In Africa, where they had military superiority, but where the climate or disease held them back, they erected heavily armed forts along their major shipping lines, but avoided the interior. In Central and South America, where the climate was more hospitable and the natives were often easily conquered, they moved in and carved up the land among adventurous nationals who hoped to establish profitable es-

*Domination by economic means.
**Britain's shoes weren't the only ones we stepped into. In the Philippines we replaced the Spanish; in Indonesia we replaced the Dutch; and so on.

tates using cheap native labor. These latter colonies, called "colonies of settlement," were the areas in which the Europeans had the most lasting, and often the most detrimental, cultural effect.

The second phase of colonization began with the defeat of Napoleon in 1815 and extended until the end of World War II. Its main leader was Great Britain, which, with France defeated and Spain in decline, became the world's supreme ruler of the seas. Between 1815 and 1914 Great Britain was the world's foremost naval power and could acquire any area accessible by sea, or deny it to others. By 1914, fully one-quarter of all humanity was under the rule of this relatively tiny island state, and it was literally true that the sun never set on the British Empire.

Alongside the British Empire grew the French, German, and United States empires, all considerably lesser, but all built in a headlong burst of economic and military energy. The key element in this explosion was the Industrial Revolution, which gave considerable technological advantage to the European states.

Let us now consider two countries, Mexico and Kenya, which illustrate the impact of colonial domination.

*Mexico*

Anyone who has read W. N. Prescott's romantic history, *The Conquest of Mexico*,[4] cannot help but marvel that a mere handful of Spaniards under the leadership of Hernán Cortés was able to subdue the vast Aztec empire. Prescott places great emphasis on the intimidating nature of the Spanish blunderbuss, plus the difference in tactics between the two forces. The Aztecs fought to capture prisoners alive, so that they could later be sacrificed to the gods. The Spanish fought to kill. Perhaps a more important factor, however, was the resentment of the indigenous Indian population against their Aztec rulers.

Cortés and his six hundred comrades stumbled upon a society that had already been colonized by the non-indigenous Aztecs. This foreign people had wandered into the Valley of Mexico sometime in the twelfth century and had eventually become the rulers of the region. Theirs was a highly stratified society, complete with a nobility, and priestly and merchant castes. The Aztecs considered themselves to be superior to the peoples they had conquered. They were the "People of the Sun," destined by their god, Huitzilopochtli, to become the masters of the world. They destroyed tribal democracy and autonomous village life, and by the time of the Spanish arrival (1519) had created a vast feudal society, complete with an hereditary ruling family, a court of nobles, and onerous taxes. The indigenous peoples had been enslaved or reduced to serfdom, and periodic wars and rebellions were common. These had all been crushed, and out of them came new victims for the practice of human sacrifice, which, according to one scholar, had reached "monumental" proportions in the few decades before Cortés.[5]

I share this early history because we tend to forget that the pre-colonial regions were not necessarily the Garden of Eden. Frequently, the Europeans simply replaced some earlier conquering people, inheriting the patterns and fruits of this previous exploitation.

In Mexico, however, the Spanish managed to make the Aztec tyranny look mild by comparison. The Spanish adventurers who came to Central America in the sixteenth century had only one thing in mind: wealth. They did not come to the New World for religious freedom, or to settle down as yeoman farmers. They came instead with visions of gold and silver, or of acquiring vast feudal estates along Castilian lines. The fact that Cortés and his men *did* manage to lay their hands on a sizeable Aztec treasure only enflamed the desire of those who followed. "Like monkeys they seized upon the gold," comments one Aztec chronicler. "They thirsted mightily for gold; they stuffed themselves with it, and hungered and lusted for it like pigs."[6]

There could never be enough gold to satisfy the craving of these fortune-hunters. So they seized upon another obvious resource of the valley—the people. Cortés established the *encomienda* system in New Spain, a system whereby an individual was granted an allotment of Indians whose labor he could exploit, and whose welfare he was to defend. But Indian welfare was the last thing on the colonist's mind, and soon Aztecs and indigenous people alike were to experience an oppression of vastly different dimensions:

> The collective tribute and labor demands of the Spanish settlers, the Crown, and the Church far exceeded the relatively puny exactions of the Aztec rulers, nobility, and priesthood. The more advanced European economy demanded a large increase in the supply of labor; the conquistadores or their sons became capitalist entrepreneurs with visions of limitless wealth to be obtained through silver mines, sugar and cacao plantations, cattle ranches, and wheat farms. The intensity of exploitation of Indian labor became intolerable. And the Indians, their bodies enfeebled by excessive toil, malnutrition, and the hardships of long journeys to distant mines and plantations, their spirits broken by the loss of ancient tribal purposes and beliefs that gave meaning to life, became easy prey to disease, both endemic and epidemic, to maladies with which they were familiar and to scourges imported by the Europeans: smallpox, influenza, measles, typhoid, malaria. A demographic tragedy of frightful proportions resulted.[7]

The net result of this ruthless exploitation was that the native population declined from seventeen million in 1522 to a mere one million by 1608.[8] Here, surely, is a piece of genocide that rivals any in history!

As news of the decimation of the population filtered back to Spain, the Crown attempted to stem the onslaught of the *encomienda* system. The Church also reacted strongly, sending numerous missions to New Spain, designed to collect the natives into local settlements with the Church as their protector. The reforming zeal of the Church waned quickly, however, and the Indians found themselves with a triple burden of taxation: monies to the Church for buildings, weddings, funerals; labor to the Spanish overlord; and taxes to the remaining Indian nobility, who played a "middleman" role in maintaining the system.

Unlike the British in Africa or America, the Spanish settlers in Central and South America often intermarried with the native population. This gave rise to a three-caste structure which can be found operating in most of Latin America to this day. First, there were the "pure" Europeans, called *creoles*. They saw themselves linked with the superior culture of the homeland, and were usually the rich and powerful. Then there were the mixed bloods, or *mestizos*, who occupied a middle role. Last came the Indians, who were relegated to the lowliest positions and the poorest land. Much of modern Latin American history can be traced to conflicts between these various classes and racial groups. Most especially in Mexico, Guatemala, Peru, Bolivia, Colombia, Ecuador, and Paraguay, we see that the poorest of the poor are still primarily drawn from the original Indian population.

As for land, that crucial resource for any agricultural people, the *encomienda* system gradually was transmuted into the *hacienda* system, whereby a wealthy family controlled a vast tract of land and hired "free" laborers to work it. In reality, these supposedly free laborers were usually tied to the land through debt to the landlord, who as their *patrón* often ruled their lives like any feudal baron. These *haciendas*, or *latafundia*, dominated the politics and economic life of most Latin American countries. In their modern agribusiness version, many still do today.

To obtain some idea of how great an impact these large landholdings have had, consider a 1960 survey of Latin American landholding which found that holdings of more than one thousand hectares represented an astonishing 65 percent of all land held for farming and grazing. At the other end of the spectrum there were over five million holdings of twenty hectares or less, which represented less than 4 percent of the land, but supported the vast bulk of the agricultural population.[9]

Even this obscures the severe problem of land distribution in Latin America. A recent survey of landholding found that the landless and near-landless made up 70 percent of rural households in Brazil, 75 percent in Ecuador, and 85 percent in Guatemala. Even in Mexico, where the revolution of 1910 was supposed to have brought about a vast reform of landholding, 60 percent of rural households were landless or nearly so. This survey of rural landholding concludes:

> The landless, the insecure tenants, and those owning marginal plots too small to support a family together constitute nearly all the poorest of the poor. . . . It is in many cases they who are born into debt and die in debt, who see up to half their infants die before age five, who live chronically on a tightwire of survival from which they can quickly fall if the weather or the international economy turns against them.[10]

*Kenya*

Half a world away from Mexico and almost four centuries after Cortés, the British began to consolidate their hold on East Africa.[11] The Suez Canal had opened in 1869, and British shipping now had a new route from India and the Orient to home. In order to protect their shipping routes, the British decided that it would be expedient to formalize their presence on the East African coast, rather than let the Germans or French claim it for themselves.

Rivalries between the European powers in Africa began to sharpen in the 1870s and 1880s, so much so that it seemed advisable to come to some mutual agreement over who got what. So in 1884 the European powers convened in Berlin and drew up a map of Africa which delineated zones of control. Germany acquired what is now Tanzania, Great Britain got Uganda and Kenya, and so on. Needless to say, the wishes of the indigenous populations were not taken into consideration, and this resulted in boundary lines that cut across tribal groupings. Many African states today are still trying to live within the boundaries that were so casually drawn at the Congress of Berlin.

The area that is now the country of Kenya had been greatly disrupted by the Arab slave trade between 1800 and 1850. Slavers went on periodic expeditions into the highlands, and tribes were set against each other as native Africans began to profit from selling their neighbors. The traditional practices of agriculture and herding were greatly disrupted by this development.

The British had had a presence in the area since 1840, but began to actively assert themselves after the opening of the Canal. They launched an extensive crusade to end the Arab slave trade, supposedly on humanitarian grounds, but also in order to mark out the territory against the French and the Germans. In 1890 the British assumed direct control of the Kenya-Uganda region, and appointed an administrator to bring things in order.

Britain, like all other European colonial powers, had the clear expectation that its colonies should (1) pay their own way, (2) provide materials and goods that would be of use to the home country, and (3) develop in ways that were complementary to the British economy. The Kenyan colonial administrators looked out over their region to determine what might be done to meet these goals. They decided that Kenya, with its moderate and well-watered highlands, was ideal for settlement by whites, and that soon the country would be exporting corn, coffee, wheat, and sisal back to England. They, therefore, concentrated their efforts on attracting settlers from Britain and South Africa with promises of cheap land and even cheaper native labor.

They found that supplying the cheap land was simple. All they had to do was "alienate" it from the Masai or Kikuyu tribes that happened to live there, order them to move into preserves, and then sell the land to prospective settlers. With this simple device, quite similar to the U.S. government's practices toward its own native population, a good 5,000-acre tract of land could be had for a mere ten pounds a year. No wonder that one man, Lord Delamere, was able to amass one million acres all for himself.

Supplying cheap labor, however, was not so easy. The Kikuyu and Masai people were self-sufficient, and preferred leisure time to working for wages. They could grow or herd enough for their own needs and had a small surplus to barter for locally made clothes, utensils, and ornaments. When they were offered money to work for a new settler, they simply shrugged. What did they need money for? And besides, the periods when the settlers wanted to hire them were the very times that the natives wanted to be tending their own crops or herds.

The white settlers found this intolerable. They had been lured to Kenya with promises of large plantations, and now they were stuck with plenty of land, but not enough hands to work it. They soon began to put pressure on the colonial administration to adopt measures that would create a willing labor force for their would-be estates. The purpose of these measures was to undermine native self-sufficiency, and to force the local people to depend on the labor market for their needs.

First, the administrators established a hut tax that had to be paid in cash. This meant that each native family had to earn money to stay out of jail, or to keep from having property seized.

Next, they cut back even further on the native preserves—far in excess of what the settlers might conceivably need—so that there was simply not enough land to meet native needs.

To this, they added import duties on the few commodities that were purchased by Africans, thus raising the price.

This was followed by a deliberate program of recruiting in which native leaders who did not produce a quota of workers were replaced. And, on the urging of South African settlers—who felt it had done wonders there—the government added a passbook system in 1915 whereby each adult African male was required to carry a passbook in which debts, criminal record, and comments by his employers could be noted. "Vagrants" who could not produce a pass or prove steady employment were subject to arrest and assignment to a work gang.

Finally, when all this still failed to produce an adequate work force, the government resorted to outright force, ordering people to work or else be imprisoned.

During the time that these drastic and culturally disruptive measures were being enforced, the white settler population of Kenya never numbered more than two thousand families—perhaps ten thousand people. Yet the black population averaged almost four million. The white minority owned 20 percent of the arable land—in fact, the best 20 percent—while the black majority had the poorer 80 percent. The white minority received agricultural loans, technical assistance, free seeds, veterinary services, lower import duties, and active government programs in health and education, while the black majority was largely ignored. In fact, the black population was being taxed to pay for the services given to the whites.

The net result of this deliberate neglect can be found in a series of figures. First, and not surprisingly, the black population in Kenya declined from

4 million in 1902 to 2.4 million in 1921. The annual mortality rate among workers was eighty deaths per thousand; the infant mortality rate was four hundred per thousand. As a British study commission on native health concluded, "In a country where men can be hired for from five to eighteen pounds a year it does not pay employers to spend large sums in keeping them alive."

Behind this harmful policy there may have been a motive other than simple white favoritism. There were Europeans in Africa—the wealthy Cecil Rhodes being their best-known champion—who dreamed of a day when whites would densely settle and develop a broad belt of East Africa from Kenya to South Africa—much as whites had done in North America. And what about the vast black population? The answer, pure and simple, is that many whites quietly hoped—or expected—that the blacks would die off. As Kenya's colonial commissioner commented in 1904, after he had pushed the Masai further back into their preserves, "There can be no doubt that the Masai and many other tribes must go under. It is a prospect which I view with equanimity and a clear conscience."

## Underdevelopment

Having reviewed the impact of colonialism on Kenya and Mexico, readers may not be surprised to learn that many Third World people argue that colonialism caused what we now term underdevelopment. That is, through the process of economic and political domination, the ruling country (often referred to as the metropolis) systematically distorted the economy of its colonies (called the periphery) so that they were increasingly incapable of balanced development.

Those who remember their American revolutionary history will recall that the British at various times enacted laws that forbade the North American colonies from engaging in industry that competed with Britain's own factories. For instance, at one time no wool, wool yarn, or cloth could be produced in the colonies except for local use. No hats could be exported—not even to a neighboring colony. For a time, no steel furnaces or slitting or rolling mills were permitted to exist. Colonies that wanted to sell goods to each other often had to ship their goods to England, and then have them shipped out to their destination, even if the destination was a colony next door. Needless to say, such restrictions were deeply resented, and had a dampening effect on commercial and industrial development.[12]

In the history of colonialism, one can find example after example of these restrictions and distortions. When the British arrived in India, they discovered a large textile industry based on small shops. Initially, they were delighted to get these cheap goods, but the attitude changed when England began to develop competing mills. The British began to impose export restrictions on Indian goods, and in Bengal they went so far as to permanently maim the hands of thousands of weavers. The net result was that between

1815 and 1832, cotton exports from India to England fell thirteen times.[13] This ruthless policy against Indian artisans caused massive unemployment and dislocation, and resulted in millions of deaths. Lord Bentinck, the British governor-general of India, reported in 1834 that "the misery hardly finds a parallel in the history of commerce. The bones of the cotton-weavers are bleaching the plains of India."[14] The net effect of this policy of enforced complementarity of the British and Indian economies was that the non-agricultural population decreased from 45 percent of the whole in early 1800 to only 26 percent by 1940. Simply put, India had been well on its way toward becoming an industrial, diversified economy. This was reversed by the British.[15]

A less obvious but equally disruptive policy of colonialism was the support for the creation of large estates and plantations oriented toward the export of cash crops for the metropolis. Thus Ceylon (now Sri Lanka) became economically dependent on exports of tea; Brazil, on coffee; Tanzania, on sisal; El Salvador, on bananas. Some countries became virtually one-crop exporters, their entire economies and the livelihood of many of their people dependent on the rise and fall of the market for their primary export.

The historian D. K. Fieldhouse argues, I think correctly, that this trend toward monoculture and the cash crop would probably have occurred with or without colonialism. The Europeans were so powerful, militarily and economically, that no country could have long withstood their demands for certain goods and materials, nor could any country have forced the Europeans to remove their own trade barriers against any products they wished to exclude. Says Fieldhouse:

> One-sided use of natural resources reflected an imbalance of power between the West and the non-industrialized areas of the world; and while this lasted no non-European society had sufficient bargaining power to impose fully equitable terms.[16]

As we move to a consideration of the post-colonial period (1945 to the present), it is important to remember Fieldhouse's statements about bargaining power and equitable terms, for this in a nutshell is what the debate over the New International Economic Order is all about.

## NOTES

1. D. K. Fieldhouse, *The Colonial Empires* (New York: Delacorte Press, 1967), pp. 229–232.

2. Ibid., p. 178.

3. Ibid.

4. W. N. Prescott, *The Conquest of Mexico* (New York: Modern Library, first issued in 1843).

5. Alonzo de Zorita, *Life and Labor in Ancient Mexico*, trans. and ed. Benjamin Keen (New Brunswick, N.J.: Rutgers University Press, 1963), editor's Introduction, p. 5.

6. Ibid., pp. 7–8.

7. Ibid., pp. 8–9.

8. Ibid., p. 9.

9. Claudio Veliz, ed., *Obstacles to Change in Latin America* (New York: Oxford University Press, 1965), pp. 81–82.

10. This quotation and the landholding figures are taken from Erik Eckholm, *The Dispossessed of the Earth: Land Reform and Sustainable Development*, Worldwatch Paper #30, June 1979 (Washington, D.C.: Worldwatch Institute), pp. 7, 10.

11. This account comes primarily from Richard D. Wolff, *The Economics of Colonialism—Britain and Kenya, 1870–1930* (New Haven, Conn.: Yale University Press, 1974).

12. Fieldhouse, *The Colonial Empires*, p. 67.

13. Eugene Toland, Thomas Fenton, and Lawrence McCulloch, "World Justice and Peace: A Radical Analysis for American Christians," reprinted in *Education for Justice*, Thomas P. Fenton, ed. (Maryknoll N.Y.: Orbis Books, 1975), p. 103.

14. Jawaharlal Nehru, *The Discovery of India* (New York: Anchor Books, 1960), p. 211.

15. Ibid., p. 212.

16. Fieldhouse, *The Colonial Empires*, p. 286.

*Chapter II*

# Economic Justice II: The Post-Colonial World

In the summer of 1974, the United Nations General Assembly held a special session, the main purpose of which was to focus on reshaping the structure of the international market. One after another, the top leaders of the Third World arose to challenge the workings of the current order and to call for major new arrangements.

This special session represented a milestone in the relations between the developed and developing worlds. It had been preceded by years of conferences, studies, draft statements, and provisional programs—inspired principally by the U.N. Committee on Trade and Development (UNCTAD). In the end, the only thing new in the special session's final resolution was the surprising degree of Third World unity around a common set of grievances and demands. With the OPEC decision to raise world oil prices by 400 percent and the developed world's increasing dependence on Third World raw materials, this united position was taken very seriously by all parties concerned.

The format for presenting Third World demands was contained in a call for a New International Economic Order (NIEO).* This call—which is essentially a call for a reform of international trade and monetary arrangements— also announced a new stage in the struggle between the lesser developed countries and the developed industrial nations.

For Third World members of the United Nations, the long struggle against colonialism was coming to an end. Soon the Portuguese empire in Africa would crumble, making it almost certain that the few remaining bastions of white control in Africa would soon follow. Now the focus would shift to the economic struggle between rich and poor, and in that debate Japan and the

---

*For the details of this call, see my discussion of the New International Economic Order in Chapter VII.

Soviet Union found themselves uncomfortably lumped together with the European capitalist nations by Third World spokespersons.

After our review of the colonial period, it is not hard to imagine some of the economic grievances and frustrations of the lesser developed countries (LDCs). But to understand fully the momentum behind the call for a New International Economic Order, we must consider the impact of neo-colonialism in the post-colonial world.

### Life in the International Marketplace

The demise of the colonial empires after World War II brought a new era in the global economy. Whereas the international economy of the nineteenth and earlier centuries had consisted of a handful of independent players, the twentieth century witnessed a multiplication of players to well over 170 by 1976. This meant that there were at least 170 governing units, each with its own currency, each with the power to erect or reduce tariffs and trade barriers, each trying to maximize its economic position in the global arena.

The importance of this development should be emphasized: *In the modern international economy, each country functions like a business. It makes no difference whether it is internally socialist, communist, or capitalist—in the global marketplace of buying and selling, each country tries to sell its products and buy the products of others on the best possible terms. Internationally, every country acts, or is forced to act, like a capitalist enterprise.*

But countries are not the only players. The huge private corporations also act in the international arena. Unlike the state-owned corporations of the socialist countries, the private companies are often remarkably free to act and react without the prior consent of their host country. Many people see these corporations as autonomous giants, able to play one country off against another, shifting factories and profits wherever suits them best. Surprisingly, of the one hundred largest financial entities in the world, fifty-four of them are countries (as measured by Gross National Product) and forty-six of them are multinational corporations (as measured by annual sales).[1]

A developing country, if it had an economy like Zambia's, would have a total GNP of approximately $13 billion. Not only would this be dwarfed by a huge economy like that of the United States (approximately $2.6 trillion in 1980) or Japan (approximately $1 trillion in 1980), but it would be small potatoes compared to many of the large multinational corporations.

In many ways, the smaller (in GNP) developing countries are like the small farmer or the small shop in the United States. If we can imagine Tim Lee's clothing store and Sally Brown's family farm—and think about how they would stack up to J. C. Penney (1979 sales, $11.3 billion) or General Foods Corporation (1979 sales, $6 billion)—then we can begin to get a sense of how powerless a developing country can be in the international economy. How would Tim fare if he needed a big loan, compared to Penneys? What kind of a bargain could Sally drive for agricultural equipment compared to the mammoth buying power of General Foods? And how much influence would Sally or Tim have with international, national, or even state legislative institutions? By themselves, very little. Joining with hundreds and thousands of people like them, they would have collective clout. This explains why countries as diverse as Cuba and Malaysia have often been able to agree on programs vis-à-vis the rich countries and the huge corporations; otherwise, they are virtually powerless.

There are major differences between Tim Lee's clothing store and Zambia, however. Zambia has one vote in the United Nations General Assembly, the same as the United States. Zambia might be wooed by the competing big powers, each offering aid, or might be playing a key diplomatic role in African affairs. But, most importantly, Zambia might be sitting on a mountain of valuable assets—oil, gold, tin, copper, good farm land, or uranium. Who knows what might be found of value?

Zambia may very well be "rich"—at least rich in potential wealth—as so much of the Third World is rich. India, for instance, has a huge supply of iron ore, about twenty-three percent of the world's known reserves.[2] Iran has recently begun to tap a huge copper porphyry belt—one that may rival the enormous deposits in Arizona and Chile.[3] And Latin America has vast reserves of oil, copper, tin, gold, zinc, lead; the list is endless.[4] Recent discoveries of huge oil reserves in Mexico and the expectation that there are large reserves in China reinforce the reality of potential Third World wealth.

But having these resources does not necessarily mean that a country can march straight into affluence. As we shall see, the path to this goal is strewn with snares and pitfalls.

## Neo-colonialism

Having spoken repeatedly of neo-colonialism, it may be helpful to give a few examples, so that the reader can see what the LDCs are facing in their path to development.*

In the 1920s two U.S. companies, Anaconda and Kennecott, bought control of virtually all the important copper reserves in Chile. Since copper was, and is, Chile's major export commodity, this meant that these two companies had control over a key factor in Chile's economy. In an article in the *Review of Radical Political Economics* economist Al Gedicks details what this foreign control meant:

1. *The loss of considerable potential income.* Initial taxation (until 1934) never returned more than 38 percent of the copper's value to

---

*The term "neo-colonialism" has also been used to refer to the continued "cultural" domination of a former colony. This happens when imported styles and tastes overshadow local mores, and when imported movies and television create myths and values that ignore or go counter to local values. This is sometimes humorously referred to as "Coca-colonization," a process to which even the People's Republic of China may prove susceptible.

Chile—the rest went to the companies and their American stock-holders. Even when taxes were raised, Chile continued to lose, because the companies cut back on production and investment—investing their (Chilean) copper profits elsewhere.

2. *The loss of control over marketing.* Kennecott and Anaconda decided where and when to sell their Chilean copper. And, as U.S. companies, they obeyed U.S. regulations and restrictions. Thus, in World War II, when the United States put a twelve cents a pound ceiling on copper prices, Chilean copper had to be sold at that price, and could not be sold to any hostile powers. The loss to Chile from being dragged into U.S. war economics was an estimated $500 million. Yet in 1933, Chilean copper had been treated as "foreign" copper and subjected to a stiff U.S. tariff. After World War II, with the heating up of the Cold War, the United States forced Chile not to sell its copper to any Soviet Bloc nations, a restriction that lasted until 1964.

3. *The loss of control over internal development.* Kennecott and Anaconda wanted copper from Chile, which then could be fabricated into products in their U.S. plants. A Chilean-owned company might have been more likely to invest in fabricating plants in Chile, thus generating other industries, and more jobs. In 1952, when Chile tried to gain control of external copper sales through a state agency—hoping for a better price—the large companies manipulated the international market so that sales plummeted. Chile dropped this experiment after three frustrating years.

In other words, the government and people of Chile were essentially left out of the integrated development of their own most precious resource. They were expected to take a back seat, claiming some part of the revenues, but essentially remaining passive participants. When the mines finally ran out, Chile would have been left with a bundle of rusted equipment and some large holes in the ground—plus whatever they had managed to save and reinvest from their cut of the profits.[5]

That Chile is not an isolated case is underscored by the report of the Kennecott Copper Corporation to a U.S. Senate committee, in which the company bragged that, while $2 billion was invested abroad in the mining and smelting industry from 1961 to 1970, some $4.8 billion came back in profits, interest, and dividends. The net surplus for the United States was $2.8 billion, a boon to our balance of payments, but a huge reinvestment loss to the overseas countries involved.[6]

For some idea of just how detrimental foreign control can be, consider the case of Iraq. In 1925 the government had granted a concession to all oil rights to the Iraq Petroleum Company—a company owned by Shell, British Petroleum, Exxon, Mobil, and two other large foreign firms. The Iraq Petroleum Company (IPC) was supposed to use its resources and technology to explore the vast oil potential, bring in wells, and market the product. The Iraqi government would get a share of the profits—at the time perhaps the best arrangement that an underdeveloped country could have gotten. But there was one hitch. The big oil companies didn't want to pump any oil from Iraq; in fact, they wanted the concession primarily in order to keep anyone else from exploring for oil. Why? Because they already had more than enough oil coming in from Iran and other locations. New finds in Iraq would have lowered the world price and hurt them all. Iraq would have gained, of course, but the companies weren't interested in what Iraq wanted or needed.

From 1925 on, IPC followed a deliberate, and secret, policy of not locating oil in Iraq. They delayed delivery of equipment, drilled shallow holes, capped wells that they had inadvertently discovered, and in general kept Iraq "down" as regards oil production. All of this, of course, while assuring the Iraqi government that they were doing their best.

After World War II, vast new stores of oil were developed in Saudi Arabia and Kuwait, again under the control of the big oil companies—so it was decided to continue to keep Iraq "down." Finally, in 1961, the government of Iraq cancelled IPC's concession in all but 0.5 percent of the country and began looking for another arrangement. They commissioned an independent study of their oil potential and found that it was considered to be fantastic. "There is every evidence that millions of barrels will be found," the study concluded, citing case after case where IPC had found oil but decided not to produce it.

IPC naturally set up a howl, claiming that its rights had been violated. But when the U.S. State Department looked into IPC's complaint, they offered little comfort to the company, reporting that:

A fairly substantial case could be made . . . that IPC has followed a "dog in the manger" policy in Iraq, excluding or swallowing up all competitors, while at the same time governing its production in accordance with the overall worldwide interests of the participating companies and not solely in accordance with the interests of Iraq.[7]

Not surprisingly, the government of Iraq finally decided to nationalize IPC's holdings and properties. This well-deserved act came only in 1972, *forty-five years after* IPC had first made promises about delivering oil from Iraq.[8]

The cases of Iraq and Chile are not unique. Rather, they are indicative of what Third World producers face in the rough and tumble world of international economics. Here, briefly, are a few more examples:

—Some sixty different countries are producers of cotton, many of them in the Third World. But when it comes to selling their cotton, they find that the world market is controlled by fifteen giant multi-commodity traders, most based in the United States and Japan. These giant traders are able to buy and sell in huge quantities, and often collude with one another to regulate or fix prices, so that the producers are often at their mercy. Even the Soviet Union, a large cotton-producing nation with a state-controlled trading arm, is forced to follow the lead of these traders. In tobacco, six large traders control 90 percent of the international market. Three companies have control of over 70 percent of the banana market; four corporations control the world cocoa trade.[9]

—In 1966, Brazil tried to broaden its coffee industry by setting up factories that could produce instant coffee from the raw beans. U.S. firms put pressure on their government, which in turn notified Brazil that it would cancel its participation in the International Coffee Agreement (an agreement designed to maintain stable prices) and would also cancel all U.S. aid. Brazil gave in, imposing an export tax on its own producers, forcing them to fold.[10] In 1976, it was reported that the United States was using its considerable weight in the World Bank (25 percent of the total votes) to oppose loans for palm oil production in several developing countries. The reason: palm oil might compete with U.S. soybean oil.[11]

The United States has not been above using its "humanitarian" aid to manipulate Third World economies as well. As a classic case study of U.S. aid loans to Pakistan has revealed, (1) the aid was used to secure control over all of Pakistan's development projects, (2) the United States recouped much of its money almost immediately through U.S. consultants' and contractors' fees—sometimes running as high as 50 percent of the allocation, (3) in granting food loans, the United States specified that the food had to be shipped in U.S. freighters, costing Pakistan twice the freight costs of other carriers, (4) U.S. cotton was dumped on the Pakistani market as a form of "aid" at a time when Pakistan already suffered from a surplus of cotton.[12]

It should be noted that such aid-tying to the donor country's industries is quite common in the world of bilateral aid. Often political as well as economic concessions are sought in exchange for this aid. Sometimes loans are granted on concessional terms, i.e., low interest and long pay back periods, but eventually these loans must be repaid. In fact, total Third World debt for government and private (bank) loans was estimated to have reached a staggering $300 billion by 1980. The interest payments on these loans is costing poor countries $35 billion a year—which explains why so many LDCs have chronic financial problems.[13]

—Finally, an example from President Julius Nyerere of Tanzania. His country has fourteen million people, living on a per capita annual income of $160—that is to say, it is one of the poorest countries in the world. Seeking to broaden the economy, Tanzania went to the World Bank for a plan to erect an integrated timber production and papermill project. When a feasibility study was first made in 1973, it was estimated that the papermill would cost $60 million. That alone would cost Tanzania all of its sisal revenues for eighteen months. Two years later, the project cost was estimated at $200 million—over three year's revenue. And after that the price of sisal dropped, meaning that the costs would be even greater.

Tanzania finds itself in a dilemma. World prices for manufactured goods are rising—largely because of inflation in the developed countries—but sisal prices are falling. Tanzania, at the bottom of the economic pecking order, can do nothing about it. As Nyerere states:

> [The] truth is that however much we reorganize our [national] economic system to serve the interest of the mass of the people, and however much our government tries to weigh the income distribution in favor of the poorest people, we are merely redistributing poverty, and we remain subject to economic decisions and interests outside our control.[14]

## The Distortions of the Present System

The twentieth century has seen the demise of the colonial political order, an event which in itself will have profound and lasting consequences for the future of humankind. Yet the colonial *economic* order remains, and with it comes a package of distortions that delay and in some cases defeat the goal of human progress.

At its most simple we can say that there are two major distortions in the present economic world order:

First, *there is an unequal division of the consumption of the world's material resources between the poor countries and the rich ones.*

Thus the United States, with only 6 percent of the world's population consumes over 30 percent of the world's petroleum, 35 percent of the world production of primary aluminum, and 24 percent of the world's copper.[15] The developed world, which consists of countries like the Soviet Union and France, altogether represents just 28 percent of the world's population; yet it possesses 93 percent of the world's telephones, 89 percent of the world's tractors, and 92 percent of the world's automobiles.[16] In other words, of every one hundred tractors, the world's poorer three billion get to use eleven, while the world's richest one billion get to use eighty-nine.

The second distortion of the present economic order follows from the first: *the rich countries have greater income—greater purchasing power—than the poor countries.*

Thus the rich 28 percent have over 80 percent of the world's income. This income means power, the power to spend on luxuries and necessities, the power to outbid the poor on the world market.

Because of this purchasing power, the United States is able to consume 15 percent of the world's petroleum production for our automobiles alone. In a poor country—like Mali or Chad—a few gallons of gasoline might power a village millet grinding mill that would save each woman four hours of backbreaking work a day, since each adult woman spends about that much time each day doing the task by hand. But the villagers of Mali and Chad can seldom afford the gasoline, much less the cost of the millet mill.

Thus the Soviet Union can afford to spend $136 per person on public education, while Kenya can only afford to spend $14; the United States can spend $273 per person on public health, while South Korea spends $5.[17]

Because of these distortions, the number one public health measure in the world today—providing clean drinking water*—proceeds at a glacial pace, while the United States and the U.S.S.R. can afford to throw away over $200 billion a year on the arms race.

## What Can Be Done?

Something is terribly wrong with our world. There are people who are hungry, people who lack the most basic health services, people who "are born into debt and die in debt." Yet the earth is rich enough to provide millions of people with more food than they can eat, with cars and campers and video-disc recorders and aluminum foil and throwaway plastic plates.

Obviously in any sane, humane world, everybody would pitch in to help those who have not even the basic necessities of life. Tools, resources, and money would be channelled to those in need.

Yet in the post-colonial world order, almost the opposite happens. Resources and wealth are taken from the poor countries and given to the rich. Pennies are spent on the desperate needs of the poor, and billions are spent on bombers, alcohol, junk food, and blow-dryers.

The call for a New International Economic Order is aimed directly at these distortions in the present system. The call envisions a new system, where industry and technology are shifted significantly to the Third World. Thus enabled to use its own resources more productively, the Third World will begin to share in the benefits of development.

Dramatic change is needed. Yet when one begins to consider what is to be done, a host of troublesome questions arise. If resources are directed to the poor countries, how do we know the leaders of these countries—the elites—won't simply grab everything for themselves, leaving the poor still poor? Anyhow, do we know that there is enough to go around? Isn't pollution already telling us that the industrial way of life is a dead end? And if pollution doesn't kill us, what about the bomb? Even if we solve all these problems, won't women still be oppressed?

These are hard questions—very hard questions. But, as world citizens, as people committed to a fair share for the world's people, they are questions that we must explore, and begin to answer. In the succeeding chapters of this book, I will attempt to explore some of these questions, as well as some proposed responses.

---

*It is estimated that water-borne intestinal diseases (cholera, dysentery, schistosomiasis) affect over one-third of humanity, and cause over ten million deaths a year.[18]

## *NOTES*

1. Authors' computations based upon *1979 World Bank Atlas* for GNP figures and *Forbes Magazine*, July 7, 1980, for company revenue figures.

2. Felix Greene, *The Enemy*, (New York: Vintage, 1971), p. 151.

3. Robert Sisselman, "Copper: Iran's Latest Desert Bonanza," *Engineering and Mining Journal*, February 1978, pp. 57–80.

4. Greene, *The Enemy*, p. 151.

5. Al Gedicks, "The Nationalization of Copper in Chile: Antecedents and Consequences," *The Review of Radical Political Economics*, Fall 1973, pp. 1–25.

6. Ibid., p. 15.

7. John M. Blair, *The Control of Oil* (New York: Pantheon Books, 1976), p. 86.

8. This is summarized from *The Control of Oil*, pp. 80–90.

9. Frederick Clairemonte and John Cavanagh, "Squeezed and Cornered," *Development Forum*, August 1978. Published by the Centre for Economic and Social Information of the United Nations.

10. Eugene Toland, Thomas Fenton, and Lawrence McCulloch, "World Justice and Peace: A Radical Analysis for American Christians," reprinted in *Education for Justice*, Thomas P. Fenton, ed., (Maryknoll, N.Y.: Orbis Books, 1975), p. 104.

11. Albert Fishlow, et al., *Rich and Poor Nations in the World Economy* (New York: McGraw-Hill, 1978), p. 136.

12. Hamza Alavi and Amir Khusro, "Pakistan: The Burden of U.S. Aid," *Imperialism and Development*, Robert I. Rhodes (New York: Monthly Review Press, 1970), pp. 62–78.

13. "Borrow or Bust," *The Economist*, Editorial, June 21, 1980.

14. Julius K. Nyerere, "The Economic Challenge: Dialogue or Confrontation?" in *International Development Review*, January 1976.

15. These figures are taken from *Mineral Commodity Summaries—1980,* U.S. Bureau of Mines (Washington, D.C.: Government Printing Office, 1979). The figure for petroleum consumption is an estimate, based on recent public statements.

16. Richard A. Falk, *This Endangered Planet* (New York: Vintage, 1972), p. 127.

17. "Socialism: Trials and Errors," *Time*, U.S. edition, March 13, 1978, pp. 24–36; figures from chart on p. 35.

18. David F. Salisbury, "World Thirst for Pure Water," in *Technology Review,* July/August 1977, pp. 6–9.

# Chapter III

# Is There Enough?

There was a time when people assumed that the world was moving on a never-ending upward spiral of material success and progress. Every year it seemed some new invention or technological breakthrough was paving the way to global affluence.

Then came the *Limits to Growth* study, in which an impressive array of scientists and public figures argued that global affluence on the scale most of us had come to expect (that is, the U.S. lifestyle, or better) was a physical impossibility. There simply were not enough resources to go around, the study claimed, and even if there were, we would pollute ourselves to death trying to use them.

Just as this study was released, the world experienced the oil shock of 1973. Long lines formed at the gas stations, prices tripled, and everywhere the conventional wisdom of growth and progress seemed to crumble in the face of a new age of scarcity.

With the collapse of the rosy vision of growth, questions were raised in the public mind. Just how much is there? Are we already overburdening the planet? Will there be enough for the poor to have better lives? What is a just global standard of living?

## How Much Is There?

At first glance, the answers seem obvious. After all, the resources of the planet are finite, and with ever-increasing consumption we are bound to run out of things someday. The fabulous Comstock Lode of silver has come and gone in the United States; the oil states know only too well that their valuable resource is limited, and will run out completely in twenty to forty years. Given this reality, it appears that a new age of simplicity and frugality is called for—perhaps even a return to an agricultural and pastoral way of life, and an abandonment of industrial civilization.

Unfortunately (or perhaps fortunately) the obvious answers may not be correct. Since the *Limits to Growth* study, there have been several challenges to its methodology and assumptions, and particularly to its gloomy projection of what might constitute a sustainable global level of living.

When pressed to come up with a realistic and sustainable standard of living for the world's people, the *Limits* study suggested that the planet might be able to house six billion people at a per capita income of $2,000.[1] That is about one-fourth of the present U.S. per capita income, a figure which suggests that the United States is "overdeveloped" in relation to the rest of the world.

On the other hand, Herman Kahn and his associates at a U.S. think tank called the Hudson Institute have made their own projections of a sustainable society. They come up with a planet populated by 15 billion people, with a per capita income of $20,000—or more than two times the current (1980) U.S. level.[2] This suggests that even the United States has some distance to go before it strains the world's resource base.

Those who have read the *Limits to Growth* probably remember a chart of "known world reserves" of various non-renewable minerals—a chart that showed silver, zinc, tin, gold, and mercury all running out in less than twenty years of growth and consumption.[3] Yet there are some fairly persuasive challenges to many of these seemingly obvious limits. Brookings Institution researcher John E. Tilton argues that "known world reserves" are a poor and misleading indication of resource availability. After all, "known" reserves means just that—reserves that have been definitely located and proved. This does not allow for new discoveries. More importantly, the size of these reserves is calculated on what can be economically extracted from ore *at the current level of technology*. New breakthroughs in technology can mean that previously uneconomical ore can be processed for the specific mineral desired.

Citing the case of copper, Tilton shows that known world reserves in 1946 were such that every speck of copper would have been used up by 1973. Yet known world reserves of copper in 1975 stood at almost five times the level of 1946. Why? Because there were new discoveries but, more importantly, because the progress of copper refining technology had made it economically profitable to extract copper from ore that was previously considered too "poor" to mine. The same process has occurred with iron ore, expanding the 1946 reserves by 400 percent.[4] Comparing known reserves of various minerals, Tilton shows that between 1950 and 1974 zinc reserves went up 210 percent, nickel 281 percent, bauxite 1,103 percent, potash 1,525 percent, and so on. The only mineral that actually decreased in those twenty-four years of consumption was tungsten, by 1.8 percent.[5] (It is important to note that Tilton focused his study on non-fuel minerals, and did not project figures for oil, coal, or gas.)

Tilton argues that, at least in theory, the *true* resource base of a mineral is that percentage which is available in the earth's crust. That is, a calculation of what can be found in common rock. Using this resource base, he concludes that we have, for example, 468 years' worth of consumption (with growth at a 5 percent annual rate) before we exhaust aluminum—as compared to thirty-one years based on the standard "known reserves" figures. Of course, getting that 468 years' worth would require digging up the entire earth's crust for processing—a rather unlikely prospect.

To add another twist, copper is a metal that is easily recycled, and at a fraction of the energy cost that is involved in producing new copper. Even at present prices, copper consumption in the United States is 45 percent recycled metal; and at higher prices this recycling would increase. Of our zinc consumption, 20 percent is recycled or scrap; iron is 36 percent; lead is 38 percent.[6]

### The Energy Factor

Professor Earl Cook, of Texas A&M, is a sharp critic of Tilton's "resource base" concept. In an article in *Technology Review*, he argues that such estimates "put extreme demands on the technological cavalry to come riding over the hill in the nick of time . . . ,"[7] and that rising energy costs will soon place a limit on what can be economically extracted. "Barring a breakthrough in the technology of energy," Cook asserts, the industralized nations will have to make "severe re-adjustments" in the next fifty years.[8] He supports his arguments by studies of silver and iron ore depletion in the United States, and contends that every mineral resource goes through a waxing and waning cycle in its availability. It is just a matter of time before all minerals in all parts of the world follow this pattern.

If Cook is right, and resources are destined to be ever more scarce, it doesn't take much imagination to figure out who the losers will be in the game of industrialization. It is the poor nations that will suffer the most from a rapid decrease in the availability of resources. The rich nations will have had their "fling," and the poor will find that the once-loaded table is practically bare, with the costs of the few remaining raw materials so high as to be prohibitive.*

But Cook's thesis is challenged at its very heart—energy costs—by Herman Kahn. Kahn and his associates see the world as going through a "transitional" stage from non-renewable to renewable energy. In seventy-five years they expect that we will have sufficient new energy from the sun, and from nuclear fusion and fission, to make expensive energy a thing of the past. This abundant energy can then be used for extracting ore, for recycling, and for new modes of manufacturing. They conclude:

> We do not mean to imply that the path to abundant energy will be smooth. Future energy projects will tend to become increasingly im-

---

*One might think that the developing countries would profit from a steep increase in the prices of industrial raw materials, since they supply so many of them. But most developing countries only supply one to five commodities in the market, and an across-the-board increase in the prices of all raw materials would make it virtually impossible for them to purchase all the other materials that they would need for large-scale and diversified production.

mense, and costly mistakes may create serious temporary local or regional supply problems lasting perhaps 5 to 10 years, higher costs, rationing, brownouts, and similar troubles.

. . . (but) the basic message is this: except for temporary fluctuations caused by bad luck or poor management, the world need not worry about energy shortages or costs in the future. And energy abundance is probably the world's best insurance that the entire human population (even 15-20 billion) can be well cared for, at least physically, during many centuries to come.[9]

Those at the Hudson Institute believe that there must eventually be some limits to growth—but that the world has plenty of room for more people and more consumption. Thus, while they agree that we will eventually need a "steady-state" economy, they feel that it can be far more affluent than many people think possible. And how do Kahn and associates think we will reach this rich plateau of material plenty? By proceeding full steam ahead, increasing the production and consumption of the already rich so that the expanding international market pulls the poor along with it.

And so the debate goes on, one side arguing that we cut back and learn to live with less; the other arguing that—in many respects—the sky is the limit.*

### Which Path to Choose?

Since these two positions seem to suggest diametrically opposed paths to development, it is important to decide who is right.

I would suggest that the answer lies not in choosing one side or the other, but in carefully assessing what we know and can apply to the world situation today.

First of all, we can see that there is no permanent, easy answer to the question of how much will be available in the long run. Resource availability depends in large part on the level of technological development, especially on the availability of cheap, plentiful energy. If Kahn is right, and we one day make the transition to an era of unlimited energy from the sun, then the age of scarcity will seem like a small disruption on the rosy path of progress.

But this "new era" hasn't come yet. It may not come for forty or seventy-five or two hundred years. It may *never* come.

*Right now*, there are limits to growth. We can imagine some marvelous invention or some great device suddenly coming over the hill to rescue us from our limits, but to count on this technological rescue, in fact to continue our resource fling while confidently awaiting for the scientists to conjure up new supplies, seems to be the utmost folly.

For example, the availability of oil seems to be placing a fairly clear constraint on our possibilities for the near future. Virtually no one is predicting that phenomenal new reserves of petroleum will rescue us from today's con-

---

*In fact, Kahn, and others, feel that the sky is not a limit, and that in the 21st century the mining of the solar system will provide us with abundant new riches.

straints, nor is anyone suggesting that alternate technologies or energy sources will save us from our present limits for at least the next twenty years, and probably longer. The "quick fix" solution of nuclear power is beginning to appear a nightmare rather than a magical solution to our energy shortage. Thus it leaves us with a clear mandate to conserve oil and use it sparingly—and wisely—for the benefit of all the world's people.

Consider the availability of the world's renewable resources—our land, waters, and vegetation. Again we find that there are rosy promises of technological breakthroughs—new "miracle" seeds, improved fertilizers, better pesticides, schemes for making the deserts bloom and growing protein in petroleum vats. But the present reality is one of environmental danger and even overburden.

Agricultural economist Lester R. Brown and his associates at the environmentally oriented Worldwatch Institute believe that we are already overstraining our global ecosystem. While non-renewable resources may be stretched out, they argue that the renewable resources are in grave danger—especially the world's croplands, fisheries, forests, and grasslands. These four systems not only provide us with food, but with all our non-mineral raw materials. Brown contends:

1. Agricultural land is rapidly deteriorating. The United States is already losing topsoil faster than it can be replaced. Highways and urbanization claim 1.3 million acres of the world's cropland each year. Over-farming is destroying millions of other acres, inch by inch.
2. The world's fisheries have been exploited up to and beyond their limits of renewal. A survey of the North Atlantic found that twenty-seven of the region's thirty fisheries are being overfished. The traditionally huge Peruvian anchovy catch has plummeted, due to overfishing, and has not only sent Peru into an economic slump, but has raised the prices of substitute foods enormously.
3. The world's grasslands are being over-grazed, turning them into deserts. The demand for milk, meat, and other livestock products is exceeding the carrying capacity of the land in one country after another. For example, the natural rangelands in northern Iraq are capable of carrying two hundred and fifty thousand head of sheep. But they are currently being grazed by one million head.
4. The world's forests are being used up at an alarming rate, sending the price of firewood in native villages up three or four times, and increasing the cost of housing in the developed world. Third World villagers are forced to range more widely for their wood, cutting down trees that form watersheds, and contributing to a devastating erosion process.

Brown's conclusion: "In economic terms, we are now consuming biological capital along with interest."[10]

## The "Basic Needs" Strategy

Since there are limits at present to global consumption, it would seem sensible for the world's scarce resources to be used wisely to help improve the lives of those who have the least. Under the old "growth-oriented" model of development, it was thought that a country could place heavy emphasis on large-scale industrial development, spending its money on airports, roads, port facilities. Then once an economic "take off" point had been reached, the overall economy would pull the poor into affluence by giving them factory work and jobs in other modernized sectors of the economy. This can be called the "top-down" model of development, one in which benefits are supposed to "trickle down" to the poor from the rich.

The problem with this model of development is twofold: first, it condemns the present generation of the poor to a life of continuing poverty, since social spending favors the rich and ignores basic health and other needs; second, the model assumes that developing countries can all become massively industrialized, ignoring the resource limitations of such a path.

Recently, it has been suggested that a "bottom-up" approach to development is more likely to help the poor. In this model, a country seeks to use scarce money and resources to give concrete benefits to the broad bulk of the population. Thus, educational funds might be spent on basic literacy programs, rather than on elite universities; on providing clean drinking water, rather than on building a shiny new airport; on materials for "self-help" housing, rather than on luxury hotels for rich tourists.

This "basic needs" strategy, as it is coming to be called in international development circles, advocates a direct concentration of world energies and resources on the glaring needs of the poor and dispossessed. It advocates a commitment of international and national resources to meeting the most simple needs of the world's people: food, clothing, shelter, adequate health, and a basic education.

Looked at from almost any angle, the basic needs strategy makes sense. It challenges a developmental emphasis on building up higher education and a technological elite, while the poor have no clean drinking water, or not enough food. It focuses on agricultural assistance to the peasant and small farmer, rather than to industry or agribusiness. It advocates basic public health measures—an adequate diet, clean water, sewage treatment—before investing in heart institutes and expensive medical machinery. In short, it holds out the hope for millions of people to take small but vital steps in their material and physical well-being.

It also promotes a wise use of world resources, attempting to direct them to areas of clear need, rather than squandering them on luxuries that our planet may literally not be able to afford.

When linked with the promotion of "appropriate" technology—which will be discussed in the following chapter—the basic needs strategy makes good ecological sense as well.

## *NOTES*

1. Donella H. Meadows et al., *The Limits to Growth* (New York: Signet, 1972), p. 171.

2. Herman Kahn et al., *The Next 200 Years* (New York: Wm. Morrow & Co., 1976), p. 55.

3. Meadows, *Limits to Growth*, pp. 64–67.

4. John E. Tilton, *The Future of Non-Fuel Minerals* (Washington, D.C.: Brookings Institutions, 1977), p. 9.

5. Ibid., p.10.

6. Earl Cook, "The Depletion of Geological Resources," in *Technology Review*, June 1975, p. 17.

7. Ibid., p. 25.

8. Ibid., p. 26.

9. Kahn, *The Next 200 Years*, p. 83.

10. Lester R. Brown, "A Biology Lesson for Economists," *New York Times*, July 9, 1978.

# Chapter IV

# The Pollution Factor

It was a warm Friday afternoon, not exactly a time when one would expect to find a school auditorium filled with working and parenting adults. But the residents in the vicinity of the Ninety-Sixth Street School were out in force, and they were anxious and angry.

Mothers rose, one after another, and sobbed out the ages of their children, or the month of their current pregnancy. Angry fathers, many still in their work clothes, demanded to know if their families were going to be separated, and if the speaker on the platform had assurances that they would have someplace to live.

The city was Niagara Falls. The date was August 4, 1978. And the man on the platform was Dr. Glen Haugie of the New York State Health Department. Dr. Haugie had come that day with the unenviable task of telling the two hundred families of the city's "Love Canal" area that their land was filled with toxic poisons, poisons that had been deposited there years ago by a local chemical company, and which now were seeping up through the earth.

Those in the greatest danger were the unborn infants, still in their mothers' wombs. It was thought that at least eleven of the eighty-two different chemicals that had been dumped in the Canal might cause birth defects, and Dr. Haugie urged the mothers to leave their homes immediately. Were others safe? Dr. Haugie didn't know; more tests were needed.

Thomas Heisner, a resident of the Love Canal area, told the assembly that two of his children had been born with birth defects. The thought that this had happened because of the dumping had him in a fury. Other residents spoke of headaches, dizzy spells, and fainting. Could this have been because of the Canal's chemicals? The answer, of course, was that it very well might have been. And in the back of each person's mind was the obvious: what have these chemicals already done to me? Will I get cancer? Or ten years from now, a rare disease? Can I ever have normal children?

A few days later the Love Canal was declared a Federal Disaster Area. All two hundred families were ordered to move out, and their homes were boarded up. Most experts agreed that it would be years before the extent of the damage to residents' health was clear.

35

In Minamata, Japan, it started with cats. They began doing strange things, twirling in circles, and acting as if they had gone mad. Then the disease began to affect the people.

What was it? At first no one knew. The people of Minamata were fishers, catching their fish in the local bay, selling it, and, of course, eating great amounts themselves. They also fed fish scraps to their cats.

The disease affected the nervous system. First, there were headaches and dizziness, then a loss of mental powers, then paralysis, then death or a life of living-death. Its more formal name was "mercury poisoning," and it came, as Japanese courts later ruled, from a nearby factory that was discharging mercury into the bay.

The fish absorbed the mercury when they fed off the sludge in the bottom of the bay. The people ate the fish, and all the while the mercury accumulated in their systems. After a while—in some cases, years—the first symptoms appeared. But by then it was usually too late. By 1975 there were 899 officially recognized victims of what was coming to be called "Minamata disease." Within the immediate area another three thousand had applied for compensation as victims of the disease; some estimated that there could be another ten thousand as yet undiscovered.[1]

### The Cycle of Poisoning

In a way, all of us live on the Love Canal. We also live in Minamata. Every one of us, no matter where we live, is subject to harmful chemicals in the air, toxins in the soil, carcinogenic substances in our drinking water, or our food, or in the walls of our homes. Every day we are subjected to dangers from the environment that are invisible, microscopic, and potentially lethal. And, of course, every day the environment is subjected to new onslaughts from us and our lifestyles. Increasingly, this pattern of mutual poisoning—people to environment and environment back to people—is becoming a worldwide phenomenon.

Let's take the question of chemical dumping as a starting point. The Love Canal was at one time a dumping ground for the Hooker Chemical and Plastics Corporation. When it had been filled, the ground was covered by landfill, and a housing project was erected on the site. When health officials began to suspect that the dumped chemicals were seeping up through the ground, the *Niagara Gazette* sent its reporters out around the county, looking for other dumping sites. They found thirty-eight of them; in some the soil was loaded with DDT, Endrin, Mirex, and other chemicals that have been subsequently banned because of their hazardous side effects.[2]

Nationally, the Environmental Protection Agency estimates that from 35 to 40 million tons of potentially hazardous waste (that's 80 *billion* pounds) are produced each year by industry. "Hazardous" means that it might be flammable, corrosive, infectious, reactive, radioactive, or toxic. Of that 80 billion pounds, only about 10 percent is currently disposed of in an environmentally adequate way.[3]

In Minamata, the mercury was being discharged into the bay by the Chisso Corporation as a byproduct of making caustic soda. The management of the factory denied that they had anything to do with the mysterious disease, even though a secret company study had already revealed otherwise—and they continued to dump mercury into the waters.[4]

How many "Minamatas" are there in the world? How many "Love Canals"? Nobody knows. One Japanese study found that there were forty-seven caustic soda plants in the country using the "mercury method" of production. As symptoms of "Minamata disease" began to appear in other parts of the country, the Japanese government took the extraordinary step of suggesting to its people that they limit their intake of fish.[5] Meanwhile, symptoms of Minamata disease began to appear among the Ojibway Indians in two areas of Ontario, Canada. The story was the same: the tribes affected were large consumers of fish; in their area was a large paper mill which was dumping mercury-laden waste into the waters.[6]

In the United States alone, the Environmental Protection Agency estimates that there are 32,000 hazardous-waste dumpsites, of which 1,200 or more may pose a danger to the public.[7] Companies find it expensive to dispose of these wastes properly—in some cases it may cost them as much as sixty cents a gallon for safe disposal.

In Thailand, government investigators acting on the complaints of local farmers found that a company that had lost two neutralization tanks for storing its chlorine discharge simply diverted the waste into the Chao Phraya River. By the time they were discovered the dumping had gone on for six months.[8]

In the New Jersey Pine Barrens, a semi-wilderness area that supplies drinking water for New York City and Philadelphia, "gypsy" chemical dumpers have taken trucks loaded with toxic chemicals and driven them down dirt roads, spraying the chemicals out the back.[9]

In an overview of the interaction of commercially produced chemicals and their effect on the environment, the United Nations Environment Programme (UNEP) found that over thirty thousand different chemicals were in use around the world, with hundreds of new chemicals being introduced for use each year. These chemicals ranged from pesticides (over one thousand different compounds are in use) to food additives to fertilizers to antibiotics — many of them are new, *all* of them are being poured into the waters, dumped into the ground, and shot into the air in enormous quantities.[10]

Pollution and industrialization seem to go hand in hand. The more we produce, the more factories we build, the more we appear to subject ourselves to new dangers. Of course, it is not just we humans who are in danger, but all life on this planet. DDT not only turns up in "unacceptable" quantities in mother's milk in Guatemala and Washington, D.C., it also can be found in the flesh of Antarctic penguins and in desert gazelles.[11]

Therefore, it should not be surprising that the *Limits to Growth* study found pollution itself was a significant "limit" on growth. Put simply, our industrial wastes may poison us long before we run out of copper, cadmium, and cobalt. Even with the best and most costly pollution-control equipment, the *Limits* study argued, we were still in danger of large-scale destruction if unabated growth continued.

Industrial wastes are only part of the picture of environmental destruction that the world faces today. Sometimes the threat to the environment can come from the thoughtless action of people using relatively simple technologies. This is often the case in Third World countries whose populations scratch out their existence on the land.

Examples from two developing countries may help clarify the picture. Nepal is a mountainous country on India's northeastern border. Its population is moving out from the valleys, where much of the land has been spoiled, onto the mountain slopes. The vegetation and soil on these slopes constitutes an even more fragile system than in the valleys, yet it is being ruthlessly exploited. The net effect of overcropping, overgrazing, and overcutting on these slopes is seen in a dramatic erosion of the soil. Every year 250 million cubic meters of topsoil are washed down the slopes into the Ganges River. Some of this soil fertilizers the Ganges Valley in India, and some of it stains the Indian Ocean for as much as four hundred miles from the shore. Meanwhile, in Nepal available land is diminishing, and a first class ecological disaster is in the making. Already 40 percent of the valley lands have been abandoned because they no longer support crops.[12]

The second example is in the tropical forests of Brazil, where lush vegetation deceives many into thinking that the soil is rich and hardy. Three decades ago a group of German Pomeranian immigrants moved from their farming in Brazil's mountains to the Atlântica forest. They cut down trees on a vast scale and turned the area into coffee plantations and pastures. With the coming of roads to the area, loggers moved in and decimated the remaining trees.

Within twenty years, one hundred square miles of forest were completely denuded. The result was that the entire ecosystem was thrown off balance. Erosion became massive; the silty runoff clogged area rivers, making them impassible. Over 450 varieties of plants and 204 species of birds disappeared from the region. With natural predators gone, pests and parasites flourished, causing many farmers to abandon their crops.

Many of the settlers have now gone. Those who remain suffer from precancerous skin lesions due to overexposure to the sun. Laments Brazilian environmentalist Augusto Ruschi, "The entire area is marching toward desertification."[13]

### The Nuclear Fix

If even the simplest technology can wreak terrible environmental destruction, what is humankind to think of the world's most deadly technological breakthrough—atomic power?

In a later chapter, I will discuss the destructive power of nuclear weapons. Here we consider the supposedly constructive side of the atomic genie—the peaceful use for the production of electricity.

Worldwide, there are about 228 nuclear power plants already built or on the drawing boards in countries outside the United States, which itself has 72 such plants in operation. France, Brazil, and the Soviet Union all have aggressive plans for further development of their nuclear power industries. Belgium, Sweden, and Switzerland already depend on nuclear plants for 30 percent of their electricity (the United States reliance is 12–14 percent).[14]

The one hundred thousand residents who had to flee from the area surrounding the Three Mile Island plant in Pennsylvania have already had cause to think twice about the "peaceful" side of the atom. Was the plant at Three Mile Island an exception? Could such an accident occur elsewhere? The answer to the latter question is a definite yes.

Consider, for example, the nuclear plant called Angra I in Brazil. When cracks began to appear in its walls, investigators found that the plant had been built on a rock shelf that was slowly drifting out to sea![15] In another case, the Philippines has been moving ahead with a nuclear plant that will be located only fourteen miles from an active volcano![16]

The danger posed by nuclear plants does not stop with the potential for a meltdown. The waste that each of these plants produces each year is highly dangerous, and may have to be stored safely for three hundred thousand years until its radioactivity dissipates.

The danger of these wastes has already been shown in a little-known accident that occurred in the Soviet Union in 1957. The Soviets have not discussed the accident in public, but through reports carried by Soviet dissidents and some CIA sleuthing by satellite, the following picture emerges.

Apparently there was a "mud volcano explosion" that was set off by radioactive wastes that were being stored in tanks in an area near the Siberian city of Sverdlovsk. The explosion may have killed hundreds of people outright and contaminated thousands of others. Satellite pictures show a series of dams and canals that have been built in the area in an apparent attempt to stop the spread of contaminated water. The area is sealed off to the public, and some thirty villages that were once listed nearby on Soviet maps are no longer listed. In all, the contaminated area appears to cover as much as four hundred square miles, an area that may be uninhabitable for untold years to come.[17]

When we consider the alarming dangers that are posed by atomic energy production, it is a wonder that this industry was ever allowed to get off the ground. Perhaps we have forgotten the promises of the industry and government officials who, when the technology was in its infancy, beguiled the public with promises of unlimited, safe energy that would be so cheap there would be no need to meter its use.

In fact, atomic power production is still in its infancy—having been rushed into use before even one permanent disposal site for its wastes had been chosen. No safe disposal site has yet been found; even so thousands of tons of deadly waste have accumulated throughout the world.

The rush to reap the dazzling benefits of nuclear power has left unanswered many very basic environmental questions that have been raised by this new technology. Like DDT, Thalidomide, Deldrin, asbestos, and a host of other destructive new technologies, nuclear power was put into use before all of its byproducts had been considered.

Bedazzled by the repeated promise of the Age of Science, we keep hoping that some wonderful miracle is just around the corner. Rather than take the time to weigh carefully the pros and cons of some new piece of technology, we have thus far allowed ourselves to be sold an endless stream of gadgets, processes, and inventions whose long-term effects, until recently, we have cared little about.

### Environmentalism and the Third World

Not surprisingly, many Third World leaders have been skeptical of the developed world's recent concern with environmentalism. They point out that just as the Third World has begun to demand its fair share of industry and industrial growth, it seems that the "haves" have found a new reason why the "have nots" shouldn't get a piece of the action.

"The rich began to talk about pollution when pollution became a danger for their children," commented one Third World intellectual. And a delegate from a developing country expressed the feelings of many others when he told the United Nations Conference on the Environment (Stockholm, 1972): "If pollution means jobs for my people, we welcome it."[18]

Yet in the years since the Stockholm Conference, environmental concern has become a worldwide phenomenon. This change is primarily due to the obvious harm that can be done by uncontrolled technology—even if that technology is only an axe that is used to fell too many trees—and because the concept of environmentalism has been broadened to include land use, water pollution, and desertification. Furthermore, some Third World leaders have been wise enough to realize that they should "learn from the mistakes of the industrialized countries," as a Nigerian official has put it.

Environmentalists have argued that one way in which we can learn from our mistakes is through not rushing to use untested technology that promises fantastic results but may bring in its wake a host of deadly side-effects. A new movement has developed to find and use what some call "intermediate" technology, and others call "alternative" technology. Perhaps the best term in current use, however, is "appropriate" technology—since that, in fact, is what it is.

### Appropriate Technology

The easiest way to understand appropriate technology is to consider two examples of its use.

There is a great difference between a high-technology approach to fertilizer production and an appropriate technology approach. The appropriate technology might be a bio-gas fertilizer plant—essentially a storage tank that collects human and animal wastes, and that uses the natural process of decomposition to produce methane gas and a fertilizer, which is full of nutrients and generally free of disease-carrying organisms.

This bio-gas converter can be installed in a village or in a person's backyard. The gas that it produces can be used for cooking or heating, and the fertilizer is inexpensive compared to purchasing commercial nutrients. In addition to the savings and the generation of energy, this technology is also more environmentally sound. Human and animal wastes are collected and purified, rather than dumped as raw sewage into waters and streams. And in cases where dried cow dung is burned as a fuel, the methane gas substitute is less polluting and less harmful to the health of the people in huts who would have inhaled the smoke from the burning dung.

This technology is being tried in India and in other Third World countries. China was so impressed with the possibilities of bio-gas technology that it trained one hundred thousand bio-gas technicians in the mid-1970s and sent them out to develop local units across the country. By May 1977 there were 4.3 million units in operation, saving the average family forty days of work a year, and appreciably reducing family fuel costs.[19]

A second example of appropriate technology is in the development of substitutes for DDT and other insecticides. When DDT was first on the market, it was hailed as a miracle spray that would rid farmers of pests that attacked their crops, and which would eradicate disease-carrying mosquitoes. This latter problem was most obvious in the case of malaria, a disease which afflicted 200 million people in 1955, and caused 2 million deaths annually.

When DDT was used to kill the larvae of the mosquitoes, its effects were so dramatic that some health officials thought the disease might be eradicated completely. Yet the illness began to reappear in significant numbers in the mid-1960s, and rampaged through some areas in the 1970s. In India, for example, reported cases went from 40,000 in 1966 to 1.4 million in 1972 to 6 million in 1976.

The reason was because the mosquitoes had developed a genetic resistance to the insecticide, as had agricultural pests which attacked crops in greater numbers after they had adapted to DDT. The choices that farmers and health officials faced were to spray more heavily, to find new and even more deadly pesticides, or to find some alternative method for dealing with harmful insects. Faced with the ecological damage to animals and humans that is caused by DDT and other pesticides, some countries are turning to appropriate technology for methods of dealing with the problem.

One approach is to use "habitat management." The mosquito larvae live in water. So draining swamps and stagnant water or changing the saltiness of the water or flushing out the irrigation trenches with fresh water from time to time will kill the larvae. Certain species of fish who eat larvae can also be introduced into the waters. There are available in nature microbes and parasitic disease agents which can be used to attack the mosquitoes.[20]

Similarly, farmers are learning to use techniques that combine changes in planting times, rotation of crops, and the use of "bug-versus-bug" strategies for insect control. New seeds that produce pest-resistant plants are also being developed.

Ecologist and physicist Amory Lovins has applied appropriate technology in planning for energy needs in the developing countries. He suggests that there are two paths to energy sufficiency. The "hard" path involves nuclear plants, national energy grids, huge capital investments, increased use of coal, and continued use of oil and gas until they run out completely. It requires an enormous outlay of money, the construction of mammoth centralized energy plants, the reliance of the citizenry on the "wisdom" of sophisticated energy technocrats, and, in general, the increased centralization of life. This path spreads pollution, urbanization, and alienation in its wake, and gives vast political power to the industrial-government-military elite.

The "soft" path, on the other hand, is based on renewable or inexhaustible resources—like the sun, the wind, and vegetation. It is locally installable and comprehensible to the average citizen. It does not require the same huge capital investments, nor the armies of inaccessible experts, nor the centralization of decision-making. It is flexible, clean, and democratic (that is, it orients the society toward local decision-making and community initiative). Lovins suggests that the energy path we choose will determine much of the future shape and quality of our life—not just in terms of pollution, but in the very makeup and organization of our communities and our political structures.[21]

The astute person with an ecological bent will recognize that appropriate technology may be something that *developed* countries could well consider for their own use. After all, one of its hallmarks is the use of local, renewable resources—and the use of renewable energy (or lessened use of non-renewable energy). Thus, the solar heating of homes and the use of corn husks for fuel in a manufacturing plant are innovations that the developed and developing worlds alike could use.

In his landmark environmental essay, *The Closing Circle*, ecologist Barry Commoner showed that most of the rich world's pollution crisis was caused not by over-consumption, but by the use of "high" technology in modern industry. The manufacture of synthetic fibers, for instance, requires more fuel and produces more waste than the use of cotton or wool—both renewable sources. Or the use of aluminum, which is not biodegradable and uses more fuel to produce than does steel or wood. Or the mushrooming use of chemical fertilizers while human and animal waste become a "disposal" problem rather than a useful resource. Commoner calculates that these various technologies have increased pollution at a tenfold rate, while consumption has only doubled.[22]

In the conceptual focus of "basic needs" and "appropriate technology" we can find goals for the future of both rich and poor countries. As oil-dependent and polluting nations redesign their industrial-economic framework, perhaps they will meet the developing nations somewhere in the middle. Somewhere between the oxcart and the nuclear power plant there would appear to lie a more sane, "soft" path into the future for all of humankind.

## Global Watch

If agricultural methodology and industrial design become less environmentally damaging in the future, then we can look forward to a lessening of the pollution crisis and a humane existence that is in harmony with the rest of the planet; but this will not come about solely through the good intentions and heightened awareness of individuals and managers. So long as there is a dollar or a yen or some other advantage gained by cutting corners and ignoring long-term consequences, there will be people who will engage in environmentally damaging activities.

Sometimes there are not such clear-cut situations as whether to dump mercury poison in the waters or not. Shall a mountain be dug up for its coal? Shall a river be dammed for its ability to irrigate and power a hydro-electric plant? Shall a pesticide that might save crops for hungry mouths not be used because of what it will do to people forty years from now?

These are not easy choices to make. With some of the choices—nuclear power and use of pesticides, for example—the whole planet may have a stake in the path that is chosen.

Pollution does not recognize national boundaries. Sometimes it may be enough that a nation or a community is responsible for making a choice or regulating a piece of technology. Other times the whole globe may legitimately be concerned. In my section on the work of the United Nations I will discuss the global efforts that are underway to meet this global problem—efforts that deserve the support of us all.

### *NOTES*

1. Karen Junkerman, "Minamata, An Ongoing Struggle," *AMPO*: Japan-Asia Quarterly Review, Oct./Dec., 1975 (Tokyo: Pacific-Asia Resource Center), pp. 62–63.

2. Donald G. McNeil, Jr., "Reporter's Notebooks: Niagara Olfactory Impact," *New York Times*, Aug. 9, 1978.

3. Pamela G. Hallie, "Curbs on Dumping of Industry Waste Grow," *New York Times*, March 22, 1978.

4. Junkerman, "Minamata, An Ongoing Struggle."

5. Matsuoka Nobuo, "Fisherman's Armada, Polluting Companies Blockaded," *AMPO*, Autumn 1973, pp. 42–47.

6. "Minamata Disease in Canada," An Interview with Ui Jun, *AMPO*, Oct./Dec., 1975, pp. 65–69.

7. Philip Taubman, "U.S. Prepares to Sue Hooker Corp. on Dumping of Hazardous Wastes," *New York Times*, May 21, 1979.

8. Inove Sumio, "Exporting Pollution," *AMPO*, Autumn 1973, pp. 39–41.

9. News report on National Public Radio's "All Things Considered," Oct. 19, 1978.

10. *The State of the Environment, 1978*, A UNEP booklet (Oxford, U.K.: Pergamon Press, 1978) p. 7.

11. Ibid., pp. 14–15.

12. Anthony Wolff, "Fragile Lands," *RF Illustrated* (a publication of the Rockefeller Foundation, New York), September, 1978.

13. "Deforestation and Disaster," *Time*, May 22, 1978, p. 95.

14. Flora Lewis, "In Europe, the Nuclear Debate Looms Even Larger," *New York Times*, Week in Review, April 8, 1979.

15. Sue Branford, "Nuclear Power Is Not a Blessing to Brazil," in the *Observer* (London); reprinted in the *Asahi Evening News* (Japan), August 29, 1979.

16. Lewis, "In Europe"; see also "Exports to the Rescue of U.S. Nuclear Firms," a letter by Philip M. Stern to the *New York Times*, April 8, 1979.

17. David Burnham, "U.S. Study Analyzes Soviet Atom Mishap," *New York Times*, Feb. 14, 1980.

18. Whitman Bassow, "The Third World: Changing Attitudes Toward Environmental Protection," in the *Annals of the American Academy of Political and Social Science,* July, 1979.

19. Dennis Hayes, "Energy for Development: Third World Options," Worldwatch Paper #15, a publication of the Worldwatch Institute, Washington, D.C., Dec., 1977, pp. 30–31.

20. *The State of the Environment, 1978,* op. cit., pp. 13–17.

21. Armory B. Lovins, *Soft Energy Paths* (Cambridge, Mass.: Ballinger Publishing Co., 1977).

22. Barry Commoner, *The Closing Circle* (New York: Bantam, 1972), pp. 143–144.

## Chapter V

# Arms and Militarism

*A siren sounded. As its wail grew in intensity, thousands of people, their bodies twisted and crumpling in a mock death agony, sank to the ground. For a minute, two, then five, there was no sound. Over five thousand people lay heaped on the concrete, experiencing the stunning reality of modern mass death.*

*The bodies lay on the plaza in front of the United Nations. Inside the U.N. building, delegates from the far corners of the earth had gathered to consider one of humankind's most fateful questions: the modern arms race. The occasion was the Special Session of the U.N. General Assembly on Disarmament, a first-of-its-kind event that reflected the growing concern of nations large and small for the world's collective safety in the face of our growing capacity for mega-death.*

*Mega-death. A phrase that means the killing of millions upon millions of people—an ability that the world's most militarily advanced nations now possess in arsenals that could wreak incomprehensible destruction in a matter of minutes.*

*After the silence was over, a tiny bell sounded, and the five thousand dead rose to life again. Their "die-in" had been part of a larger peace gathering that had tried to add a sense of urgency to the deliberations inside.*

*If a nuclear bomb had in fact hit Manhattan—one bomb of twenty megatons—seven million people would have died instantly. A hole twenty stories deep and half a mile wide would have been blasted out, and winds of one thousand miles an hour would have lashed out from the center. A huge firestorm would have reduced the rest of the city to cinders, and people forty miles away would have suffered first degree burns. The fallout from the bomb would have covered an area of 4,800 square miles, killing perhaps millions of others—some in great agony—and devastating the land.*

*That would be the effect of one bomb of twenty megatons. The world stockpile of nuclear weapons is now about 50,000 megatons—enough to make 2,500 such bombs.*[1]

## Nuclear Madness

The reality of modern nuclear warfare is so astonishing, so barbaric, so absurd, that it is almost impossible to comprehend. Our legitimate concern with the pollution caused by factory smokestacks and city sewage seems insignificant compared to what pollution and destruction could be wrought by forty minutes of nuclear war. Our alarm over the cancer-producing tendencies of modern food additives seems to be reduced to nothing in the face of a world where every child is born with 25,000 pounds of dynamite earmarked for its sole destruction.*

From any angle, the degree of global militarization and overkill capacity is absolutely insane. So insane that even the word "insane" is too mild to describe it. Perhaps "mega-insane"?

Yet it is just such mega-insanity that occupies the thinking of top military planners in the United States and the Soviet Union, each wondering whether it has more survivability than the other, or if it has a nuclear capability "that inflicts more damage on the opposition than it can inflict on you."[2]

The danger posed by nuclear war is almost impossible to comprehend. One recent simulation of a full-scale nuclear exchange estimates that 140 million Americans and 113 million Soviets would die as a result.[3] The United Nations has estimated that an attack of 20,000 megatons on the United States would eventually kill as much as 95 percent of the population.[4] What does survivability mean after such a holocaust?

Even if there is never an exchange of nuclear weapons, the conduct of the arms race and the maintenance of military establishments does damage daily to every citizen on this planet. Day in and day out, billions are being spent on arms and the military—money that is desperately needed for the planet's true needs. Not only is money wasted, but precious resources are consumed, both national resources and the resources of the human mind.

From 1945 to 1976, the world expended six *trillion* dollars on arms and the military (in 1975 dollars).[5] Each year the world's military expenditures ($350 billion in 1976) equals the annual income of the 1.8 billion people who live in the poorest nations.[6] Right now, over 400,000 engineers and scientists in the world are engaged in direct military research, and they represent 25 percent of the planet's scientific workforce.[7]

Imagine if this kind of money and this kind of brainpower were devoted to solving the problems of hunger, disease, and pollution!

Ruth Leger Sivard, a researcher for the Rockefeller Foundation, has tried to imagine what could be done with just 5 percent of the world's military budget for 1976—a mere $17.5 billion. Here are some of the ways that this money could be put to good use, with an annual price tag attached to each item:

*50,000 megatons = 100,000,000,000,000,000 lbs. of dynamite.

—A vaccination program to give protection against infectious diseases to all infants. ($600 million)

—A program to extend literacy to all adults by the end of the century. ($1.2 billion)

—A preventive and community-oriented training program for a sharp increase in the numbers of medical auxiliaries. ($250 million)

—Increased development aid to improve the capacity of the Third World to grow its own food and prevent malnutrition. ($3 billion)

—An expanded minimum-shelter program, incorporating self-help construction, for the urban poor. ($750 million)

—Supplementary feeding to insure full development for 200 million malnourished children. ($4 billion)

—Supplementary feeding for 60 million malnourished pregnant and lactating women to protect their health and reduce infant mortality. ($1.5 billion)

—Major increase in the number of primary schools, with the addition of 100 million new places. ($3.2 billion)

—Hygienic water supply systems, toward the goal of clean water for all humanity by 1990. ($3 billion)[8]

Quite a shopping list! Yet it represents only 5 percent of world military spending. What a different world we would have if the nations were willing to devote only a portion of their military expenditures to social projects; but the sad fact remains that the rich nations who make these huge outlays claim that they "can't afford" to give more for development aid, and thus a worthwhile program like the World Health Organization's plan to eradicate malaria in the world (total cost: $450 million) is dragging due to lack of funds.[9]

Let us now turn to a consideration in greater depth of the political realities that lie behind the military expenditures of both developed and developing countries, taking special note of the role that the United States plays in this deadly drama.

### The Deadly Triangle

As the year 1984 approaches, an endless succession of articles will assault the public, each one claiming that "1984" can be found here, there—everywhere. Perhaps nowhere will the prophecies seem more true than in the area of global great-power rivalry. Writing in the 1940s, George Orwell foresaw a world divided between three superpowers: Oceania, Eurasia, and Eastasia. These three giants make war with each other in alternating alliances of two against one; thus last year's foe may be today's gallant ally.

Orwell's three powers are, of course, rather thinly disguised portraits of China, the Soviet Union, and the United States–Western Europe. Thus, when Chinese Prime Minister Deng Xiao-ping made his historic visit to the United States in January 1978—during which time he donned a ten-gallon hat, ate barbecue, denounced Soviet hegemony, and was rewarded with a national poll that showed that Americans liked China a whole lot better than the Soviet Union—one can say that Orwell's prediction came in right on cue.

It is now fairly easy to predict that the rest of the century will be taken up with the power struggle between China, the Soviet Union, and the United States. In this version of "The Great Game," virtually every area of the world becomes a battleground for military, economic, or diplomatic struggle. As the Balkans were an area of constant rivalry between the European powers in the nineteenth and early twentieth centuries, so now does every non-aligned area become Balkan-like in its potential for turmoil.

The Soviet invasion of Afghanistan brought this situation into a harsh light. I was working in the international selection of a large humanitarian organization, and as the world began to respond to the shock of the Soviet invasion, reports of anxiety and shifting power alignments began to pour in from all corners: Western Europe was fearful of what might happen in Yugoslavia; Israel was worried that the United States would force it into an unfavorable settlement with the Palestinian Arabs—because of our eagerness to win Arab friends in the Middle East; India feared our rearmament of Pakistan; China searched for new military technology to offset the Soviet-India alliance; Cuba lost a chance for a United Nations Security Council seat because of its closeness to Soviet policy; on and on the shock waves traveled.

Everywhere in the media there was talk of war. Analogies were made with Hitler's March into Austria, with Mussolini's invasion of Ethiopia, with the Japanese invasion of Manchuria. All of a sudden the Salt II agreement was on the shelf, the U.S. military was being granted its most optimistic Christmas wish list, the Indian Ocean was transformed from a potential zone of peace into a zone of war. All because the Soviet Union had moved into a barren borderland of mountains and desert.

Afghanistan was no plum for the Soviet Union—far more likely is it to be a quagmire—but the invasion showed how delicate is the balance between the global giants.

"When you live in the sea, you must accommodate to the whales," Pakistan's General Zia told Western reporters who had asked him what he planned to do with the Soviets on his doorstep. The Afghanistan crisis showed that, in reality, all of us are living in dread of the whales—including the average citizen of the United States, or the USSR or China. Whether one lives in the belly of the whale, or simply nearby, a major lurch of the leviathan can harm us all.

### The Chinese Potential

There is a significant disparity between our three world giants, however. In *1984*, each of the three powers was a match for the other; this is not true—not yet—of the real world's Big Three.

In the real world of megatonnage and electronic delivery systems, China is very much a third-rate power. While the Big Two have been able to spend $2 trillion on "defense" in the 1960–75 period, China—with a GNP similar to that of Italy's—spent the equivalent of $130 billion.[10] Though China does have a small force of nuclear bombs and missiles that can reach as far as the European USSR and Australia, these weapons-carriers are considered by the CIA to be fifteen to twenty years behind U.S.-USSR technology. In fact, most Chinese weapons—whether rifles or bombs—are copies of weapons that were built by the Big Two in the 1950s. China's navy is also not competitive with that of either the United States or the USSR.[11]

At present, China is absolutely no threat to the continental United States. Nor is China much of a rival—in arms—for the Soviet Union. But what China lacks in arms, it makes up in numbers of troops, so many (3.4 million regulars) and so well trained that the CIA concedes that either of the superpowers "would be unable to totally overwhelm the PRC on Chinese soil."[12] The Soviet Union obviously regards the Chinese as a threat—if not to the whole country, then to portions along their huge common border. To defend against this threat, and to pose a counter-threat, the USSR has 650,000 soldiers stationed along the border, including six armored divisions, and large stocks of nerve gas. Nine percent of its offensive missiles, and 16 percent of its defensive missiles are aimed at China.[13]

The real danger posed by China, however, lies in the future. During 1978, China began actively bidding for modern military technology from the West. In a reversal of a long-standing U.S. position, President Carter accepted a "neutral" stance toward military sales to China by our European allies. This resulted in sales of anti-tank and anti-aircraft missiles from France, and Harrier jet fighters from Britain.[14] In the wake of the Afghanistan crisis, the United States moved even closer to arming China, allowing direct U.S. sales of military equipment like trucks and radar, though still holding back on weapons sales. A secret Pentagon study "leaked" to the press surveyed, in lurid detail, what the United States might do if it decided to upgrade China's military. The Pentagon thought it could do a pretty fair job of increasing China's defense capabilities for a modest $63 billion, including in that package 8,600 medium tanks, 10,000 armored personnel carriers, 6,000 air-to-air missiles, 240 fighter-bombers, and so on.[15]

Unlikely? As Orwell suggested, very little is unlikely in the deadly triangle. It was only yesterday that the Chinese were considered a deadly menace. As one scholar put it, "the public image of China was altogether portrayed in livid primary colors: a red nation of blue ants programmed to sweep over the world like a yellow peril."[16]

Then it all changed. Richard Nixon, a man who had built his career on anticommunism, did a complete about-face by personally extending the hand of friendship to that archrevolutionary, Mao Zedong.

Today the United States and China are friends—or at least quasi-friends—a relationship cemented by a mutual antipathy to the Soviet Union and by Chinese admiration of western technology.

But tomorrow? In *1984,* Orwell portrayed a three-power system in which today's friend was tomorrow's enemy, and vice versa. In the warm glow of our "China card" triumphs in foreign policy, some observers have suggested that China has a "Russian card" that they can play on us. That is, China could decide to shift to more friendly relations with the Soviet Union, and all of a sudden the deadly triangle would be loaded against us.

## The Big Two

Regardless of China's long-run potential, the major military rivalry in the world remains that between the United States and the USSR. The Cold War between these two powers has been such a fixture of modern existence that it seems hardly possible to believe that we were once—however briefly— friends.

The high spot of that friendship was, of course, World War II. The Soviet Union became our valiant ally, pitted desperately against the German onslaught, fighting heroically at Stalingrad, suffering losses and privations in the Allied effort. In a Bicentennial assessment of U.S.-Soviet relations, former Ambassador George F. Kennan described the rather abrupt change in public image that World War II brought:

> Gone, as if by magic, were most of the memories and impressions of the past. Forgotten, now, were the Russian purges, along with the reflection that the men now running Russia's war effort and diplomacy were the same who had conducted those bloody persecutions. Forgotten, too, were the cruelties only recently perpetrated by Beriya's police establishment upon the innocent population of Eastern Poland and the Baltic states. . . . In place of all this there emerged, and was systematically cultivated in Washington, the image of the great Soviet people, animated by the same noble impulses of humane indignation and yearning for a future free of all tyranny by which Americans conceived themselves and their allies to be animated, fighting with inspiring heroism and grandeur against an opponent in whose repulsive political personality all the evil of an imperfect world seemed to be concentrated.[17]

But the glow didn't last very long. After all, the U.S.-Soviet-British alliance was a rather unlikely triangle in the first place. U.S. capitalists and Soviet communists had conceived a mutual suspicion from the very beginning of the Russian revolution in 1917, though common interest in slowing Japanese expansion in Asia had finally caused the Roosevelt Administration to "recognize" the Soviet regime in 1933. The British and the Americans seem fairly natural together, but in the interwar years they were in intense economic rivalry as the world's chief capitalist contenders. In fact, some historians have made the case that the United States was far more distrustful of British post-war economic and territorial ambitions than it was of Soviet ambitions—at least in the early stages of the Alliance. There is no question that Roosevelt often felt he and Stalin saw eye to eye against an obstinate

Churchill. As for British-Soviet relations, it is generally agreed that each country regarded the other as an archrival in the interwar period, and that neither would have been saddened to see Germany fight the other to a bloody standstill.

The Allied victory in 1945 marked the beginning of a new era in international relations. Germany, Italy, and Japan were occupied and defeated. The Free French had played a gallant, but peripheral role in the victory, and owed their renewed lease to the Big Three. China—the part controlled by Chiang Kai-shek—was corrupt, militarily weak, and considered by most to be a vassal of the United States.

Of the three main victors, the United States came out of the war in the best position. Our economy had recovered from the Depression, and we even had $29 billion in gold reserves—77 percent of the entire world's reserves. Our principal economic rival, Great Britain, was in a shambles. Britain had started the war as an internationl lender with $16 billion in its portfolio. It ended the war $12 billion in debt. Its gold reserves were a mere $12 *million*. Its factories were either bombed out or in a great state of wear. Britain could no longer afford to keep up its 1.4 million-member army or its vast navy, nor could it afford its formal and informal empire. In fact, without substantial U. S. economic assistance, Great Britain could hardly have stayed afloat at all.[18]

The Soviet Union also emerged from the war badly crippled. Twenty million of its people had died in the war, a calamity of stunning proportions. Many of its cities had been destroyed, as had a large number of its factories. The task of rebuilding was enormous.

Militarily, there was no question as to who had emerged with the greatest strength. The United States had assembled a huge war machine with 17.3 million men and women in its ranks; we had a large and modern air force and navy; we had an intact industrial base and good supply lines, and we had the Bomb. The Bomb, of course, was nothing compared to the arsenal we now possess, but to American planners it was a superweapon, and its possession was said to have given "an entirely new feeling of confidence" to President Truman in his conduct of foreign policy vis-à-vis the Soviet Union. As the American statesman Bernard Baruch put it, "America can get what she wants if she insists on it. After all, we've got it—the bomb—and they haven't and won't have it for a long time to come."[19]

Somewhere in the middle of the hot war of 1939–45 the "cold" war between the United States and the USSR began. The standard American version, of course, is that the Soviet Union returned to its diabolical crusade to spread communism—as evidenced by its "swallowing" of Eastern Europe and the surprising (but predictable) victory of Mao's communism in China. In fact, tension between the Allies during the war over a division of the spoils—who would control Italy, who would control Greece, what about Iran's oil—was so great that many people thought that immediate war between the United States and the Soviet Union was likely. As General Andrew

Goodpaster put it, describing the birth of the NATO alliance, the question on the military's mind was not "Will there be a war?" but instead, "In what month will war start?"[20]

A "revisionist" view of the Cold War often stresses the U.S. determination to assert a Pax Americana all over the globe. The Soviet Union, it is claimed, had an interest only in a defense zone around its European borders—from which it had been attacked repeatedly—and thus it moved to assure friendly governments in Poland, Czechoslovakia, East Germany, and so on. Aggressive America, however, wouldn't stand for such reasonable requests (after all, we had moved to assure "friendly" governments in the Caribbean for years) and, emboldened by the Bomb, decided to roll back the Soviet hold in Europe.

However one decides to place the blame for the Cold War—and, of course, there is also a "both sides are guilty" school of thought—the central fact that emerged from the war was a world divided into two camps, one dominated by the United States and one dominated by the USSR.

And—to show that Orwell didn't get his ideas from thin air—the public image of the Soviet Union in America again changed overnight:

> Unrequited love now turned only too easily to unreasonable hatred. . . . The real personality of Russia, in all its vast complexity, was often lost to view; and in its place, assuming in many respects the aspect of the late-departed Hitler, there emerged one of those great and forbidding apparitions to the credence in which mass opinion is so easily swayed: a monster devoid of all humanity and of all rationality of motive, at once the embodiment and the caricature of evil, devoid of internal conflicts and problems of its own, intent only on bringing senseless destruction to the lives and the hopes of others.[21]

Those of us who have lived through the era of détente have had a chance to experience a similar turn of public opinion from Cold War to "thaw" to Cold War again. Two days after the Soviet invasion of Afghanistan I was rather humorously reminded of this abrupt change when a letter arrived in the mail. "Greetings from Moscow!" it said on the outside, and on the inside was a computer letter urging me to subscribe to *Sputnik* magazine. "Every issue of *Sputnik*," I was told, "is like a trip to the Soviet Union." A self-addressed postage-paid reply card was enclosed for my convenience.

Obviously the Soviet Ministry of Information was taking a cue from the capitalist direct mail experts. Like everybody else, they had no doubt rented a mailing list from some magazine, and like everybody else they had enclosed a glossy four-color pamphlet that told their story—it even had a pretty blonde on the cover in a bathing suit!

One wishes that the ups and downs of U.S.-Soviet relations were always so harmlessly apparent. One wishes that bullets and bombs weren't part of the picture.

## The Arms Race

Surprisingly, both sides in the Cold War began their post-World War II struggle with a mutual disarmament. The United States kept its strong navy and air force, and its worldwide string of bases, but its ground forces shrank to 670,000 men and women by 1947. The Soviets also demobilized, going from 11.3 million under arms to 2.8 million.[22]

As the Cold War continued, however, both sides began to rearm. The Soviet Union, while pooh-poohing the atomic bomb, went on a crash program to develop its own, and by 1954 had a stockpile of 200 warheads (the United States had 600).[23] Both sides began with bombers as their chief means of weapons delivery, but as the race went on they graduated to inter-continental ballistic missiles (ICBMs) capable of striking a target in either country within scant minutes after launching. By 1960 the United States and USSR were each spending about $40 billion annually on defense, and by 1970 it was generally conceded that the USSR had reached parity with the United States in terms of nuclear destructive capability.[24]

Today, each side possesses a sufficient arsenal of bombers, missile-launching submarines, and ICBMs to reduce the other side to ashes. In fact, each side has an insane overkill capacity, as though it wants to stir the rubble four or five or ten times over.

For instance, just one U.S. missile-carrying submarine can launch nuclear warheads against 160 to 224 Soviet targets. This alone would be a devastation of life and property beyond anything ever known in human history. Yet the United States has forty-one of these submarines, and is planning for new ones that are each capable of launching 408 warheads.[25] On the Soviet side, one land-based missile is capable of delivering eight or ten warheads to U.S. sites. At last count the USSR had 1,477 of these missiles. A recent strategic study has estimated that both sides together may possess 29,000 long-range nuclear weapons by 1985.[26]

Since a force of 500 such weapons would be sufficent to bomb either side into total ruination, it may be wondered why both sides continue to arm at such a feverish pitch (the stockpile of nuclear weapons doubled from 1972 to 1977).[27] The answer, in miltary theory, is that each side wants to make sure the other is deterred by its weighty arsenal. So long as both sides are convinced that even with a massive and unexpected attack the other would still be capable of retaliating with unharmed missiles and causing unacceptable destruction, then neither will be tempted to use the weapons. This is referred to as "mutually assured deterrance" or, appropriately, MAD.

The danger, we are told by military spending advocates, is that one side or the other might arm sufficiently to allow for a first strike that would totally wipe out the other's capacity to respond. For instance, what if the USSR were able to launch an attack that caught all of our missiles in the ground and destroyed them, stopped most of our bombers, and sank most of our subs?

On top of that, they evacuate their urban population to the woods so that we can't kill as many as we thought we could in retaliation? All of these what-ifs are highly implausible—most would say impossible—but preparedness advocates on both sides make their careers by worrying about what the other side might be even remotely capable of doing.

For example, U.S. hawks have generally favored the development of the MX missile system, a $60 billion project that would tear up large chunks of Nevada and Utah in order to place 200 missiles on undergound tracks where they would be shuttled over an area of 25,000 square miles in order to escape detection. This proposal in turn gives Soviet hawks new reasons to argue for a greater build-up on their side.

Students of both countries have suggested that each nation is saddled with a cancerous "military-industrial complex" that constantly yearns for more dollars or more rubles, for more power and more prestige. On the U.S. side, most of us are familiar with the interconnections between the military and the large corporations. With an annual procurement budget that has risen to over $40 billion, the Defense Department finds it easy to make and keep influential friends in the business community. Major business contractors in turn farm out subcontracts to hundreds of smaller firms throughout the country—firms that can be counted on to lobby their local member of Congress if cuts are threatened. "Of course I'm in favor of military budget cuts," our local Congressperson told us recently, "but you talk to a representative from Florida where they've got two military bases in his district, or a Senator from Washington State where they've got Boeing and see what *they* tell you." As he shared his sentiments with us, he and the rest of the Philadelphia congressional delegation were fighting tooth and nail with the Virginia delegation to get the contract for refurbishing the USS *Saratoga*.

Interestingly enough, the Soviet Union's military-industrial complex appears to be equally formidable in national politics. Helmut Sonnenfeldt, formerly a top Kissinger aide, has suggested that every time there is a crisis in leadership in the Soviet Union, as when Stalin died or Khrushchev was deposed, the military plays a substantial kingmaker role in the inter-bureaucratic wrangling for power. He finds a great increase in new military programs after the succession is firmed, by way of payoff to the military. He concludes, "It seems fair to say that none of Stalin's successors could consolidate or even attain power against the sustained opposition of the military elite."[28]

Some analysts have even suggested that in the bureaucratic struggle for a share of national resources, the military on both sides often—deliberately or not—support each other's interests. Commenting on the dubious value of the 1974 Vladivostok arms limitation agreement, the *New York Times* editorialized: "[it] appears to be an agreement between the military on both sides—achieved through the intermediaries of the chiefs of government—to permit the buildups each desired. . . ."[29]

Richard Barnet, author of *The Giants*, has this opinion:

The military establishments in the United States and the Soviet Union are no doubt each other's best allies. The Soviets accommodate Pentagon budget planners by surfacing submarines, parading a new weapons system in Red Square, or writing bellicose articles in military journals. (Some Congressional doves are convinced of a conspiracy.) Soviet military planners in turn, a Soviet general once told me, feed on the bellicose statements and extravagant budget projections that emanate from time to time from the Pentagon.[30]

In the meantime, we common citizens are left with two military establishments armed to the teeth and hungry for more. And the entire world has to live with the danger that some confrontation, or a mistake, will launch a global war that would rain radioactive death on all of us. Plus we and the Soviets continue to spend enormous quantities on arms—money that could be far better spent on social needs.

Some people argue that mutual deterrence may not be such a bad state of affairs. Both sides, they say, would be mad to pull the nuclear trigger, and thus we have reached a state of balanced terror in which global war is unthinkable. But what will happen to the nuclear balance when China becomes a full-fledged power? Behind China there are some fifteen other countries that already possess enough fissionable material to produce their own atomic bombs.[31] Surely we need to put a stop to the arms race before it is too late.

### The Third World

How has the Third World fared in the midst of the Big Power competition? For one thing, the very term "Third World" was coined to express the collective existence of countries that didn't want to line up on the U.S. side (the ("First World")) or the Soviet side (the "Second World"). Since the Third—or nonaligned—World also happened to overlap significantly with the poorer nations of the globe, the term has continued in usage.

The term "Third World" should serve to remind us that in the post World War II era, the competition between the two camps was so severe that a vast portion of the globe found itself buffeted between one side and the other.

After World War II, the United States embarked upon a policy of "containing" the Soviet Union. Having stepped into the British imperial shoes in the Mediterranean and in Southeast Asia, we soon began supporting the colonial and neo-colonial status quo. When independence-minded leaders arose in the colonial countries, they often found themselves opposed by U.S. foreign policy—especially if their leaders had been in any way inspired by the example of the Soviet or Chinese revolutions, and most especially if they threatened to challenge the role of our multinational corporations in their local economies. The United States was now the guardian of global capitalism, and we didn't want anybody upsetting our apple carts (or copper concessions, or oil deals, or investments).

As anti-communist John Foster Dulles put it, with 1.6 billion people in the Third World exposed to communism, a large scale infection might shift the world balance "to a one-to-three ratio against freedom." "That," he went on to say, "would be an almost intolerable ratio given the industrialized nature of the Atlantic community and its dependence upon broad markets and access to raw materials."[32]

With freedom as the moral cover for access to raw materials, the United States pursued a policy in the post-war era that was deliberately designed to support leaders in the Third World who would be convinced of the nobility of being on our side. To this end we gave strings-attached aid, supported and maintained military coups, supported counter-guerrilla wars in Indochina and Africa, and—when necessary—launched full-scale military invasions of countries like Vietnam and the Dominican Republic. Not surprisingly, the Soviet Union countered with covert and overt attempts to win friends and keep its Eastern European status quo intact. China, too, has entered the international competition in various ways, though its influence has been felt more as an example of Third World development than through large-scale aid or covert operations.

There have been some decided advantages for the Third World as a result of the Big Power competition. A multi-polar world means that many countries have room to maneuver one side against another, playing this one against that for favors or protection. Certainly the U.S.-Soviet competition for Third World affection had a positive impact on decolonization, and it may well have kept economic aid at higher levels than they otherwise might have been.

There are also negative sides to the competition. The devastation of Vietnam went far beyond that of a "normal" civil war because of Big Power intervention on both sides. Cuba found that the Soviet Union could be a friend in need, even a protector for its revolution, yet the subsequent U.S. economic boycott has seriously hurt Cuba's economy. Czechoslovakia found that its room to experiment with liberalization was severely hampered by its status as a Soviet client. Chile learned that the United States would, even after détente, "not sit idly by" and watch a former client "go communist," as former Secretary of State Kissinger expressed it.

In addition to the terrible waste of world resources and brain power that is sunk into the arms race—money and time that could be infinitely better used to solve the world's real problems—the Third World is also suffering because it is increasingly being encouraged to arm by the competing superpowers, and by greedy arms merchants (often these very same governments).

In 1955 the total number of jet combat aircraft supplied to the Third World numbered about one thousand planes, most of them cast-offs. By 1975 there were 11,000 combat planes in the Third World, many of them of the most modern make. The number of tanks in 1955 was about 2,500; by 1975 the inventory was nearly 25,000. The value of weapons shipped to the Third World increased from $1 billion in 1956, to $8 billion in 1975 (in constant 1975 dollars).[33]

The greatest bulk of this aid has gone to the Middle East, that perennial hot spot. A full 50 percent of military imports have been shipped to that region, an increase of 800 percent since 1956. The greatest leap, however, has occurred in Sub-Saharan Africa, from $1 million in 1956 to $432 million in 1976, showing that big power competition can raise the military stakes rapidly in an area of new interest.[34]

The United States heads the list of arms merchants, with cumulative sales (1961–75) of $40.9 billion,[35] and with current sales to the Third World running at a brisk $8 billion a year.[36] The Soviet Union, by comparison, comes in at a cumulative $26.5 billion; and France, the United Kingdom, and China all have total sales of less than $4 billion in that fourteen year period.[37]

These sales consist of modern jets, tanks, medium-range missiles, naval ships, helicopters, modern rifles, tear gas, electronic equipment, cluster bombs, chemical agent rockets, and so on. Not a very nice array of things to be giving our friends to fling at their neighbors, and an altogether dangerous way to cement alliances.

Commenting on the U.S. package-deal decision in 1978 to sell advanced jets to Egypt, Saudi Arabia, and Israel, Russell Baker of the *New York Times* asked humorously why we couldn't show these countries we liked them by sending candy and chocolates? Or, he asked, what if we had locked the planes under guard at Fort Knox, and sent each country vouchers stating that they now had "fifty warplanes worth of American affection"?

Alas, Baker lamented, no one seems satisfied until they have tangible proof of our esteem. "In short, the only tenable policy for assuring people we like them is to help them shoot each other more efficiently."[38]

The sad aspect of arms sales to Third World countries is that these countries cannot in any way afford the luxuries of a modern armed force. Some countries are drawn into military purchases because their neighbors are arming themselves. Some are forced into such purchases by their own local military elites who want to be able to acquire prestige by possessing sophisticated armaments. Still others are drawn in because of the backdoor bribes that are available for compliant politicians.

For whatever reason, or combination of reasons, the poorest nations can little afford to get caught up in the arms race. A brief consideration of Iran— a country that is rich in comparison to most Third World nations—will illustrate this point.

From 1953, when our CIA helped restore Shah Mohammed Reza Pahlevi to the throne, until 1979, when his own people drove him from power, the United States regarded Iran as a significant ally. This long-term interest in the Shah received an added boost in the 1970s. Reacting to the quagmire of Vietnam, President Nixon proclaimed a new policy—dubbed the "Nixon Doctrine"—whereby the United States would rely on regional powers to police their own areas with the logistical support of the United States. The countries chosen for this role were Indonesia, Iran, Nigeria, and Brazil—none of them particularly noted for their democratic institutions or respect for human rights, but all of them noted for their pro-U.S. views.[39]

Iran ranked high in our esteem as a new influential country, and responded to our favors by supporting U.S. Middle East policy, shipping oil to Israel, allowing U.S. listening posts along the Soviet border, and leaving an open door to U.S. trade and investment. Iran also happened to have a lot of money, derived from the four-fold increase in oil prices that OPEC had decreed in 1973. It turned out that the Shah had an endless appetite for military equipment, so much so that Iran was spending two dollars on American products in the 1970s for every one dollar we spent on its oil.[40]

During the heyday of U.S. military sales to Iran, some $20 billion in arms, ammunition, and technical assistance was contracted (1950-1977).[41] In fact, over 25 percent of all U.S. sales abroad in that period were earmarked for Iran. What did the Shah buy? The list seemed endless: tear gas masks, armed helicopters, revolvers, hand grenades, F-14 *Tomcat* jet fighters, F-4E *Phantom* deep-strike fighter-bombers, *Spruance*-class heavy destroyers, *Tang*-class submarines, and so on.[42]

The Shah bought so much and so fast that his troops hardly had time to uncrate the goods, much less be properly trained in their use. Hence, the companies that sold the equipment were also granted contracts to train the Iranians for its use, and often used American employees to operate key parts of the package—such as radar. By the time the whole show came crashing down, the United States had thousands of military and para-military people in Iran, helping to keep the army active and the air force in the air.

In the meantime, the Shah and his secret police ran a tight ship, jailing, torturing, and executing those who opposed his policies or his dictatorial methods. As a new upper class of civil servants, business people, and military leaders enjoyed the fruits of this rapid modernization, the poorest peasants saw their country's oil being spent on bombs while they didn't even have clean drinking water. By 1974, Iran had become the seventh highest world power, in terms of military spending, but eighty-second in literacy, eighty-second in life expectancy at birth, and one-hundred-and-sixth in infant mortality per 1,000 live births out of a total of 138 countries. By way of contrast, Israel—which has been under a much greater military threat than Iran—spent only two-thirds of what Iran did on arms, was ninth in life expectacy at birth, and tied for first in literacy.[43]

Here in a nutshell can be seen the tragedy of military spending—the waste of precious resources, the displaced priorities, the inattention to social needs, the emphasis on the military and its needs and wishes, the atrophy of democracy, and the stifling of democratic aspirations. In the Third World today, some 40 percent of the countries find themselves under formal military rule, and even more are under some form of quasi-military dominance.[44]

Too often, the United States has looked to the military leaders of Third World countries to represent "our" interests. Too often have we supplied them with arms, trained their leaders, quietly whispered or even shouted our support for military coups. We, at least, are rich enough to afford an oversized military establishment—though we pay a price in inflation, unmet social needs, and potential nuclear destruction. But in the Third World, where every dollar spent in arms is a dollar not spent on the people's most basic needs for food, shelter, health needs—the cost is astronomical.

## *NOTES*

1. These figures are taken from the opening chapter of Richard McSorley, *Kill? For Peace?* (Washington, D.C.: The Center for Peace Studies, 1977).

2. Remarks of presidential candidate George Bush, quoted in Anthony Lewis, "Thinking About the Unthinkable," *New York Times*, Feb. 14, 1980.

3. Cited on the *ABC Evening News*, April 17, 1979.

4. McSorley, *Kill? For Peace?*, p. 17.

5. *Economic and Social Consequences of the Arms Race and of Military Expenditures*, Updated Report of the Secretary General (New York: United Nations, 1978), p. 24.

6. Ibid., p. 5.

7. Ibid., pp. 46, 28.

8. These examples are taken from Ruth Leger Sivard, *World Military and Social Expenditures, 1977* (New York: Rockefeller Foundation, 1977).

9. *Economic and Social Consequences*, p. 27.

10. Sivard, *World Military*, p. 7.

11. Testimony of Admiral Stansfield Turner and others, June–July 1978, reprinted in "Allocation of Resources in the Soviet Union and China—1977," Hearings of the Joint Economic Committee of the U.S. Congress, pp. 64–67.

12. Ibid., p. 67.

13. Drew Middleton, "China's Military Problems on Two Fronts," *New York Times*, Jan. 28, 1979; Drew Middleton, "Soviet-Vietnamese Treaty May Alter Sea Strategies," *New York Times*, Oct. 8, 1978.

14. David K. Shipler, "China Has People, U.S. Has Machines, Russia Has Fear," *New York Times*, Week in Review, Jan. 28, 1979.

15. Drew Middleton, "Pentagon Studies Prospect of Military Links with China," *New York Times*, Jan. 4, 1980.

16. Frederick Wakeman, Jr., "The Real China," *New York Review of Books*, June 21, 1978.

17. George F. Kennan, "The United States and the Soviet Union, 1917–1976," *Foreign Affairs*, July 1976, p. 678.

18. This description is taken from Sidney Lens, *The Forging of the American Empire* (New York: Thomas Y. Crowell, 1974), pp. 336–337.

19. Ibid., p. 343.

20. Richard Barnet, *The Giants: Russia and America* (New York: Simon and Shuster, 1978), p. 126.

21. Kennan, "The United States and the Soviet Union," p. 680.

22. Barnet, *The Giants*, p. 107.

23. Ibid., p. 108.

24. Ibid., pp. 112–113.

25. Ibid., p. 115.

26. Ibid., p. 102.

27. Ibid., p. 103.

28. Helmut Sonnenfeldt, "Russia, America, and Détente," *Foreign Affairs*, Jan. 1978, p. 277.

29. Cited in Barnet, *The Giants*, p. 104.

30. Ibid., p. 106.

31. "World Armaments, the Nuclear Threat," (Sweden: Stockholm International Peace Research Institute, 1977), p. 21.

32. Walter LaFeber, *America, Russia, and the Cold War, 1945-1966* (New York: John Wiley and Sons, 1967), p. 177.

33. "World Armaments," pp. 14, 15.

34. Ibid., p. 13.

35. Sivard, *World Military*, p. 9.

36. "Carter Cuts Back Exports of Arms," *New York Times,* Nov. 30, 1978.

37. Sivard, *World Military*, p. 9.

38. Russell Baker, "More Than Words Can Ever Say," *New York Times*, May 20, 1978.

39. Seymour M. Hersh, "Ex-Analyst Says CIA Rejected Warning on Shah," *New York Times*, Jan. 7, 1979.

40. Nicholas Gage, "U.S.-Iran Links Still Strong," *New York Times*, July 9, 1978.

41. "The Crisis in Iran." A background paper by the Institute for Policy Studies, 1978, p. 2. (Available from IPS, 1901 "Q" St. N.W., Washington, DC 20009.)

42. Ibid., p. 13.

43. Sivard, *World Military*, p. 11.

44. Ibid., p. 7.

# Chapter VI

# Social Injustice

Long before the nation state had assumed its present power, people in all parts of the world and throughout history often suffered oppression at the hands of others. Sometimes the basis of discrimination was race or color; sometimes it was ideology or belief; sometimes it was caste or economic position; sometimes it was because of one's sex or age. Often the powers of the state, or the military, or the established religious institutions were used to reinforce and legitimate this discrimination.

This form of injustice has been termed social injustice, because it occurs *within* a society, and between various social groupings. It has as its root the dislike or rejection of another human being or group of human beings because they are different. Some of its forms are obvious and well-known to us all—racism, sexism, religious persecution, caste discrimination—and some are so subtle that we fail to recognize their existence until the victims speak out.

### Is It Our Business?

Many nations feel that their internal social problems are nobody else's business, and that outsiders have no right to meddle with these situations. This claim has recently been made by some Third World leaders against Western feminists who have been critical of the status and treatment of women in some developing societies. We are told that these feminists don't understand the actual situations, and that they are imposing their cultural standards on another country. If such denunciations came solely from Third World men, we could perhaps discount them, but sometimes they are made by Third World women.

Take another situation. Soviet leaders feel they have the duty to protect young children from being taught "superstition" and "religious fanaticism" and therefore have opposed the formation of Sunday schools. Religious leaders in other countries denounce this as a blatant denial of the freedom of belief. Are they right? Even if they are, is it any of their business what the Soviets do or don't do inside their own country?

61

I would argue strongly that it *is* very much our business as citizens of this planet to be concerned about blatant and harmful forms of social discrimination and injustice, wherever they occur. And, of course, people in other societies have every right to raise questions with us as U.S. citizens about injustices within our own borders.

There are limitations and potential problems with this attitude which shall be mentioned at the close of this chapter. First, let us consider the realities of these problems.

### Religious Discrimination

On April 27, 1979, Georgi Vins and four other Soviet dissidents were freed from their prison cells, given new suits, and placed on a plane for New York. They were being exchanged for two Soviet spies who had been held in U.S. prisons. The crimes for which the five dissidents had been convicted were many and various, yet through each of their histories ran a common thread of religious persecution in the Soviet Union.

Georgi Vins, a leader of the officially outlawed reform Baptists, had been convicted of harming Soviet society through the conduct of religious activities. Valentyn Moroz, a Ukranian intellectual and nationalist, ran afoul of the government after he wrote a series of articles protesting the persecution of the Uniate Church. Edvard S. Kuznetsov and Mark Dymshits were imprisoned because they tried to hijack a plane to take them to Israel—a plan born of the frustration that Soviet Jews experience when they are denied the right to freely emigrate. Aleksandr Ginzburg is a practicing member of the Russian Orthodox Church who took his Jewish mother's last name to protest anti-Semitism during the Stalin era. Because of his dissident activities, his health has been nearly destroyed.[1]

When the Jewish activists, Dymshits and Kuznetsov, tried to hijack a plane to Israel, they did so out of a history of persecution of religious Judaism that goes back before the 1917 Revolution. The Soviet Union once had a large and religiously active Jewish population. When it incorporated the Baltic Republics and the West Ukraine during World War II, it added some two million more Jews. While there are still millions of Jews in the Soviet Union today, their religious practice has been reduced to its lowest point in history. Today the city of Moscow, with over 500,000 Jews, is allowed to have one synagogue. In all of the Soviet Union, there are no more than forty active rabbis, and the number of synagogues has been reduced from three thousand in 1917 to perhaps fifty today. Official Soviet commentators publically denounce Judaism as "an enemy of progress" and the observance of the Jewish Sabbath (by not working) is considered a crime. Even the making of *matzos*—the unleavened bread that is used during Passover—is illegal.[2]

Jews who practice their faith are subject to ridicule, loss of jobs, denial of schooling, and harassment. Jews who apply to emigrate to Israel have often been turned down, and their careers ruined. Jews who speak out against this discrimination, or who defend other activists, are often sent to prison for "anti-Soviet activities."

Like the Jews, Baptists have been routinely persecuted—most especially those who meet "illegally." Since any prayer meeting held anywhere but in an officially recognized church is considered illegal—and since the government often refuses to recognize a congregation—there are ample opportunities for the authorities to harass Baptists, Catholics, Jews, and others. Georgi Vins is part of a movement called *Initsiativniki*, or Action Baptists. They believe, as Lenin proclaimed at the beginning of the revolution, that there should be no state control over their religious practice, and many refuse to register. It is estimated that hundreds of their leaders are in jail; some having been sentenced for the crime of illegally printing copies of the New Testament.[3]

When the Bolsheviks came to power in 1917, they were especially concerned with breaking the power of the Russian Orthodox Church—an institution that had been intimately and officially intertwined with the Czarist regime. Many other denominations were left alone during the first ten years of communist rule, but as Stalin consolidated his power, no independent centers of authority or potential opposition were left untouched. In 1929 a new set of laws was promulgated that still serves to restrict religious practice.

Here is what religious persecution has meant in the Soviet Union:

—All Sunday Schools are outlawed. Organized teaching of religion to children in any guise is suspect and/or illegal. Some parents who have tried to teach their faith in the home have been accused of "spiritual rape" and their children have been taken from them.

—All religious publications, including the Bible and the Torah, are severely restricted, while the state has poured millions of rubles into the teaching of scientific atheism. Most *Yeshivahs* and seminaries have been closed. Jews, for example, have been allowed only one *Yeshivah*, and only 3,000 Jewish prayer books have been allowed to be printed since 1917.

—The government has engaged in a systematic campaign to close or "consolidate" churches. For example, over 10,000 Orthodox churches, half of those existing, were closed between 1960 and 1964; 2,700 Baptist congregations were closed in the same period. All monasteries and convents have been closed.

—Finally, hundreds of thousands of religious believers and leaders have been sentenced to long terms in prison, or internal exile, for illegally operating as priests or ministers, or illegally holding a prayer meeting, or for circulating slanderous religious documents, or for the performance of deceitful acts with the aim of arousing religious superstitions among the public.

Along with this official discrimination has gone an unofficial persecution by fellow citizens. Children of believing families are sometimes taunted at school by other children and by teachers. Religious employees have lost their jobs when their employers found out about their faith. Housing has sometimes been denied to known believers, as have been promotions, and entrance to universities, technical schools, or scholarly societies. Even though these forms of discrimination are officially outlawed, there is no evidence that anti-religious zealots have ever been punished in the courts.

Those people who are shocked at religious persecution in the Soviet Union might do well to remember that religious tolerance has more often been the exception rather than the rule in human society. We do not have to look back very far to find numerous examples of religious persecution—the Nazis, for example, with their holocaust of six million Jews; the Hindi-Moslem strife at India's independence in 1948, which uprooted and made refugees of 15 million people (200,000 of whom died along the way); the Soviet *pogroms* against the Jews in the late nineteenth and early twentieth centuries. In fact, human history is littered with the corpses of those who professed a differing faith and has seen endless battles between religious adherents. The struggle between Catholics and Protestants in Northern Ireland, for example, is just the latest incident in a struggle that saw Europe devastated by the Thirty Years War, France crippled by a civil war between Huguenots and Catholics, Spain made into a nightmare by the Inquisition.

Religious tolerance has been a hard-won principle in human existence—a principle that is firmly enshrined in the Universal Declaration of Human Rights, and in constitutions around the world (including that of the Soviet Union), yet it is still a principle that is constantly under threat.

Communist regimes are often singled out for their religious persecutions, though tolerance varies greatly from religiously centered Poland to the harsher regimes in the Soviet Union and China. But the communists are not the only persecutors of the religious, as several other examples will quickly show.

—In the summer of 1978, over two hundred thousand Moslems fled from Burma's western Arakan region into Bangladesh. They told stories of persecution by Burma's Buddhist majority, and of being forcibly evicted from their homes. Burma, in turn, charged that the refugees were really interlopers from Moslem Bangladesh who were fleeing identity checks. Whatever the story, some thousands died in the refugee camps in Bangladesh—many of them children.[4]

—Jehovah's Witnesses have been severely persecuted in Central Africa, most especially in Malawi. Because of their beliefs, most Witnesses will not salute a flag, sing a national anthem, or fight in the army. They also do not join political parties, nor do they vote, since they believe that all governments are run by satanic forces. They do pay taxes, however, and they are usually model villagers and workers.

In Central Africa, where there has been a strong emphasis on nation-building and adherence to a one-party state, Jehovah's Witnesses have become decidedly unpopular. The sect is banned outright in Ethiopia, Tanzania, Zaire, and Uganda, and has been banned until recently in Kenya. In Mozambique, all Witnesses have been arrested and sent to re-education camps. In Zambia, Witnesses have been beaten and killed, their churches have been burned down and their property confiscated. Adults have been fired from their jobs, and some have been arrested for refusing to sing the national anthem; some children have been suspended from school.

In Malawi, the persecution has been the worst. There President-for-life Dr. H. Kamuzu Banda, has taken personal affront at the Witnesses' refusal to join his political party. His government has launched a program of harassment and arrests and has encouraged local party members to attack the sect. Hundreds of Witnesses have been killed, some in horrible ways. Their property has been confiscated or destroyed. They have lost their jobs, their homes, and any protection under the law. In the past twelve years, some 21,000 Witnesses have fled to Zambia and Mozambique seeking refuge, only to be returned by these governments. A 1976 study reported that some five thousand Malawi Witnesses were being held in barbed-wire detention camps, and the rest were being hunted down by a relentless government and a zealous citizenry.[5]

—In Latin America, most states are under some form of military control. This control has been accompanied by the systematic oppression of all opposition groups leaving the Roman Catholic Church as one of the few institutions in which social change or advocacy for the poor can take place. Because most political and labor leaders have been exiled, jailed, or killed, the priests and nuns of the continent are often the sole voices raised on behalf of the oppressed and downtrodden. Sensing that the churches are a source of potential opposition and criticism, military leaders have begun to try to bring the churches into conformity with government policy.

Sometimes this pressure to conform is subtle—as when the archbishop in Nicaragua was told in 1977 that visas for foreign priests would be allowed if he had his picture taken with (Somoza) government officials. Sometimes it is covert and violent, as in Argentina and El Salvador, where priests have been gunned down in their homes or offices by unidentified gangs. And sometimes the action is blatant, as when Ecuadorian troops crashed into the midst of a meeting and hauled seventeen foreign bishops and thirty Ecuadorian bishops and priests off to jail, charged them with holding a "subversive meeting," and ordered the foreigners out of the country. (Three Chilean bishops who attended the meeting were "welcomed" off the plane in Chile by a government-organized rock-throwing crowd. It is thought that the arrests in Ecuador may have been part of a continent-wide attempt by the Chilean government and its military allies to embarrass dissident clergy).[6]

In our brief survey we have seen that in right-wing and left-wing governments alike, religious practice can be severely suppressed, especially when a sect or group seems to offer any opposition to the government. Whereas religious persecution in the past was often undertaken by or on behalf of an opposing religious group, today most of the repression of religion comes from secular sources—primarily the government, the military, or the Party. The motivation for this oppression stems not from theological differences, but from political fears. In states that are organizing themselves along totalitarian or authoritarian lines, few independent centers of thought are allowed to continue. Schools and universities are taken over, independent trade unions are banned, political parties are destroyed, and independent religious expression is attacked.

Thus it is difficult, perhaps impossible, to separate completely the repression of religion and the repression of other elements in a society. Conversely, any pressure on a government to recognize a greater degree of personal and political freedom will often, if successful, make religious practice more free.

## Race and Caste

Brazil has the largest African population outside of Africa itself. By U.S. standards, one-third to one-half of Brazil's 115 million citizens would be considered black—most of them descended from slavery. (Brazil was the last nation in the West to abolish this institution in 1888.) But Brazilians do not classify themselves in such black-white categories, having intermarried more readily than their North American neighbors. As a result, there are more than twenty different terms to describe the various color-shades of this society. Nevertheless, a broad form of racial discrimination does exist in Brazil— made worse, perhaps, by the government's attempts to deny its existence.

For instance, newspaper want ads frequently ask for job candidates who have "good appearance." Black Brazilians have come to learn that this is a code phrase for light-skinned. In the province of Bahia, officials have complained that the majority of families who want to adopt are only interested in blue-eyed, straight-haired children. A popular national television serial recently included the beginnings of a romance between a black plantation foreman and the owner's white daughter. The script was re-written after protest calls came in from incensed viewers.

Not surprisingly, this pattern of unofficial discrimination—so reminiscent of the United States—has kept most black Brazilians at the bottom of the economic order. The *Jornal do Brazil* recently estimated that only 3 percent of college students were black, and only 2 percent of public employees were black. Black literacy is estimated at 26 percent as compared to 53 percent for whites.

In spite of these obvious indicators of social injustice, Brazil's military government continues to argue that Brazil is a paradise of racial harmony—a model for other nations to emulate. To make sure that this image is not sullied, black activist groups are systematically discouraged and media attention to racial problems is strictly censored. This attitude is not unique to racial problems, however, and the military has generally censored any social comment or protest.[7]

It is not uncommon for one group of people to discriminate against another. In fact, intergroup harmony is usually the exception. As we shall see when we discuss caste in India, there are many ways in which a particular people can be oppressed or excluded because they are "different." Much of the attention to racism in the twentieth century has centered on the attitude of whites toward peoples of other colors—and justly so, since an insufferable attitude of racial superiority accompanied the European colonizers as they set out to conquer the globe.

This legacy continues in Central and East Africa today in the tensions between black Africans and Asian immigrants. The Asians—who live in Kenya, Malawi, Tanzania, Zambia, and Uganda—are primarily descended from Indian immigrants who moved to Africa in the late nineteenth and twentieth centuries. Because they were citizens of the British Empire, these Indians were allowed free immigration to Britain's African colonies, where many of them became shopkeepers and traders. The whites who had settled in Central and East Africa were none too happy to have Indians moving into their territory, and tried to have them excluded. That failing, they made sure that Indians were not able to purchase land and set up their own plantations, since only whites were to have that privilege.

Finding themselves in the midst of a society strictly divided between black natives and white rulers, the Indians and other Asian immigrants tried to carve out a space for themselves. To this end they agitated against racial laws that placed them in the same category as blacks, and often they were successful in winning a middle position in the social structure. Denied access to land, Indians took up mid-level posts in business and government and strengthened their hold on commerce.

When independence came to black Africa, the Asians found themselves in a very awkward position. Many of their leaders had backed the cause of independence, but the mass of Asians were fearful of what the black-led governments would do with them. At independence, most Asians were offered the opportunity to become citizens of their new nation, but many decided to keep their British citizenship just in case they might want to leave. Black African leaders resented this ambivalent attitude, and soon the Asians found that citizenship offers became more stringent.

The greatest conflict came, however, as black leaders tried to Africanize the government services and the business management of local companies. Many of the middle positions that blacks were qualified for were occupied by Asians. Something had to give, and not surprisingly it was the Asian minority that lost out. Work permits were granted preferentially to blacks; Asians were fired or passed over for promotions; Asian shopkeepers experienced difficulty in getting import licenses, and so on. The greatest blow came in Uganda, where Idi Amin ordered all Asians out of his country and their property confiscated.

Similar conflicts have occurred in West Africa, where Syrian and Lebanese immigrants were brought in by the French and allowed to settle into merchant roles, and in Southeast Asia where Chinese and Indians have played a comparable role in trade. Often their position in commerce is resented by customers and competing traders, which has in turn led to riots and forced expulsion.[8]

By far the most publicized, and perhaps the worst, case of current racial oppression can be found in white-dominated South Africa. There, racial discrimination is official government policy, imposed by a thorough police-state apparatus.

The Republic of South Africa is the last bastion of white supremacy in Africa. In this country some 4.5 million whites keep a strict control over 20 million blacks. Using the army, the police, and the courts, the whites have erected a strict system of *apartheid* ("separateness") which guarantees to them 87 percent of the land and 75 percent of the national income. While whites claim that they are aiding the blacks in development, government expenditure for black education is only $45 per black pupil compared to $696 per white pupil; and there is only one doctor for every 44,000 blacks as compared to one for every 400 whites.[9]

Until very recently, South Africa's *apartheid* system was very much like the segregated system of the American South before the 1960s: there were "whites only" drinking fountains, restaurants, and hotels; "whites only" hospitals and schools; even "whites only" ambulances that would not pick up a stricken black in the street.

Under the weight of external and internal pressure, some parts of South Africa's "petty *apartheid*" system are being changed. But the more profound system of discrimination remains. Blacks are denied, *by law*, the right to most skilled and managerial jobs; blacks are required at all times to carry a passbook that gives their address and work history. Failure to have a valid passbook can and does result in a jail sentence (250,000 blacks were prosecuted under this law in 1976). Legally, blacks are allowed to reside only in one of twelve "bantustans," areas that have been reserved for blacks as so-called homelands. To live and work in the other 87 percent of the country—the white part—requires a special permit. Often permits are given only to a worker and not to his or her family. Family members are expected to stay in the bantustan, and if they try to leave, they are subject to arrest.

All of this, of course, fits very nicely into a national scheme to keep blacks at the bottom of the economic pryamid while whites keep the best jobs, earn the greatest incomes, and grab the greater share of the profits from South Africa's abundant mineral resources.

Naturally, this system is resented by South Africa's blacks, and they have demonstrated and rioted against it. These demonstrations, many of them peaceful, have been met by government arrests and worse. In Windhoek, the police opened fire on a peaceful demonstration and killed eleven; in Sharpeville, police killed sixty-eight and wounded over two hundred who were demonstrating against the pass law; police again opened fire on student crowds in the Soweto riots, killing hundreds. Whites and blacks who speak out against the *apartheid* system are arrested and detained, often without formal charges and with no legal right of recourse.

Thomas Manthata is a black staff member of the South African Council of Churches. For his work against *apartheid* he has been detained three times; the last time he was kept in solitary confinement for 230 days, and then released without ever being charged with any crime. Sometimes critics are "banned," a form of house arrest in which they are not allowed to travel, write, give talks, or receive visitors without specific government permission. This happened to Fatima Meer, the president of the Association for Sociology in Southern Africa and a faculty member at Natal University. Her banning began in 1976 and was supposed to last for five years.[10]

The government and the police have far-ranging powers in South Africa. Under various internal security laws, they can detain people for weeks, months, years, without ever having to go to court or bring formal charges, or even to notify the family of the prisoner's whereabouts. Naturally, such unchecked power leads to even greater abuse, and reports of torture are common. Amnesty International reported that in 1976 at least eighteen prisoners died under "mysterious circumstances." The case of Mapetta Mohapi, a black organizer, provides a good example of how the security system is abused:

Mr. Mohapi was alleged by security police to have hanged himself with a pair of jeans on 5 August 1976 while detained *incommunicado* at Kei Road police station in King William's Town. A doctor who represented the Mohapi family at a post-mortem held soon after his death was detained on 12 August and held without charge until late December 1976. The doctor, Dr. Mamphela Ramphele, was banned and restricted to an isolated village more than one thousand kilometers from King William's Town in April 1977. At the inquest held on Mohapi in March 1977, his wife claimed that an alleged suicide note produced by the police was not in her husband's handwriting. The inquest was then postponed until September 1977.[11]

Finally in our survey of discrimination based on race or caste, let us consider the case of the Untouchables (*Harijans*) in India. These people are relegated to the bottom of the social structure; they are, in fact, outside the formal caste structure, though they really form a fifth caste by themselves. In 1977, it was estimated that there were 93 million Untouchables, about 15 percent of India's population.[12] These people are primarily landless and work in the "lowest" occupations—waste removal, disposing of dead animals, and working with leather (which violates the Hindu attitude toward the sacredness of the cow). They are considered so impure that in some provinces even the sight of an Untouchable could ritually pollute a higher-caste Indian. Certainly they were not to be touched—hence the name—nor were they to be allowed to live in the villages, drink from the common well, or enter the temples.

In the traditional Indian mind, it made little difference what work an Untouchable actually performed. An Untouchable might never have performed dirty work—could, in fact, be a doctor or a professor—yet that person would still be considered unclean. Thus when India's former defense minister, Jagjivan Ram, dedicated a statue in the state of Uttar Pradesh, he no sooner got out of town than a group of high-caste Hindus had it washed down with sacred Ganges water to purify it from his supposedly defiling touch.[13]

India's Constitution completely outlaws Untouchability, making its observance a crime. This has been followed up by a series of specific laws that forbid discriminatory practices as well as an affirmative action program that reserves jobs, university posts, and seats in the legislatures for Untouchables, or "former Untouchables" as one author calls them. Special Welfare Departments were set up with the task of improving the lot of the ex-Untouchables, and the government has also committed itself to redistributing land to these people.

The laws, however, are hard to enforce. Virtually all of the police who might enforce them are themselves from a higher caste, and often look the other way when crimes against Untouchables are committed. Thus when a nineteen-year-old Untouchable boy was accused of having stolen two dollars and was taken by a mob and beaten for an hour and then burned alive, the local and state police did nothing about it. Even when the national government intervened, the killers received only three- to seven-year sentences.[14]

Government surveys have found that progress in attaining justice for the Untouchables has been slow. For example, a survey of 179 villages in Madhya Pradesh state showed that Untouchables were barred from the village well in 124 localities. Some 48 of the 128 temples were closed to them, as were 11 of the 39 restaurants. No barber in any village would cut an Untouchable's hair.[15] Another survey stated that Untouchables could be found in only 2.8 percent of the upper grade and 3.1 percent of the middle grade civil service jobs, even though 12 percent of the jobs were supposed to be reserved for them.[16] And still another found that the Untouchable's literacy rate (15 percent) was half that of the general population.[17]

There are some small rays of hope for Untouchables, however. In the cities, it is much harder to maintain strict caste lines, and persons can often leave their pasts behind them. One Indian sociologist is optimistic in the long run, because Untouchables look like everyone else. If their economic and educational level is raised, he argues, "Then the Harijan problem will be less tough to solve than the black problem in the United States."[18]

We have surveyed several instances of race and caste discrimination in various parts of the world. Should we ask ourselves what we, as world citizens, might do about these situations, the answer all too often is discouraging. After all, what could a concerned Indian activist do about black-white relations in the United States? At first glance, the answer seems to be not much. Like so many social problems, the solution usually lies in the way local people behave toward one another, most especially when the right laws are on the books—as they are in India and the United States—but are being ignored by the people.

The situation is quite different, however, when discrimination and repression are *official government policy*—as in the case of South African *apartheid* and Malawi's persecution of Jehovah's Witnesses. In these cases it is entirely possible for action to pressure the government into changing its stance. The international campaign against South Africa's present policies is a classic case in point.

South Africa has been condemned repeatedly by the United Nations for its flagrant racism and denial of human rights. In the General Assembly, South Africa has been, in effect, denied its seat, and there has been a call for a total economic boycott of the country. The Security Council has called for a mandatory boycott of military trade with the Republic, but has not called for a mandatory economic boycott (the U.S. representative usually vetoes such resolutions). The voluntary economic boycott has been honored by many oil producing countries, and when Iran's new leadership announced that it would begin compliance, the source for 90 percent of South Africa's oil consumption was cut off.

So far the United States and Great Britain—South Africa's two main trading partners—have exerted very little pressure on the regime for change. While black South African leaders have asked for an economic boycott, the United States has refused to discourage any but military trade; that is, until the Congress ordered the Export-Import Bank to stop loans that supported *apartheid* in October 1978.

With $1.8 billion in corporate investments, $2.5 billion in private loans, and $2 billion in individual investments, the United States has been a mainstay for the South African economy. Perhaps because of this investment, and because some U.S. leaders regard South Africa's vast mineral wealth as being as crucial to our economy as Saudi Arabia's oil, U.S. presidents have been most reluctant to threaten our cozy relationship with this repugnant regime. Many business and government leaders argue that U.S. investment helps to liberalize the South African government. However, former Senator Dick Clark, an African specialist, found from his study that "the net effect of American investment has been to strengthen the economic and military self-sufficiency of South Africa's *apartheid* regime."[19]

## National Minorities

The right of self-determination is a principle that has received strong support in the UN Charter and in UN pronouncements against colonialism. But the concept of self-determination is a broad one, broad enough to have justified the right of secession of the American Confederacy in 1861, broad enough to fire the imaginations of Basque separatists in Spain or French separatists in Quebec.

The United Nations defined self-determination very precisely in its 1960

Declaration on the Granting of Independence: "Any attempt aimed at the partial or total disruption of the national unity and territorial integrity of a country is incompatible with the purposes and principles of the Charter of the United Nations."

In other words, the General Assembly was proclaiming the right of colonies to liberate themselves from the European powers, but not the right of tribes, ethnic groups, or national minorities to liberate themselves from the newly created states. It was Africa that the General Assembly had in mind, since Africa's boundaries had been arbitrarily drawn by the Europeans and were the most subject to challenge by internal dissidents. Yet this restriction on the right of self-determination was one that could easily be welcomed by many old and new countries in the world which were themselves composed of conglomerates of people.

Self-determination is a term that can have an appeal to hundreds of oppressed groups around the world. With the rise of the nation-state as the most powerful arbiter of domestic life, it should not be surprising that many subnational groups within today's boundaries hope to one day take on the trappings and privileges of nationhood. After all, there is nothing sacred about present national boundaries, nor does there seem to be any size or population level that can be called a prerequisite for the creation of a state. No wonder, then, that Woodrow Wilson's Secretary of State, Robert Lansing, should have objected so strenuously to the president's use of the term, "self-determination" during the peace negotiations at Versailles. "The phrase is simply loaded with dynamite," Lansing said. "It will raise hopes which can never be realized. It will, I fear, cost thousands of lives."[20]

In fact, millions of people have died in struggles for self-determination in the six decades since Lansing's statement. Hundreds of thousands died in the anti-colonial struggles that arose in China against the Japanese or in North Africa against the French. In a very unpublicized civil war in the Sudan, it is estimated that 500,000 died in the fighting between 1963 and 1972, and another 500,000 died because of war-related disease and famine.[21]

The Palestinian struggle with Israel is often phrased in terms of self-determination. The Quebec separatist movement, the goals of Native Americans in the United States and Latin America, the nationalist movements in the Ukraine and Soviet Georgia—all of these are moved by desires for greater self-determination, though the ultimate goal may not necessarily be the creation of a separate state. Behind these struggles we can see a complex planetary struggle over the way in which groups of people are going to be governed.

Let us consider a few examples of this struggle.

## Spain

Supposedly, the kingdom of Spain was unified in the sixteenth century under the rulership of the kings of Castile. Yet for centuries thereafter, a strong sense of local identity was maintained in many of Spain's provinces.

This was especially true in the Basque and Catalan regions in the north, each of which had continued their own separate language and customs.

During the Spanish Civil War (1936–1939), many Basques and Catalans supported the losing side—the Republicans—because they had been promised greater local autonomy. When Franco won instead, large areas belonging to the Basques and Catalans became virtually occupied territory.

Franco decided to put an end to Basque and Catalan nationalism once and for all. To this end, he outlawed local nationalist groups and rounded up their leaders. His government closed down virtually all of their cultural institutions, forbade the teaching of either Basque or Catalan in the schools. He even went so far as to ban the use of either language outside the home, so that people were commonly arrested for speaking their native tongue. All publication in either language was stopped, and local priests who might harbor nationalist sentiments were transferred to other areas. Catalans and Basques who responded to this campaign with petitions or protests, however mild, were arrested, harassed, intimidated. Franco also took steps to keep Basques and Catalans out of the army and out of the government.

Needless to say, this discrimination was not appreciated in the Basque and Catalan regions, and a strong spirit of resentment ran just below the surface. This resentment was expressed through petitions, strikes, and a refusal to vote. Among the Basques, government policy was also resisted by assassination and armed struggle. When a local police chief was assassinated by Basque nationalists in 1968, the government ordered a total crackdown and used mass arrests and torture to try to break the movement. This massive response was not only unsuccessful, it gave a greater solidarity and more publicity to Basque nationalism.

In 1973, the Basque militants "changed the course of Spanish history" by assassinating Franco's chosen heir, Admiral Luis Carrero Blanco. He was perhaps the one man who could have continued Franco's iron rule, and his death led to sweeping democratic reforms after Franco also died. Spain now has a democratic structure and has promised the Basque and Catalan regions greater cultural and political autonomy.

The struggle over Basque and Catalan nationalism is not over, however. Some Basque militants are convinced that only complete independence will meet their aims, and in 1978 they carried out fifty killings and numerous robberies to publicize and finance their cause. On the other hand some former guerrillas have run for office and have been elected under the new constitution. Both the Basque and Catalan regions responded heavily to the 1977 voting for parliament, returning significant blocs of delegates who support greater autonomy. Hopefully, the cause of these two distinct peoples can now be worked out non-violently through the legislature.

There is one other factor that has propelled Basque and Catalan nationalism: both regions were among the first to industrialize, and both have standards of living that are higher than most of the rest of Spain. This has contributed to a certain pride, some would say arrogance, toward the more rural and poorer areas. It has also meant that these regions feel that they have nothing to lose financially, and perhaps a lot to gain, by going their own way.[22]

## The Soviet Union

For a look at another country with explosive nationalist passions, consider the Soviet Union. The Union of Soviet Socialist Republics, as it is formally called, is the largest country in the world. Its vast land mass spreads from Europe all across Asia, and encompasses a varied collection of peoples— from Buddhist Buryat Mongols to Moslem Uzbeks to atheist and Orthodox Russians. This polyglot empire was put together out of the military campaigns of the czars, and in many cases today is still held together by military might.

Russia's turn-of-the-century revolutionaries were only too aware of the fact that their empire had been put together by the sword and gun; thus they promised to allow self-determination for any Republic that desired to go their own way after the overthrow of the Czar. Lenin thought that a number of provinces would break away after the Revolution, but he expected the revolutionary struggle to continue in them nonetheless. Lenin and other Bolshevik leaders may still have been surprised at how rapidly this breakup began after they came to power. The list is quite extensive and illustrates conflicts of nationalisms that are alive today: Latvia, Estonia, Georgia, the Trans-Caucasus, Armenia, Aserbaijan, the Ukraine. All split off within the first two years of the revolution.[23]

It soon became apparent to the Bolsheviks that nationalism was a greater force than they had expected, and, more alarmingly, that revolutionary governments would not automatically seize control in the new republics. This, in turn, prompted a change in policy. As Stalin put it in 1923, "There are instances where the nation's right of self-determination conflicts with another, higher principle, namely the right of the working class to consolidate its rule once it has seized power."[24] As he spoke, the banner of the working class had already accompanied the Red Army in its re-occupation of most of the new Republics. This occupation had gone so well that the USSR was formally created by a vote of the All-Russian Soviet Congress on December 27, 1922.

The Soviet Constitution envisioned a federated system designed to give a great amount of local autonomy to the republics. The national government was responsible for defense, foreign policy, public health, education, and justice, but much of the administration was to be left to local decisionmakers. The USSR was to be ruled by the Congress of Soviets, elected through indirect representation from all the republics, but as Stalin consolidated his power this supposedly decentralized and democratic system became a sham.

During the 1920s, however, many Soviet Republics enjoyed a golden era of cultural resurgence. In the Ukraine, local leaders were brought into positions of power, books were printed, scholars were given a high degree of freedom, and the Ukranian language was adopted as the official language for state functions. In the Crimea, leaders who spoke the Tatar language were in command, and Tatar was made an official language alongside Russian. Tatar art and literature flourished, and Tatar schools were opened.

This golden era ended abruptly with a campaign to purge all "bourgeois nationalists" from positions of power. Leaders in the Ukraine, the Crimea, and elsewhere were rounded up and sent into exile. In their place were put men and women whose loyalty was to Moscow, to the Party, and to Stalin. Leading artists, writers, and scholars were also purged, and censorship of local publications became more strict. In many areas, peasants were rounded up and shipped off to Siberia or the Urals; some 30,000 to 40,000 were deported from the Crimea alone. And a campaign against Moslem clergy was launched.

These initial purges were followed by the mass purges of the 1930s in which millions of citizens were charged with a variety of "crimes" and shipped off to concentration camps or executed. These purges consolidated Stalin's power, but at the cost of creating vast resentment all over the country.

It should not be surprising, then, that many Soviet nationalities welcomed the German invasion of the USSR. In the Baltics and the Ukraine, Hitler's troops were welcomed as liberators, and many young men signed up in the army to fight against the Soviet troops. When it became apparent that Hitler had no more intention of liberating these areas than Stalin had, bands of guerrillas were formed which fought first against the Germans and later against the Soviets. In the Ukraine, armed resistance to Soviet occupation lasted until 1950.[25]

As Soviet troops again occupied the Ukraine, Latvia, Lithuania, and Estonia, thousands and hundreds of thousands of people were rounded up and forceably resettled in the vast Northeast Territories. Of the Crimean Tatars, some of whom had fought for the Germans and some of whom had fought for the Soviets, *all* families were gathered and shipped off to Uzbekistan. This forced resettlement involved 250,000 people, about half of whom died in the eighteen month transition. Even today, while the Soviet government has officially cleared the charges against the Tatars, these people are still not allowed to return to their homeland.[26] Along with the Tatars went many Volga Germans, Ukranians, Georgians, Balkans, and others. Reports from the Siberian camps indicate that by far the largest proportion of prisoners came from the Ukraine.

The successful close of World War II brought the USSR back to its imperial size. Lost was Finland, granted independence in 1918, but regained were the Baltic Republics of Lithuania, Latvia, and Estonia. Borders satisfactory to the Soviets were also negotiated with Poland and Romania, and these two nations together with East Germany, Hungary, Czechoslovakia, and Bulgaria formed a pro-Soviet buffer zone. Since pro-Soviet leaders in these countries were brought to power with the aid of the Soviet Army, and since they are kept in line with the threat of armed intervention, they are sometimes referred to as captive nations, along with the Baltic Republics.

Many outside observers believe that the Soviet Union is sitting on top of a nationalist volcano. They cite the Hungarian and Czechoslovakian uprisings, the dramatic reforms in Poland, and the continuation of nationalist sentiment in many of the provinces of the USSR itself. Certainly, the Soviets give every evidence of fearing separatist tendencies. Valentyn Moroz, who was one of those traded for the two Soviet spies, was convicted for "anti-Soviet" agitation because of his support of Ukranian nationalism. When Ukranian friends mounted a petition campaign on his behalf, they were also jailed. Mykhaylo Osadchy, a Ukranian writer, was sentenced to two years at hard labor for his "anti-Soviet" writings, released, then re-arrested in 1972 and sentenced for an additional ten years.

These few cases are but a sampling of the many convictions that spring from nationalist sentiment, giving evidence that such feelings still run strong in many parts of the USSR to this day.

The trend toward centralization and homogenization that modern technology introduced is also met by a strong countertrend toward localism, small-group identity, and sub-nationalism. In a way, there is much to be said for both trends. The large, centralized state possessed the power to redistribute wealth and administer an even-handed justice to all citizens. The large state is able to tap the resources of its many peoples, and its economy can be founded upon a diversity of trade and manufacture. The small state can be homogeneous and close-knit, like a family. Its leaders can be more easily reached by a majority of people, and its sense of national identity can be strong. And since small states can field only small armies, some people feel that they pose less of a threat to world peace.

Is there, in fact, a just solution to the problem of conflicting national and sub-national groups? Can we find a rule or recipe that will apply to all situations? I rather doubt it. What we can advocate, however, is the non-violent resolution of conflicts. Separatists should have every opportunity to argue their case—a freedom that is routinely denied them—and mechanisms should be found whereby a people can opt for national independence. The Canadian struggle over Quebec's future, which has largely been waged through peaceful means, will provide an example from which we can all learn.

### Women

The oppression and subjugation of women is unquestionably the most significant social problem that the world faces today. Not just because women are almost everywhere relegated to secondary status, not just because women are still routinely denied legal and economic rights, not just because violence against women is common—and commonly goes unpunished. It is for all of these reasons, and for one glaring fact: *In almost every situation where a people is oppressed, the women suffer more.* Are there people who are hungry? In most poor populations, women suffer more greatly than the men. Why? Because the more highly valued men and boys are fed first, and the women and girls are fed with what is left over. Thus in India, where this practice is common, there is a higher rate of female mortality. The result is that the ratio of females to males has sunk from 970 women per 1,000 men in 1900 to 930 per 1,000 in the 1970s.[27]

Are there workers who are underpaid? In many parts of the world women are routinely paid less than men for the same work. Thus in Mexico, it was found that male coffee harvesters were paid $1.26 a day, on the average, while women were paid 94 cents. In maize harvesting, men got 63 cents a day, while women received 38 cents.[28] Many employers prefer to hire women, feeling that they are a more docile labor force, and that they will accept lower pay and worse standards than men. In South Korea, women are heavily employed in the textile industry and are expected to put in a ten-hour day for six to seven days a week. Their pay is two-thirds of the minimum wage (less than $62 a month).[29]

Is there a world literacy problem? Over 60 percent of the 800 million illiterates in the world are female, and their number is increasing faster than that of men. Why? Because as one Moroccan parent put it, "Of what use is school to a girl? She doesn't learn anything useful and she doesn't earn anything. She will marry and that is her future."[30]

Simply put, women suffer by being part of an oppressed group, and they suffer at the hands of the men in that oppressed group. To put it more correctly, women suffer because of patriarchal attitudes, since often older women are also the agents of the repression of younger women.

To have a better idea of what women's oppression can mean, let us consider the story of Roshana, a young woman who lives in a village in Bangladesh. Here, in her own words, is the story of how she was married:

One day eight men from Katni came to my father's house. I was very embarrassed. I covered myself with my sari so they couldn't see my face. But then my uncle showed my neck to them and pulled up my sari to show my feet and ankles. I felt like dying. I had to read the Koran to them too. After I left, one of the men told my father that the old man who wanted to marry me had three tin roofs and many duns of land. The next day the men sent word that they approved of me and that the marriage would take place that night. That's how I married my husband.

It was all a lie. Where are the tin roofs, tell me! Where is all the land? My husband is a poor man who works as a carpenter. What will I do when he can't work any more? Or if he dies?

It's terrible to live with a man like my husband. He has no love for anyone. (*She takes a piece of iron pipe from the table and grips it tightly in her hand.*) Look at this! My husband beat me with this. All the neighbors came running when they heard me screaming. I had a fever for a week and my body was sore all over.

I told my father about the beating and he complained to my husband. Now my husband doesn't beat me so often. But he has other ways to hurt me. He says he is going to divorce me because I'm not pregnant yet. We've only been married ten months. He worries that if I don't have a baby soon, it will be too late. He's an old man. He only has one daughter and he doesn't want her to inherit everything. He blames it on me that I'm not pregnant. Other people laugh and say it's his fault. Do you know of any medicine which makes you have babies? I'm unhappy here but I don't want to be divorced. No one will look at me if that happens. They'll say, "She must be at fault if her husband divorced her."[31]

Here in one woman's story we have almost every aspect of the oppression of many Third World women: an expectation that their primary and perhaps only role is as mother and housekeeper, their subjection to the rule of their father or uncle or husband, their vulnerability to violence, their lack of protection under the law.

Perhaps the most shocking common problem of women is their subjection to violence and brutality. In almost every land, and from every class, women are beaten by their fathers, husbands, and lovers, and very little is done to protect them. In pre-revolutionary Russia, it was customary in peasant weddings for the bride's father to present the groom with a whip, as a symbol of his authority. The whip was then hung over the bed as a reminder of what would befall the disobedient wife. While the Soviet Union has made considerable progress in women's liberation, wife-beating is a problem to this day.[32]

While broad statistics are not available for the United States, a Cleveland study found that 37 percent of women applying for divorce listed physical abuse as one of their complaints, and in San Francisco police have estimated that 50 percent of their calls were to stop domestic violence.[33] The FBI has estimated that wife-beating is the least reported crime in America, and that it outnumbers rape cases by 3 to 1.[34]

Women suffer, in addition, because of the sexual double standard that can be found in most societies. Men are allowed to have plentiful sexual relations, but women are expected to stay virgins until they are married. In Algeria, and in less urban areas of many Moslem societies, a woman who loses her virginity can be killed by the male members of her family.[35] In many societies, a woman who is not proven to be a virgin on her wedding night can be automatically returned to her parents by the husband, and the marriage annulled. This custom is practiced in parts of Brazil, and many of the rejected women are also turned out by their families—their only option then being a life of prostitution.[36]

One of the most astonishing and outrageous customs related to this all-consuming desire to regulate female sexuality is the widespread practice of clitoridectomy, sometimes misleadingly referred to as female circumcision. Widespread in Africa, Indonesia, and some parts of the Middle East, this operation involves the removal of the female clitoris, usually from young girls aged five to seven, and usually with a razor blade or unsterilized knife. Not only is the operation painful and traumatic, and not only is it often accompanied by infection and childbirth problems, but it also makes intercourse unenjoyable and often painful.

As hard as it may be to believe, the obsession with controlling female sexuality is carried to such lengths that in a few countries (Mali, Ethiopia, Sudan, parts of Egypt and Kenya) the clitoris is removed and the vulva is closed by sewing the labia majora together, leaving only a small opening the size of a matchstick.[37] The husband is then accorded the privilege of slitting the area open with a knife on the wedding night. Some husbands, it is reported, re-sew the area if they are going on long trips, and in the Sudan some women keep the area sewn up, re-sewing it after every childbirth.[38]

## Women and Socialism

The news about the condition of women in the world is bad, but not all bad. In many socialist countries remarkable progress has been made, enough to show how far other countries—including the United States and Western European nations—have to go. In my studies, I have been most impressed with the progress that has been shown in countries that have experienced a Marxist revolution, so much impressed that I would tentatively advance this thesis: *Far beyond any other social group, women have benefited the most from Marxist revolutions.*

Having been justifiably critical of totalitarianism and human rights violations under Marxist regimes, I have found it intriguing that the cause of women has apparently fared so well in Communist revolutions. The Union of Soviet Socialist Republics is far and away the leading example of this progress. In the sixty-plus years since the 1917 revolution, the status of women in Soviet society has undergone a fantastic revision—so much so that the USSR can safely claim to be in a class by itself on this issue. One measure of this progress can be found in employment statistics for women. While we here in the United States struggle with affirmative action programs for women, the Soviet Union has been pursuing affirmative action in education and employment for years. Here are some employment figures for women that contrast the Soviet Union and the United States:[39]

### (% of Total in the Occupational Category)

|  | USSR | U.S. |
|---|---|---|
| High School Principals | 25% | 1.4% |
| Physicians | 72% | 9% |
| Engineers | 30% | 2% |
| Judges | 33% | 2% |
| Associate Professors | 20% | 7% |
| Elected Officials* | 47% | 0.5% |

*Soviet elections tend to be pro forma endorsements of candidates who have been nominated from above, as was the case in Poland before the reforms of 1980-81. This listing comes from William M. Mandel, *Soviet Women* (Garden City, N.Y.: Anchor Books, 1975), and the categories are the author's, not mine.

Throughout the Soviet Union, women can regularly and routinely be found in professions and leadership positions that are almost exclusively male in the United States—heads of universities, presidents of Republics, factory managers, supervising engineers. Yet the Soviet Union began its revolution with a record of patriarchalism as great as any country in Europe. Women were kept in the home, kept from school, married by arrangement, and subject to regular physical abuse. In the predominantly Moslem portions of the USSR, women wore horsehair veils, without eyeslits, and were forbidden to remove them even in front of visiting women, for fear that the visitor might describe the face to her husband.[40] The Moslem women were routinely married, or even sold, at the age of nine to twelve, and once married they were kept in "reclusion" in the house all day.

Government officials responded to this system by passing laws that banned these practices, by launching a massive literacy and education campaign, and by encouraging local women to remove their veils and speak out against their repression. The Central Asian men responded with violence, beating the women who dared to attend public meetings, burning schools and books and beating teachers. In the Uzbek Republic, the first two women who dared to appear in a theater with their faces unveiled were killed; in 1928 alone there were 203 anti-feminist murders reported in that Republic.[41]

Similar reactions occurred in Tadjikistan, Turkmenia, and Azerbaidjan. Yet the current vice-president of Tadjikistan is a woman, as is the vice-premier. The veil is gone, as is the practice of reclusion, and women are in school in equal proportions to their numbers. In Turkmenia, 30 percent of the Communist Party's Central Committee is female, as is 38 percent of city and town government.[42]

There is still a long way to go in the Soviet Union. Despite great progress, women have not achieved job equality in many professions, and they do not have the political power that Soviet men do. Many local and regional posts in government are administrative and appointive rather than political and truly elective. While bureaucratic posts have a fair amount of power, the greatest decision-making power is concentrated in the Communist Party, where women make up only 22 percent of the membership. A key post of power—the first secretary of the Party in a Republic—is so far held in all cases by men, and the Central Committee of the Party has only 14 females out of 360 members (about 4 percent, and exactly the same as the proportion of women in the U.S. House of Representatives). Finally, the Presidium (Politburo) which represents the pinnacle of Soviet power, has had only one female member since 1917.

Soviet women also complain that male dominant attitudes still hang over in the family as well. Educated young women in Central Asia say that their husbands still expect them to stay at home and have lots of babies. Soviet women in general say that Soviet men refuse to do cooking, childcare, and housework, which means that a working woman really has two jobs—one at home and the other at the work place. One study has found that this double burden means that a woman has two hours less leisure time a day than her husband and gets one and a half hours less sleep each night.[43] Such a pattern, in addition to being unfair, is detrimental to the woman's health.

Yet there is little to complain of in the Soviet Union that isn't also true of the United States and Western Europe. And, in many cases, the Soviet record is far better. This record is echoed in the Eastern European countries, where female education and employment is generally far better than in Western Europe. The Soviet record is also emulated in the Marxist nations of Cuba, Guinea-Bissau, and in China—though it is nowhere yet equalled.

The women's cause is far from hopeless. Women are realizing that male leadership, despite its promises, can rarely be counted on to initiate drastic reforms without the constant prodding and persistent action of women. In Algeria, in Kenya, in Syria, in Iran, women are discovering that they must unite with each other across tribal, regional, and national lines in order to gain their rightful place in society.

Can a national women's struggle be aided from the outside? The answer will depend on the particularities of the ongoing struggle. Where there is a strong local women's movement, Western women's involvement may be rejected and resented as another form of cultural imperialism. Yet other local women may welcome aid, publicity, and pressure from outside. Is there a growing international women's movement? The answer that feminists give is a resounding yes, though the barriers of race and class—and memories of all-too-recent colonial domination—mean that communication is often slow and painful.

## Conclusion

We have surveyed four major areas of social injustice, and it is time to restate our question: Is this any of our business?

Interestingly enough, most of the countries in the world have already answered this question in the affirmative by affixing their signatures to the United Nations Charter and to the Universal Declaration of Human Rights. In these documents the signatories pledged themselves to cooperate with the United Nations in the "promotion of universal respect for and observance of human rights and fundamental freedoms." The Universal Declaration spells out these rights—economic, social, and political—and says that they cannot be denied due to race, color, sex, language, religion, political or other opinion, national or social origin, property, birth or other status.

Having agreed to this commendable listing of rights, most countries proceed to discriminate as they see fit, and denounce outside complaints as interference in their internal affairs. Concerned world citizens should not be fooled by such rhetoric.

On the other hand, the argument can be made that the logical avenue for complaint and action should be through the United Nations and other international bodies. If the United Nations will not—or cannot—act, then international citizens' actions may be indicated.

Of course, the primary responsibility for change rests with the people of the country involved. This is true not only for situations of social injustice, but also for actions to promote development, stop pollution, challenge militarism, or feed the poor. Having said that, let us now turn to a consideration of the United Nations and its role in addressing the problems that have been stated in this and previous chapters.

## *NOTES*

1. These biographies appeared in the *New York Times*, April 28, 1979.

2. Cornelia Gerstenmaier, "The Jews as a Religious Minority," *Religious Minorities in the Soviet Union*, Report #1 of the Minority Rights Group, 3rd edition, London, 1977, pp. 18–20.

3. Michael Bordeaux, "Baptists and Other Protestants", "The Jews as a Religious Minority," pp. 15–18.

4. William Borders, "Bangladesh, Sad Haven for Fleeing Burmese," *New York Times*, June 3, 1978; and James P. Sterba, *New York Times*, "At a Camp for Burmese Refugees, Death Is Routine," March 2, 1979.

5. Tony Hodges, "Jehovah's Witnesses in Central Africa," Report #29 of the Minority Rights Group, London, 1976.

6. For details, see Penny Lernoux, *Notes on a Revolutionary Church* (New York: Rockefeller Foundation, 1978), and Penny Lernoux, *Cry of the People* (New York: Doubleday, 1980).

7. This information was taken from David Vidal, "Many Blacks Shut Out of Brazil's Racial 'Paradise,' " *New York Times*, June 5, 1978. See also Anani Dzidzienyo, "The Position of Blacks in Brazilian Society," Ben Whitaker, ed., *The Fourth World* (New York: Schocken Books, 1973), pp. 162–187.

8. Yash Ghai and Dharan Ghai, "The Asian Minorities of East and Central Africa," in Whitaker, *The Fourth World*, pp. 24–72.

9. Leslie Rubin, "South Africa: Facts and Fiction," *UNESCO Courier*, Nov. 1977.

10. Both cases cited in *Banned and Detained in South Africa*, published by the International Fellowship of Reconciliation, Alkmaar, Holland, 1978.

11. *Amnesty International Report 1977,* London, 1977, pp. 98, 99.

12. Barry Kramer, "India's Outcastes," *Wall Street Journal,* Oct. 24, 1977.

13. Cited in Harinder Boparai, "India's Ex-Untouchables," *Review of the International Commission of Jurists*, June 1978, p. 41.

14. Ibid., p. 41–42.

15. Kramer, "India's Outcasts."

16. Boparai, "India's Ex-Untouchables," p. 42.

17. Kramer, "India's Outcasts."

18. Ibid.

19. This quote and the investment figures come from the Sept. 11, 1978 issue of the *International Bulletin*.

20. N. Gordon Levin, Jr., *Woodrow Wilson and World Politics* (New York: Oxford University Press, 1968), p. 248.

21. Leslie Rubin and Brian Weinstein, *Introduction to African Politics* (New York: Praeger, 1974), p. 172.

22. This discussion is derived primarily from "The Basques and the Catalans," Report #9 of the Minority Rights Group, London, 1977. Some facts are from James M. Markham, "Death Is a Way of Life for Some Basques," *New York Times*, Dec. 10, 1978.

23. Georg von Rauch, *A History of Soviet Russia,* 6th ed. (New York: Praeger, 1972), pp. 80–87.

24. Ibid., p. 84.

25. Details for the above discussion come from von Rauch, *A History of Soviet Russia*, and Roland Gaucher, *Opposition in the U.S.S.R., 1917–1967* (New York: Funk and Wagnalls, 1969).

26. Ann Sheehy, "The Crimean Tatars and Volga Germans," in Whitaker, *The Fourth World*, pp. 270–305.

27. Hobart Rowen, "India's Submerged Women," *Washington Post,* Dec. 4, 1977.

28. Kate Young, "Employer Power," *The New Internationalist,* Oct. 1977.

29. "The U.S. and South Korean Textiles: A Closely Woven Fabric," a fact sheet put out by the American Friends Service Committee, 1501 Cherry St., Philadelphia, PA., 19102.

30. Patrick Montgomery, "Slavery—Old Evil Lingers On," *One World,* June 1977.

31. Betsy Hartmann and Jim Boyce, "Roshana," *The New Internationalist*, Oct. 1977.

32. Hedrick Smith, *The Russians* (New York: Ballantine Books, 1977), p. 171.

33. Wayne King, "Problem of Battered Wives Draws Increased Attention," *New York Times*, Dec. 3, 1977.

34. Ibid.

35. *WIN News*, Winter, 1979, p. 50.

36. Ibid., p. 41.

37. *WIN News*, Autumn, 1978, p. 41.

38. *WIN News*, Spring, 1978, pp. 6 and 48.

39. Figures drawn from William M. Mandel, *Soviet Women* (Garden City, N.Y.: Anchor Books, 1971), pp. 124–140.

40. Ibid., p. 179.

41. Sheila Rowbotham, *Women, Resistance and Revolution* (New York: Vintage, 1974), p. 149.

42. David K. Shipler, "A Modern Soviet Woman Emerges from the Islamic Veil," *New York Times*, Jan. 8, 1979.

43. Rowbotham, *Women, Resistance and Revolution*, p. 165.

# Chapter VII

# The United Nations—
# In Weakness and in Strength

Pollution . . . hunger . . . nuclear weapons . . . economic injustice . . . the list of world-sized problems seems to go on and on. No surprise, then, if the would-be world citizen feels alarmed, overwhelmed, and discouraged.

Fortunately, there are signs of hope: positive accomplishments that can give us inspiration and help guide our efforts.

In the next two chapters I will discuss some of these signs of hope, beginning with the United Nations and concluding with a look at what we as world citizens can do.

Anyone who has visited the United Nations headquarters in New York recalls the architecture as suitably impressive and in keeping with the notion of modern world government. The high steel-blue tower of the Secretary General's staff headquarters (the Secretariat) matches in grandeur any of the tall, modern corporate headquarters that dot Manhattan and manages to convey a sense that thousands of serious-minded bureaucrats are dutifully at work managing the complex affairs of global government. There are the required guards at each door and a pass system to keep visitors in check—just enough security to make one feel that something important is happening here.

Set against the Secretariat building is the low but sweepingly grand structure that houses the General Assembly. This is where most visitors will find themselves, carefully ushered about by multilingual guides from far-off lands, stopping in front of this mural or that statue, reading the lofty words that speak of Peace, Equality, Justice. Perhaps our party of visitors will get a chance to see the General Assembly in action—world-straddling debate in a superb but understated grand hall, capped with a domed ceiling.

That dome, one writer reminds us, is very significant. It is meant to tie the General Assembly to a host of other meaningful structures: the Pantheon, St. Peter's, the U.S. Capitol, Hagia Sophia. "Since ancient times," this writer goes on, "the dome is a symbol of religious or secular authority with universal if not utopian aspirations."[1]

The UN has more than its share of utopian and universal aspirations. While it has managed to become almost universal, it has come nowhere near the realization of its utopian hopes. It is not democratic, it has not brought world peace, it has not brought justice. Instead it passes lofty resolutions, which its members seem to ignore routinely; it condemns human rights in selected countries, while other massive violators of human rights are left unmentioned. It is, in so many ways, a massively disappointing institution.

And yet it is the only world government we've got. Its many weaknesses reflect not the incompetence of its administrators, or the lack of high ideals and global vision—they are instead reflective of its constituent members, who, organized into nation-states, have tried to make sure that this world institution never has the power to interfere with national self-interests.

Even so, there is a vitality, an idealism, and—most important—a growing planetary need that keeps the United Nations going, and growing. The very existence of global problems, and the need for global patterns of cooperation and communication to avoid greater ills, mandate an organization like the United Nations. The sheer realities of pollution, economic strain, and constant threats of armed conflict have forced the world's nation-states to mute their sovereign sensitivities and agree to work together in the United Nations framework. Therefore we can point to accomplishments, to achievements, and to positive trends in the development of our global government. These, indeed, can give us signs of hope for humanity's future.

### That Motley Assembly

By 1980 the United Nations had 152 sovereign members, each of whom could cast one vote in the General Assembly—a situation that means that Grenada, with 110,000 people and a Gross National Product of $50 million, has the same voting power as the United States, with its 214 million people and GNP of $1.7 trillion. No wonder the United Nations was referred to by one British statesman as "a motley assembly."[2] This one-state one-vote system means that an absolute majority of votes in the General Assembly can be gathered from nations who represent only 4.4 percent of the world's population; and a two-thirds majority can be had by countries representing only 10 percent of world population.[3] To make things worse, there are some fifty sub-microstates with populations under 100,000 who might conceivably be admitted to the United Nations.[4] Were these states to be added, the United Nations would find itself with 130 states (out of 201) with populations of less than five million.[5]

The General Assembly is supposed to be the more democratic organ of the United Nations—as contrasted with the Security Council—and yet none of its members is elected to be a representative of the people back home. Rather, delegates are appointed by the home government, and they must vote according to instructions from the state that sends them. Furthermore, less than one-third of the UN delegates come from countries that can be described as democracies. A rough estimate by this author, based on a world survey of political and civil liberties,[6] places the average United Nations member state at about five on a seven-point scale, seven being the worst. That means that a typical UN member, in terms of democratic freedoms, would be a state like South Korea, or Indonesia, or Iran under the Shah.

Turning to the Security Council, we find a body that is elite in the extreme, granting five special members the power to veto any major recommendation, resolution, or call for action. The Security Council was designed to be the upper chamber of a two-house UN system. It has the right to pass resolutions that are binding on the whole UN membership—including the imposition of economic or military sanctions on a member or non-member state. General Assembly resolutions, on the other hand, are only recommendations (the exception being the UN budget) and can be ignored by member states. In practice, however, both bodies only have the power to recommend, since there is no effective mechanism to enforce the decisions that they make. Voluntary compliance is the byword at the United Nations, and only in cases where the real world powers (especially the United States and the USSR) happen to agree do the sanctions of the UN system take real effect.

Thus, we have a relatively weak governing institution for the planet, with two undemocratic legislative assemblies, where one chamber is dominated by a big-power veto system, the other by the one-state one-vote system that gives small powers an overwhelming majority of votes. To this we should add that the executive, the UN secretary general, is elected by the member states, not by the world's people—and is dependent upon big-power sanction for any but the most discrete independent initiatives. Completing the picture is the judicial organ—the International Court of Justice—which has the power to rule on all manner of cases, but which can only consider items that are referred to it by the UN, or by states in which all national parties agree in advance to consult the court.

By now most U.S. readers will be comparing the UN government with our own, and finding it but a shadow of the powerful national mechanism that we have erected. After all, our president (comparable to the UN secretary general) is independently elected, and has the power of the veto. Plus the chief executive has enormous initiatory powers, especially in foreign policy, and often tends to dominate the legislative process as well. Our legislature is democratically elected, and our House of Representatives (comparable to the General Assembly) is truly representative of the population on a one-person one-vote system. Even our Senate (comparable to the Security Council), with its one-state two-votes system is at least democratically elected and does support the interest of state constituencies that might be overwhelmed by the population-centered House. Finally, our Supreme Court can hear cases that challenge willing or unwilling member states, and that can be initiated by aggrieved individuals—unlike the International Court of Justice.

### The Young Federal Nation

The United Nations suffers by comparison with the U.S. government as we find it today. If we compare the United Nations to the *infancy* of the new American Republic, however, we will learn more about the United Nations, and be more realistically appreciative of its accomplishments.

The central government of the United States of America was "small potatoes" in those days. It lived a hand-to-mouth existence, and by 1800 could boast of revenues totalling only $5.7 million.[7] It was small even in contrast to its member states, to whom the greater portion of power was given.

By virtue of their joint Declaration of Independence, each of the thirteen colonies had become a sovereign or semi-sovereign state. The first form of central government, under the Articles of Confederation, reflected this new status. The key to the confederated system was the equal power of each state, and the deliberate weakness of the joint government. Just as in the General Assembly, each state had one vote—regardless of size, wealth, or population. Just as in the General Assembly, the delegates to the central government were chosen by the state government, not by a popular election of the people.

As we know, the Articles of Confederation were found to be too weak to sustain the common union of the new states and a stronger compact was drawn up in 1787—our present Constitution. We find even here remarkable parallels with the United Nations. The new government that took power in 1788–89 still gave substantial recognition to the powers and prerogatives of the member states. While the House of Representatives was popularly elected by proportional representation, the Senate had its members chosen by each state legislature (a practice that did not end until the adoption of the 17th Amendment in 1913). Each state had two Senators, and thus two votes. The Senate, not the House, got the power to ratify treaties, and the power to approve or disapprove all significant presidential appointments, including appointments to the Supreme Court. In addition, all legislation had to have Senate approval. Since the Senators were elected by the legislatures of the member states, this gave enormous power to the constituent states.

Few of us today realize that the president was not to be popularly elected (and technically still isn't), but instead was to be elected by the states. The device for such an election was the Electoral College. Each state legislature appointed members to the Electoral College, the number being determined by the number of Senators and Representatives in its Congressional delegation. The Electors then voted for their choice for president, and the ballots were counted by the central government. If one person had a clear majority, then that person would be president. Thus the president was chosen, in effect, by the state legislatures and not by popular election.[8]

Finally, we need to recall one more set of important facts. Not only was the new central government still weakened by state control, but those states themselves were only mildly democratic in their internal governing structure.

In 1790, no woman could vote. Furthermore, most states required that a voter own property. This meant that only middle- and upper-class men could vote, and the state legislatures reflected the power of this small elite.

Those who aren't knowledgeable about early American history are often surprised to learn how undemocratic and elitist our federal system was at the outset. Liberty? It took one hundred years and a bloody Civil War to free the slaves, and then black Americans were free in name only. Justice? Lynching, the slaughter of the native population, Jim Crow laws, denial of women's rights—all of these gross injustices existed parallel with our lofty rhetoric and shining ideals.

We should think twice before we are too hard on the United Nations. If we count the League of Nations experiment (1919–1945), world government is only in its seventh decade. If we think the United Nations is weak, so was the U.S. government in its infancy. If we think the member states of the United Nations are often cruel and corrupt, so were many of the American states in the 1850s, when slavery and debt slavery were rampant, and state legislatures were routinely "bought and sold as sausages or fish are in the market."[9] If we are often frustrated that the United Nations does not do something about torture, injustice, poverty, we would do well to remember that only in the last few decades has our own government tried to do something about many of our most glaring social ills.

There is great hope in this analysis. Not, perhaps, for the miseries of today, but perhaps for some of those of tomorrow, or the next day. A justice-promoting global government is only a hope for this, the second generation to live with world institutions, but in twenty, or fifty, or one hundred years the citizens of that era may look back and marvel at how weak planetary government once was, just as we can look back and marvel at how narrow was the base that launched our experiment in national democracy.

### Growth and Change at the UN

Continuing our parallel with the growth of the U.S. central government, it is useful to recall that not only was the U.S. federal government lacking in democracy, it was also lacking in power. While it did have far more power than was granted under the Articles of Confederation, it still played a modest role in national development and welfare until the surprising growth of the twentieth century.

In 1900, the federal budget was a mere $400 million, quite a growth from the $5.7 million of 1800, but "insignificant" compared to the $4.3 billion budget of 1925. That in turn is dwarfed by the $615 billion budget of 1981.

The massive, complex U.S. national government of the 1980s would have astounded our founding fathers. The "imperial presidency" with its awesome powers and its command of the U.S. strategic nuclear arsenal; the "welfare state" with its vast social security, public assistance, aid-to-education programs; the "regulatory government" and its power to compel corporations and individuals to do this or stop doing that—all of these realities of our present system are major innovations of the past fifty years.

These greater powers each came about as a result of evolutionary tendencies and revolutionary developments. The revolutionary developments were unique and somewhat unexpected: the atomic bomb, the Great Depression, World War II.

Similarly, we can look to both evolutionary and revolutionary developments in the future of the United Nations system. The revolutionary developments can only be guessed at—World War III, an ecological disaster of massive proportions, the sudden appearance of hostile little green people from Vega 5—but the evolutionary developments can be studied and even predicted.

In the discussion of UN achievements that follows, we can ascertain some of the evolutionary trends that are at work in our global government, trends that can give us some glimmer of hope.

## UN Peacekeeping

If there was any one factor that drove the world's nations to take a second stab at global government, it was the specter of war. As the founding nations met in San Francisco, the battles of World War II still raged on. The United States, foremost in the ranks of the victors, was determined to cement a new world order that would save its citizens, and others, from the ravages of World War III, or even lesser wars.

Thus, the first item in the Preamble to the United Nations Charter speaks of determination "to save succeeding generations from the scourge of war," and then continues to speak of "uniting our strength to maintain international peace and security," and "ensur[ing]. . . . that armed force shall not be used, save in the common interest."

This precedence given to peace continues in the body of the Charter, Article I clearly stating that the purpose of the United Nations is to "take effective collective measures for the prevention and removal of threats to peace, and for the suppression of acts of aggression or other breaches of the peace. . . ."

Finally, the commitment to peacekeeping is given flesh in Chapter VII of the Charter, which empowers the Security Council to use armed force to change any situation which it determines is a threat to the peace.

Yet here we are, almost four decades after the founding of the United Nations, and wars and threats to peace have continued unabated. We have not yet had World War III—though we have come close—and civil wars and limited wars have taken as many lives as were lost in all of World War II.

Year after year there has been war somewhere on the planet, causing many people to become bitter about the UN's inability to keep the peace. The UN's inaction in face of Vietnam's invasion of Kampuchea (Cambodia), of China's subsequent invasion of Vietnam, and its weakness in dealing with the Soviet invasion of Afghanistan, are only the most recent examples of UN helplessness in situations of clear aggression.

In fact, the UN is not helpless. It does have the legal power to intervene militarily in conflicts, provided there is a strong enough agreement in the Security Council or the General Assembly. The Security Council has the power to use armed force or economic sanctions or blockades against any aggressor state or to interpose itself between two warring states. Once the Security Council decides to undertake an action, it can require all UN members to cooperate, it can direct the UN secretary general to implement its orders, and it can ask the General Assembly to fund the operation through a legal assessment that is binding upon all members.

Though any proposed Security Council action runs the risk of a veto by any one of the Council's five permanent members—France, Great Britain, China, the United States, and the Soviet Union—still there have been times when the Security Council has been able to take common action. In 1964, for example, it authorized a UN peacekeeping force for civil-war-torn Cyprus, and the force is still there, trying to mediate between the opposing Greek and Turkish factions. The Security Council has placed peacekeeping forces in Lebanon (1978), the Sinai (1973), and the Congo (1960). It has also dispatched non-combatant observer teams to the Balkans (1946), Kashmir (1947), the Golan Heights between Syria and Israel (1973), and elsewhere.

In the event of a deadlock in the Security Council, the General Assembly has the power—under the controversial "Uniting for Peace" Resolution—to override the Security Council and call for action on its own. In 1956 this power was used by the General Assembly to condemn the Soviet invasion of Hungary and to call for the removal of Soviet tanks and troops. The secretary general was directed to go to Hungary to ascertain whether the rights of the people were being violated, but the new Soviet-supported government of Janos Kadar refused him entry. No peacekeeping force was established, however, because the United States and others were not willing to go to war over the issue.[10]

The Resolution was also used to send troops to the Sinai during the 1956 Suez crisis in which Great Britain, France, and Israel invaded Egypt in order to keep it from seizing control of the Canal. The UN Emergency Force, UNEF, supervised the withdrawal of the invaders and patrolled the area to keep conflicts from recurring. UNEF successfully fulfilled this role until 1967, when Egypt asked it to withdraw. New fighting broke out thereafter.[11]

### The Congo Debacle

The Congo intervention in 1960 is the most ambitious peacekeeping effort that the United Nations has ever undertaken. At its height, twenty thousand UN troops were in the country. The UN military presence lasted for four years (1960–1964). Unlike the Korean intervention—which was just a cloak for U.S. involvement—the Congo operation had initial support from a broad cross-section of the world community. It began when the elected government of the newly independent Congo (now Zaire) found itself faced simultaneously with a rebellion of its native police, a secession of its richest province, and a partial re-occupation by Belgian troops.

The Congolese government asked for international aid, and the United Nations was quick to respond. Within days, the first detachment of UN troops arrived, the Belgians left, and a kind of peace was restored. But the UN troops, under the direct command of the secretary general, soon found themselves in a very awkward position. The Congolese central government wanted the UN troops to use force to end the Katangan secession, yet the UN had no clear mandate to do so, and some of its European members opposed such a move.

To further complicate matters, the two chief politicians of the central government—Prime Minister Patrice Lumumba and President Joseph Kasavubu—had a falling out and each fired the other from office. As each party rallied its internal supporters, the member nations of the United Nations began to line up behind their favorite candidate. The USSR and the leftist bloc in the United Nations supported Lumumba. The United States, Western Europe, and the more conservative Third World countries tended to support Kasavubu. And a smaller, but influential, bloc supported the leader of the breakaway province of Katanga—Moise Tshombe. The secretary general was hopelessly caught in the middle of these factions.

The situation deteriorated further. Lumumba was kidnapped and murdered. Some people charged that the United Nations, which had been guarding Lumumba's house, was implicated in his death. Meanwhile, President Kasavubu was deposed by a military coup. There was now no legal government from the UN point of view. The secretary general (Dag Hammarskjold) tried to reconcile the competing Congolese factions, but earned the ire of the USSR, which demanded his resignation. What had begun as a bold demonstration of UN peacekeeping power had deteriorated into an international debacle.

After great effort, the UN troops were directed to put down the Katanga secession, and UN officials patched together a coalition government which lasted long enough for the UN to get out.[12]

What had the United Nations accomplished in the Congo? It can be argued that, had the United Nations not intervened, Katanga under Tshombe would have made good on its secession, and that would have crippled the country. It can also be argued that UN action prevented unilateral action by the Soviet Union or the United States which might have led to a Vietnam-style confrontation, or worse. Further, it may well be that a great amount of bloodshed was avoided by the intervention of UN troops. And finally, it is worth noting that the UN did set up a technical aid program that supplied experts and administrators to replace the colonial Belgians and that trained the native peoples to succeed them.

But the Congo involvement also put the United Nations on the firing line between the United States and the Soviet Union and between conservative Third World countries and more radical ones. Instead of showing how useful the United Nations could be in a violent confrontation, it showed how easily military intervention could threaten the very fabric of the UN.

What the Congo intervention shows is that the United Nations is capable of action when its members agree, though continued agreement is necessary to complete the task. Once again, the cooperation of the United States and the Soviet Union, as the world's foremost military powers, is essential in keeping a local situation contained. When rivalry replaces cooperation, the danger of a fatal rift in the United Nations shows itself in glaring light.

From an evolutionary point of view, there are several developments that should be noted in the UN's peacekeeping history. First, there was the very significant seizure by the General Assembly of the power to act when the Security Council is stymied. The Assembly's power—under the "Uniting for Peace" Resolution—has been used several times since 1950, and could be used again. Second, the World Court ruled that General Assembly assessments for the Congo operation were legally binding on the members, though the General Assembly has decided for the moment not to press the point. Third, there emerged the prominent role of the secretary general as commander-in-chief of the UN forces in the Congo. While this resulted in great controversy, it also set a precedent for future action. Fourth, the United Nations has been able to finance itself even though the Soviet Union and others have refused to pay for some major bills, as in the Congo operation.

### Nuclear Arms

If ever there were an issue that would seem to draw upon universal consensus, it is the issue of the nuclear arms race. There is no place on earth that is safe from the potential destruction of a nuclear exchange, no matter how peaceful the people, no matter how innocent. Not surprisingly, the General Assembly, most of whose members do not possess nuclear weapons, has expressed itself strongly on the subject of the arms race, calling it "the most important (question) facing the world today."[13]

Here, too, there are some accomplishments that the United Nations can point to: a treaty banning nuclear weapons in the Antarctic (1959), another banning such weapons in outer space (1967), another barring nuclear weapons in the ocean seabeds (1972), and a treaty that declares Latin America to be a nuclear weapons-free zone (1967). These treaties have at least limited the placement of nuclear weapons, if not their numbers, their range, or their destructive power. Only in the case of biological weapons has the United Nations actually been able to promote disarmament—that is, the actual reduction and destruction of existing weapons.[14]

Why is the record of the United Nations on disarmament so skimpy? Because, as Alva Myrdal (Sweden's UN disarmament expert) learned after years of sincere efforts, the superpowers do not want to disarm—and even if they do, they do not want to let the United Nations in on their process of serious negotiation.

Among the UN negotiators, those from the nonaligned nations have been able to apply a global outlook. The proposals they have made could not, in sober analysis, be said to go against anybody's interest, not even those of the superpowers and their allies. But all their attempts have been thwarted because of the resistance of the superpowers. More and more a pattern has become visible: though seeming to struggle against each other, the superpowers are in a kind of conspiracy, dividing between them the responsibility for saying yes and no. They apparently want to continue their arms race, to make mutual concessions, minor as they are, within bilateral negotiations, undisturbed by the majority of nations.[15]

According to Myrdal, the USSR and the United States have consistently backed away from any substantive negotiations within the United Nations framework, preferring to hold bilateral SALT-type talks that do not have to take the opinions of other nations into account.

In 1978, the General Assembly held a special session of its entire membership to try to put some pressure on the nuclear powers to disarm. As a result of this session the United Nations' Disarmament Commission was given new life and a mandate to seek treaties establishing nuclear-weapons-free zones in Africa and the Middle East. The smaller Committee on Disarmament, which has forty members, was strengthened and urged to tackle the disarmament issue head-on; its goal: a "general and complete disarmament under effective international control."

The United Nations alone does not have the power to force these countries to give up their arsenals of destruction, but an aroused citizenry does. Only a strong national and international citizens' peace movement possesses the potential to effect disarmament, and while the United Nations may be weak in this area, we can at least take heart that it will be a firm and determined ally to such a movement.

## Decolonization

Over the last half a century we have witnessed the demise of colonialism as, one by one, former colonies have gained their political independence. Increasingly, these former colonies are now trying to loose the bonds of economic dependence as well.

It would be incorrect to give the United Nations full credit for these developments, but it is also impossible to ignore its very significant role in the process of decolonization and liberation. As we shall see, weak though it might seem, the anti-colonial forces have been able to use this world organization as an important ally in their struggle for change.

It seems in hindsight that an end to colonialism was somehow inevitable. Like slavery and the leeching of blood as a cure for illness, colonial domination was a wornout idea, no longer compatible with the modern mind. If, in fact, we now feel that way about colonialism, it is a testimony to the rapidity with which ideas can change. Less than one hundred years ago, colonialism was still quite popular in the European mind: explorers were opening the "dark continent" of Africa, Cecil Rhodes was dreaming of a white empire in southern and eastern Africa, the United States was discovering that its own Manifest Destiny justified the occupation of Cuba and the Philippines. These were the times when Europeans and their American cousins felt called to take up the "white man's burden" and bring the unenlightened nations out into the sunshine of our higher civilization. Behind their "selflessness," there lay the base motives of greed and hunger for land—factors that played a key role in bringing on World War I and World War II.

By the beginning of World War II, there were still some eighty colonial territories on the planet—representing almost one-third of the world's population, and dominated by just eight European nations and the United States.[16] Even before the United States entered the war, President Roosevelt and his chief advisers had already begun to think about the world they desired to see emerge at the end of the conflict. On one thing they were clear: the post-war world should be wide open to the benefits of healthy competition, meaning that the United States should have equal access to previously closed trading areas. Since most of those areas were under colonial domination, a policy of anti-colonialism had the twin advantages of meeting America's idealistic desires as well as its materialistic ones.

Thus, when Roosevelt and Churchill met off the coast of Newfoundland in August of 1941 to draw up a statement of common war aims, the resultant Atlantic Charter contained a commitment to "respect the right of all peoples to choose the form of government under which they will live," and expressed the desire "to see sovereign rights and self-government restored to those who have been forcibly deprived of them."[17]

The British view of the desirable post-war order was rather different from the American view. Churchill and his associates hoped to retain their hold on the British Empire, including their trade advantages, and they expected to be the pre-eminent power in Europe. Not surprisingly, they insisted that the self-determination clause in the Atlantic Charter applied to the independent nations that had been captured by the Axis powers, and did not apply to the colonies. The Americans disagreed, arguing that the principles of the Charter applied to "the world as a whole—in all oceans and all continents."[18]

Throughout the course of the war, the struggle over the colonial empires continued between the British and the Americans. In order to bolster their position, the British also championed the cause of the French colonial empire, and they took whatever steps they could to help the French restore their rule in former colonies that had been occupied by others during the war. For example, the British had taken control of the French island colony of Madagascar, off the coast of Africa, in order to deny it to either the Germans or the German-controlled French government at Vichy. In 1943, they allowed De Gaulle's Free French troops to take over their position. The Free French then used military force to put down a native independence movement, killing somewhere between 80,000 and 220,000 people in the process. The British also supported the Free French in their "pacification" of Algeria, Tunisia, and Morocco—campaigns that left 45,000 dead in Morocco and 7,000 dead in Tunisia.[19]

By the end of the war it was obvious that Great Britain was not going to be a commercial threat to the United States; that in fact, it was going to need a considerable infusion of funds just to stay afloat. The new threat was the Soviet Union, with whom relations were steadily deteriorating. As the Cold War began to develop in the midst of the hot war, the United States began to realize that Great Britain and a revitalized Europe would be important assets in any future conflict.

Roosevelt had thought that he and Stalin could work out their differences and cooperate in the post-war order. Whether he could have done so is a moot point, since by the time of the founding conference of the United Nations in San Francisco in 1945, Roosevelt was dead. In his place was Harry Truman, a man who was determined not to let the Soviets, or any other left-wing movements, challenge the American world order. The word went out to the U.S. delegation at San Francisco that a hard stand in favor of the independence of colonies was to be dropped. The French delegation was quietly assured that the United States had no intention of challenging the military reimposition of French control in Indo-China, a complete about-face from Roosevelt's sentiments.[20]

Even though the fifty-one nations that adopted the UN Charter were hand-picked by U.S. planners, the Anglo-American alliance faced problems when the question of the colonial empires came up. Over half the delegations were from former colonies, and emotions against imperialism and western domination ran high. To this bloc could be added the Soviet Union, its allies, and the anti-colonial leadership of Australia's delegation. Together they formed a solid majority in favor of a strong stand against colonialism.

The issue was joined on May 12, 1945, when the representatives from the Soviet Union and China (still under Chiang Kai-shek) announced that they wanted the word "independence" inserted in the Charter. More than that, the Soviets argued for "full national independence and self-determination in all colonial areas," a view that alarmed the colonial powers, and that forced the United States to choose between the "old" powers, and the new anti-colonial bloc. The choice, as outlined by U.S. delegate Harold Stassen, was to side with the colonialists, because "we . . . did not wish to find ourselves committed to breaking up the British Empire."[21]

The U.S. delegation then began lining up the votes. China, then an American ally, was persuaded to drop its suggestion. The Philippines was pressured, the Latin Americans were told that the United States needed votes to combat Soviet propaganda, and so on. In the end, a much weaker series of measures was passed:

—First, the word "independence" was dropped from the Charter chapter on the colonial empires, urging their rulers instead to "develop self-government . . . according to the particular circumstances of each territory and its peoples and their varying stages of advancement."

—Second, the colonial powers were pledged to submit information on the social, economic, and educational developments in their colonies. These reports were to be given to the secretary general, and not to the Trusteeship Council, and this meant that accountability was very limited indeed.

—Third, the Trusteeship Council was given power only over the mandated territories* and any territories that might be detached from the Axis powers. In the next few years, ten territories—all of them former League mandates—were placed under trust agreements with the Trusteeship Council. The Council was given the power to review progress in the trust territories, to receive and discuss petitions from individuals in these areas, and to make periodic inspection visits. All of these powers were improvements over the very weak League system.

On the whole, the San Francisco conference could be judged a failure with regard to liberation from colonial domination. The remarkable story, however, is the way in which the anti-colonial bloc used the limited powers under the Charter to transform the United Nations into an important force for promoting independence.

The key to this development lay with the increased activity of the General Assembly. As new members were added to this body, it came more and more to be led by a strong pro-independence bloc. Less and less was the United States inclined to try to corral votes on behalf of the colonial powers, especially since the Soviet Union was making a lot of political mileage from its strong anti-colonial stands.

From 1946 to 1960 the United Nations was only mildly involved in anti-colonial activities. It did successfully block the attempt of South Africa to incorporate the mandated territory of South West Africa (now Namibia), and it supervised the polling in several mandated countries that voted for independence (British Togoland, French Togoland).

These first few years of activism were nothing compared with the heightened advocacy that began in 1960. By that time, the General Assembly had grown to almost one hundred members, many of them newly independent. After considerable debate and re-drafting, the General Assembly adopted a remarkably strong "Declaration on the Granting of Independence to Colo-

*After World War I, the colonies of the defeated powers were given to various victors who were "mandated" the responsibility for their social and economic progress. Some of these colonies were to be granted independence, others could be held for an indefinite period. When the United Nations was established, the League of Nations' mandates passed on to the new organization. Palestine and Southwest Africa are examples of such territories.

nial Countries and Peoples." Among its major points were statements that seem light-years beyond the equivocal wording of the Charter:

1. The subjection of peoples to alien subjugation, domination and exploitation constitutes a denial of fundamental human rights, is contrary to the Charter of the United Nations and is an impediment to the promotion of world peace and cooperation.

2. All peoples have the right to self-determination, by virtue of that right they freely determine their political status and freely pursue their economic, social and cultural development.

3. Inadequacy of political, economic, social or educational preparedness should never serve as a pretext for delaying independence.[22]

Here, then, is an extraordinary statement, one that would never have had a chance of adoption at San Francisco, but which breezed through the General Assembly by a vote of eighty-nine in favor, none opposed, and nine abstentions. Among the abstainers was the United States. Its entire delegation had urged a yes vote, only to be overruled by President Eisenhower after a personal appeal from British Prime Minister Harold Macmillan.

What had happened in the fifteen years since the founding of the United Nations? The answer is that the General Assembly had declared its own independence and refused to have its vote determined by any of the great powers. Furthermore, a host of former colonies had won their freedom, and the momentum was in favor of liberation. Africa especially was becoming rapidly de-colonized, and the African-Asian bloc was most active in pressing for a stronger UN role. The colonial powers were on the defensive, as witnessed by the fact that none of them had even dared to vote against the strongly-worded Declaration, but rather had abstained.

Other methods that the United Nations has used in its activism are fascinating extensions of the organization's surprising power to act. These methods have established interesting precedents for the future. For instance, the General Assembly established a Special Committee to oversee implementation of the Declaration on the Granting of Independence. Unlike previous committees, the Special Committee had a majority of anti-colonial members, and chose its leaders from among the most active. This committee has taken a vigorously aggressive stance, challenging colonial regimes, meeting with representatives of liberation groups, holding hearings in disputed territories, urging the General Assembly and the Security Council to greater action.

Under the leadership of the Special Committee, the United Nations has taken the following steps to combat the remains of colonialism:

—The Security Council asked all members not to recognize the white Rhodesian declaration of independence, and asked the colony's administrator, Great Britain, to retake control of the country (1965). In 1966 the Security Council, for the first time ever, called for mandatory economic sanctions against Rhodesia.

—The General Assembly revoked the League mandate to South Africa for South West Africa (Namibia) and established a Special Committee for South West Africa, which was to determine how the United Nations could take control of the area (1966). This was followed by a series of actions, including re-naming the area Namibia in accordance with the wishes of the liberation movements (1968). The Security Council followed up with a declaration in 1970 that South African occupation of Namibia was illegal. It subsequently urged all states to cease all support for South Africa's claim.

—The Special Committee on De-colonization sent a special mission to the liberated areas of Portuguese Guinea (now Guinea-Bissau) and declared that the liberation movement had de facto control of the country. The General Assembly (1972) affirmed that the national liberation movements in the three Portuguese African colonies of Guinea-Bissau, Mozambique, and Angola were the "authentic representatives of the aspirations of the territories' people" and asked that all agencies within the UN system include representatives of these groups in their meetings.

It would be a mistake to give the greatest credit to the United Nations for the rapid process of decolonization that occurred after World War II. More important factors, perhaps, were the economic and military weakness of the colonial powers; the Cold War struggle between the United States and the USSR, in which the United States did not want to lose credibility with the new nations; and the violent and nonviolent resistance of the colonized peoples themselves. The United Nations played a secondary role in decolonization, yet it was an important and, at times, crucial role. The United Nations, and especially the General Assembly, became an important center for anti-colonial activity, adding a legal and a moral framework to the movement that was virtually unassailable.

### Setting the Pace for the Planet

In recent years the United Nations has developed a special role as a promoter of good causes for the planet. Lacking the power to pass binding global legislation, the United Nations has become a shaper of the world's agenda for social change.

A pattern of action has emerged which looks something like this: A group of nations (or even non-governmental advocacy groups) who feel strongly about an issue bring it to the General Assembly. If enough member states feel the issue is important, the General Assembly may call for a World Conference to be held on the topic, or hold a Special Session itself to consider the issue, or refer it to a committee with a request for a proposed Declaration by the General Assembly. If a conference or Special Session is held, the issue (world hunger, for instance) is given broad global publicity—world awareness of the problem is heightened; usually a declaration or statement is issued that calls for national and international action.

All of the above (concern to conference to statement) can be considered

Stage I of the United Nations' advocacy role. It might be called a process of gaining global consensus on an issue, an agreement by the representatives of the world's nations that, yes, discrimination against women is a bad thing or, yes, the arms race poses a grave danger to humankind. Having accomplished this (and it may take five or ten or even twenty years to get to this point) the United Nations is now in a position to be an advocate for action. Thus we come to Stage II.

In Stage II, the United Nations assumes the task of persuading the nations of the world to live up to their own rhetoric. The United Nations may set up a special program or agency whose sole purpose is to achieve compliance with the new consensus. Model legislation is drawn up for states to consider adopting; regional conferences are held at which country delegations are asked what they intend to do about this problem; international covenants and treaties are developed which nations are asked to sign, thus binding themselves through international law. This completes Stage II.

Having completed Stage II (consensus to formal national agreement) we come to the third stage of action, and that, quite simply, is to pressure the nations to follow through on what they have agreed to do. To this end, the United Nations cajoles, upbraids, encourages, calls for reports, deplores, publicizes—whatever it can think to do to keep up the momentum for change. Some have called this a role of upholding the world's conscience. I would suggest that the term "keeper of the consensus" might be more accurate, since at times the United Nations has been unable to achieve a working consensus about matters that to some are morally objectionable.

A brief example of this process can be found in United Nations action against racial discrimination. In 1969 an International Convention on the Elimination of All Forms of Racial Discrimination was signed by the requisite number of nations to make it binding on these and all future signatories. This Convention obliges each state to end official acts of discrimination and to prohibit such practices by non-governmental groups and clubs.

Having drawn up the Covenant and promoted it, the United Nations then turned to enforcement. This compliance is monitored by a special Committee on the Elimination of Racial Discrimination to which each state must furnish a report of compliance, and whose representatives must then appear to defend their report (and their country's behavior) under detailed questioning by a panel of eighteen experts who are serving not as country representatives, but in their personal capacity—meaning that they are more free to ask tough questions. Similar committees have been established to deal with human rights reports from countries that have signed the appropriate covenants, and to monitor country compliance with a covenant against discrimination against women.

Of course, there are countries that do not choose to sign these covenants, and others who sign and then ignore their duties. In these instances the United Nations tries to use its other mechanisms to shame or even coerce the maverick to comply. Through a World Conference in 1978, for instance, the United

Nations has tried to focus attention on renegade South Africa. The Conference adopted a Programme of Action to combat racial discrimination, one part of which included a call to the United Nations to adopt mandatory economic sanctions against this gross violator of human rights.

## Action on the Environment

One of the more encouraging stories to come out of the United Nations system in the past decade is the way in which environmental concern has been enhanced by UN advocacy.

When the United Nations decided to hold a World Conference on the Human Environment, many Third World countries were skeptical—even hostile. They felt that environmentalism was a luxury that only the rich, industrialized nations could afford, and they feared that ecological concern might be a weapon that the rich nations would use to halt development in the poor nations.

Yet these attitudes have changed. So much so that one observer who was an organizer of the 1972 conference has termed the 1970s a decade of "revolutionary" change in world environmental concern.[23] The United Nations deserves a great deal of credit for this change in attitude, since it has broadened the concept of environment to include such Third World concerns as unclean water and destruction of soils.

The United Nations established a special body, called the United Nations Environment Programme (UNEP), and gave it a home in Nairobi, Kenya—thus making it the first United Nations global body to be headquartered in a developing country. UNEP was charged with the role of being a catalyst, that is, an agent that stimulates action by others. It was given a modest budget and a small fund with which to stimulate new programs or to conduct experimental projects.

Aided by an increased world awareness of environmental problems, UNEP has been remarkably efficient in its use of small resources. In 1972 there were only eleven developing countries that had agencies that addressed environmental concerns; by 1979 that number had grown to eighty-seven countries, many of whose programs were set up with UNEP assistance and advice. Further, as these agencies have hired staff, UNEP has helped to train them. Finally, when a country is ready to consider adopting environmental laws, UNEP can help them design legislation that suits their needs.

Environmentalists are pleased that as a result of the United Nations' efforts to heighten world concern they can now point to developing countries who are taking the lead in ecological action. Venezuela, for example, created in 1976 a Ministry of Environment and Renewable National Resources that has broad powers to challenge pollution and environmental deterioration. This ministry has established citizen boards in each municipality that act as watchdogs over ecological crime, as well as being educators of the general public. The government has also launched a national reforestation campaign that in its first three years was able to plant 65 million trees.

UNEP has also been able to play a creative role in bringing countries together to address common problems. A fine example can be found in UNEP's convocation of the Mediterranean border states to agree on joint environmental action. Prodded by UNEP, these seventeen countries (Albania has not participated) have worked out and signed a covenant on protecting the sea from chemical dumping and other hazards. Seven pollution monitoring stations have been set up to alert the signatories to problems, and France has developed a Blue Plan for the entire area which will help guide future efforts. UNEP has started to play a similar role in the Caribbean and in the Persian Gulf.[24]

Another special contribution of UNEP has been in the area of global information sharing. The Global Environmental Monitoring System (GEMS) is a UNEP project that coordinates the monitoring of several other United Nations agencies in the environmental areas of climate, health, oceans, and renewable natural resources. One part of GEMS, for example, is a World Health Organization program that will establish over three hundred stations around the world to monitor water pollution.[25]

And so the work of UNEP goes: setting up an experimental rural energy center in Sri Lanka, planning and hosting a World Conference on Desertification (Nairobi, 1977), launching a yearly observance of World Environment Day (June 5). Surely in the UNEP we can see a sign of hope for global problem management.

## The New International Economic Order

Having begun this book with the question of economic injustice, it may be fitting to close my chapter on the United Nations with a consideration of what the UN has done to fashion more just global economic structures. One wishes that, as in the case of the environment, we could point to rapid and determined actions. Unfortunately, we cannot.

Certainly the United Nations has placed itself firmly on the side of the poor and the hungry. In the case of refugees, for instance, the United Nations feeds and cares for hundreds of thousands around the world. The World Food Programme has taken the lead in responding to famine. The United Nations Development Programme gives aid to development projects. UNICEF tries to help poor children and their parents.

What about the deeper, structural problems that the developing world faces? What about the rules of the game that are stacked in favor of the rich countries? What has the United Nations done about these?

The answer is that the United Nations has tried to meet the question directly in the General Assembly and that it has managed to achieve the beginnings of a global consensus on these questions. Moving to implement this consensus, however, is going to be difficult in the extreme.

In 1974, the UN General Assembly held an important Special Session on global economic structures. After weeks of behind-the-scenes negotiating (really after years of debate prior to this session) the Assembly adopted a

Declaration on the Establishment of a New International Economic Order (NIEO). The Declaration called for the following:

1. Greater international control over the large private corporations, so that they cannot easily use their superior wealth and inside knowledge to unfair advantage in relations with the Less Developed Countries (LDCs).
2. Arrangements between developed countries and LDCs that insure the stability of prices of raw materials. And that the prices of raw materials be linked to the prices of manufactured goods.
3. Encouragement for producers' cooperatives, like that of the oil-producing countries, among Third World countries.
4. Recognition of the right of a nation to control its own resources, including the right to nationalize the holdings of a foreign corporation. (Not without compensation, however.)
5. Reform of the International Monetary Fund and World Bank, to give the LDCs greater voting power (at present six rich countries control 54 percent of the vote, with the other 46 percent divided between 108 countries), and the creation of a Special Drawing Rights system that favors Third World development.
6. Support for industrialization in the Third World, with a target of 25 percent of industry being located there by the year 2000 (the current figure is 7 percent).
7. Greater aid to the LDCs, and on better terms. Review of debts owed to rich governments, and cancellation of these wherever possible.
8. Better "terms of trade" between LDCs and developed countries, in particular the reduction of tariffs and barriers against Third World manufactured and finished goods, and the acceptance of the Third World's right to protect fledgling industries from severe international competition.
9. Support for the transfer of modern technology to the Third World, by companies, by governments, and by international agencies.
10. A "Special Program" of aid and assistance for the poorest of the developing countries—sometimes referred to as the Fourth World.

There are many other details and recommendations in the Program of Action, but these ten are among the most important. The fact that these proposals are not radically new, or even particularly revolutionary, reflects the compromise nature of the document, as well as the realities of global power distribution.

The Declaration on the New International Economic Order is not a piece of binding legislation. Rather, it is a platform for continued debate and negotiation. It represents not the culmination of discussion, but a summation and a restatement of goals—and it sets the stage for a global debate that may well reshape the lives of all the world's people.

The struggle to bring a new international economic order will be fierce.

The NIEO document calls for dramatic and painful change—painful to those countries, and companies, who are profiting from the present system. These reforms could mean that citizens of the wealthy countries will have to pay more for imported products, as they have for oil. They could mean that manufacturing employment would rise in the poor countries while falling in the rich countries. In other words, it could mean more inflation and fewer jobs in countries like the United States, Canada, and those in Western Europe.

The debate about the New International Economic Order is going to be part of our lives and our children's lives. It is, in reality, a world discussion about how our planet's economic life is going to be organized, and the complexity and importance of it for human well-being cannot be too highly emphasized.

It represents an attempt to undo some of the injustices of the past, and to give a better life for all in the future. It is, in reality, the centerpiece of a conscious global agenda for humankind. Such a debate, and the changes it may bring, is of vital concern to all the world's people.

It seems eminently appropriate that the United Nations take the lead in this project. For all of its weaknesses and shortcomings, the United Nations is the one forum that brings us all together, and which—with a better degree of consistency than most governments—asks us to consider what is fair, what is moral, what is just, and then to act on that considered judgment.

As citizens of our nation, and as citizens of the world, we need to respond to the global agenda that is taking shape through the United Nations. We need to do this for the sake of global justice—and for our own sake as well.


### NOTES

1. Stephan G. Xydis, "The General Assembly," James Barras, ed., *The United Nations: Past, Present, and Future* (New York: Free Press, 1972), p. 98.

2. William Roger Louis, *Imperialism at Bay* (New York: Oxford University Press, 1978), p. 472.

3. Author's calculations based upon 1976 population estimates by the World Bank.

4. Elmer Plischke, "Microstates: Lilliputs in World Affairs," *The Futurist*, February 1978.

5. Ibid.

6. "Survey of Freedom, 1978," *Freedom at Issue*, January–February, 1979.

7. *Encyclopedia Americana*, 1970, vol. 15, p. 289.

8. Taken from *The Encyclopedia Americana*, 1970, vol. 4, pp. 412, 413, vol. 7, p. 659.

9. From a description of the corrupt Massachusetts legislature at the close of the nineteenth century, Thomas W. Lawson, *Frenzied Finance* (New York: Greenwood Press, 1968), p. 140. (Originally printed in 1905).

10. This account is taken from *Everyman's United Nations*, 8th edition (New York: United Nations, 1968), pp. 190–193.

11. See fact sheet on "The UN and the Middle East," published by the United Nations Association, New York, 1977.

12. This account of events in the Congo is taken from two sources: Roger Hilsman, *To Move a Nation* (New York: Dell Publishing Company, 1967); and *Everyman's United Nations*, 8th Edition.

13. *United Nations Today*, published by the United Nations for United Nations Day, October 24, 1979, p. 36.

14. Ibid., p. 37.

15. Alva Myrdal, *The Game of Disarmament* (New York: Pantheon, 1976), p. xvii.

16. *Everyman's United Nations*, 8th edition, p. 143.

17. Quoted in Sidney Lens, *The Forging of the American Empire* (New York: Thomas Y. Crowell, 1974), p. 329.

18. This statement was made by Sumner Welles, Under Secretary of State, in 1942, and was duly noted by the British. Cited in Louis, *Imperialism at Bay*, p. 155.

19. Lens, *Forging*, p. 331.

20. Louis, *Imperialism at Bay*, p. 552.

21. Ibid., p.537.

22. The full text is cited in *The United Nations and Decolonization*, a UN publication, 1977.

23. Whitman Bassow, "The Third World: Changing Attitudes Toward Environmental Protection," *The Annals of the American Academy of Political and Social Science*, vol. 444, July 1979.

24. *Uniterra*, February 1980. Published monthly by UNEP, Nairobi, Kenya.

25. *The United Nations Environment Programme* (Nairobi, Kenya: UNEP, 1979), pp. 26, 27.

# Chapter VIII

# Citizen Action

If the United Nations were capable of solving all the world's problems, there would be no reason for me to continue my discussion. But, as we have seen, the United Nations does not have this sweeping capacity, and perhaps it never should. After all, many of us are already unhappy with the red tape and bulkiness of our own central government—just imagine the size of its bureaucracy if the United Nations really ran the world.

Bureaucracy aside, many people fear the possible repressive powers of a strong world government and worry that they would find themselves or their country coerced into unpleasant compliance with the global *dictat*. Better, it is argued, to have a weak global government that can act only on the basis of clear and overwhelming consensus.

Thus some people are relatively happy with the United Nations in its present form: a global debating forum with limited programs and powers. Change, they say, can come as a result of voluntary compliance of nations, and through the pressure of world opinion.

I am intrigued by this term "world opinion," as though somehow the planet had a mind of its own. What it generally seems to mean is quite similar to the term "public opinion" in the United States; that is, a summation of the feeling of a majority of the people, as expressed in countless face-to-face interactions, through organized group action, and via the media. Therefore an appeal to world opinion is an appeal to a world citizenry, asking them to express themselves to the institutions of power.

Thus the final statement of the UN Special Session on Disarmament (1978) expresses the hope that its deliberations "will attract the attention of all peoples, further mobilize world public opinion and provide a powerful impetus for the cause of disarmament."

This call is directed at you and me. It is directed at the citizen of Egypt and the citizen of Jamaica. It is a call to all of us to do what we can to promote human betterment—in this case the issue is disarmament, but it could be pollution, racism, hunger, or human rights. It implies an interactive process whereby the citizens of the planet engage themselves with their own national government as well as with others. It asks that we take up the duties of world citizenship and that we give some allegiance to humankind. It is not an easy call—there are so many claims on our time, so many competing loyalties to consider—but it is a call to which we should respond.

Many of us are used to the idea that we have a certain responsibility for our neighborhood, for our community, and for our nation. Only in recent years has it become apparent that we also have a responsibility to humankind, and to our planet. In this chapter I would like to consider the responsibilities that we have as U.S. citizens who are also part of a global system. I shall argue that we must work to make sure that our nation is part of the solution to world ills, rather than part of the problem, and that in addition to influencing our own national behavior there are also ways in which we can join with international citizens' movements for change.

## Human Rights

In recent years I have come to be convinced that a key contribution which citizen activists can make to the process of building a better world is *through promotion of a greater respect for human rights*. In using the term human rights, I am using it as most of us understand it: the right to speak freely, to dissent, to practice one's faith, to join with others to promote change, to urge one's government to do or not to do something—all without fear of reprisal.*

Why are these rights important? Because in every society there are people who are ready and willing to organize for social change and social betterment. Every society has its natural leaders, its innovative thinkers, its healers of civil strife, its promoters of justice. In human terms, it is quite natural for such people to develop their leadership skills in creative interaction with their people, and to be drawn from every class and strata.

These people are the union leaders, the outspoken clergy, the peasant organizers, the students, the minority-group leaders. They are the ones who see the need for change and who are willing to put their time and energy into bringing it about. Nine times out of ten they set about their goals peacefully, armed with nothing stronger than their ideas and the hope that they can convince others to join them. Yet in country after country these people— these creative, energetic, idealistic people—are hunted down, imprisoned, tortured, and even murdered.

We read about these people in the paper every day: dissident professor arrested in Czechoslovakia, union organizer "disappears" in the Philippines, bishop is gunned down in El Salvador. For every one we hear about there are hundreds—even thousands—who may suffer a similar fate; thousands who are murdered, or arrested and tortured, or forced into exile.

Truly, a society that systematically silences such people is committing a

---

*I am using human rights primarily to mean civil and political rights. The United Nations— through its Universal Declaration of Human Rights—has said that employment, an adequate diet, and decent health care are also important human rights.

form of suicide. A world that allows such people to be silenced is a world that is destroying its own future.

One would think that the United Nations would be in the forefront of world human rights leadership; that it would be a natural ally of the dissidents and idealists who share its universal values. Yet, in its four decades, the United Nations has done very little to press its member states to respect the civil and political rights of their citizens. This is because the official and legal delegates who represent the countries at the United Nations are in fact representatives of whatever elite happens to control their national government. Too often these elites are the very ones who are systematically violating the human rights of their own people, and over the years they have made sure that the United Nations' role in promoting human rights is a very weak one indeed.

Only on rare occasions does the United Nations directly challenge a human rights-violating country. This has happened with Chile and South Africa, for example, since the elites who run these countries have few friends among the other elites who comprise the United Nations' membership. Yet other gross violators like Malawi, Brazil, Czechoslovakia, and China (to name but a few) have gone unchallenged. This double standard on human rights is one of the greatest weaknesses of the organization—particularly when it attempts to mobilize world opinion behind its moral leadership.

People who care about human rights fortunately do not have to wait for twenty or fifty years to go by before the United Nations is truly effective in this vital area. As world citizens we can act in our own capacity, and in league with others, to promote better human rights observance. In fact there is already a worldwide citizens' human rights organization which has been able to play a more meaningful role in challenging human rights abuse than any other international body. This group is called Amnesty International.

## Amnesty International

In early 1961, a small band of British lawyers and others who were concerned about the worldwide patterns of unchecked human rights abuses met to consider what they could do about it. They conceived of a campaign, conducted through the media and by word of mouth, a campaign to pressure governments around the world to release their dissidents and political prisoners—to grant them an amnesty.

How did they propose to pressure these human rights-violating regimes? Simply put, they hoped to do it by bringing their violations into the light of day, by encouraging newspaper and magazine stories about these practices, by deluging government officials with hundreds and thousands of letters calling for the release of prisoners by name. In other words, they wanted to mobilize world opinion and shame the governments who conducted such evil practices.

They decided to term the people they were concerned about "prisoners of conscience," meaning those who had been imprisoned for their beliefs or opinions. Since they were fully aware that governments of the left, the right, and the center were involved in human rights abuses, they made it a rule to always keep a balance of publicity on particular cases of abuse.

They started with just an idea, and with a meager budget and a volunteer staff. They had no governmental backing, no official mandate—only the mandate of their own consciences. They hoped that their idea—of promoting human rights through citizen action—would be effective, and that it would spread through the universality of its moral basis. In this hope they have been richly rewarded, perhaps far beyond what most of them may have dared to dream.

Almost immediately their idea began to take hold. An initial appeal that appeared in the British Sunday paper *The Observer* and in *Le Monde*.was picked up by newspapers around the world. Offers of help, of volunteer time, of encouragement began to pour in from all sides. By the end of the year Amnesty groups had been formed by people in Belgium, Greece, Nigeria, Burma, and seventeen other countries.

The founders soon realized that they had more than a one-year-long campaign on their hands (their original intention). They had a full-scale world movement. "We had underestimated the intellectual capacity and the conscience of the public," one of the instigators later wrote.[1] Thus they quickly called an international meeting in Luxembourg and agreed to found an ongoing organization.

The heart of the work of Amnesty International is individual and group volunteer action on the grassroots level. Wherever possible, interested individuals are urged to form an "adoption group" which then "adopts" two prisoners from countries of different political systems. The group then engages in a number of activities to secure the release of their adopted prisoners: by letters to government officials, by stimulating media attention, by visits to the embassies, by petitions and vigils, by pressure on international bodies. They also correspond, wherever possible, with the prisoner and the prisoner's family, in order to let them know that somebody cares. Sometimes groups have raised money to send to the families of these prisoners, or have helped a released prisoner to relocate and find employment in a new country.

In addition to the adoption groups, and to its network of individual members around the world, Amnesty International has also established special groups of professionals who intercede on behalf of their colleagues and groups on campuses and among religious congregations. Further, Amnesty International has launched a worldwide campaign to publicize and help eliminate the practice of torture, and to end the death penalty for all prisoners—whether they are prisoners of conscience or not.

Today Amnesty International has grown into an organization with over 150,000 members in over one hundred countries. In Sweden alone there are 250 adoption groups, and there are many hundreds more in other parts of the globe. Amnesty International now has an International Secretariat, based in

London, with a staff of over 140 people who are daily engaged in the painstaking research that has made the organization effective and universally respected—or feared.

By its own calculations, Amnesty International has helped to free over 13,000 prisoners of conscience since its inception in 1961. But it has done much more than this. By its very existence, Amnesty International has brought to the foreground a terribly vital human issue that can no longer be ignored by the governments of the world. Who can say how many prisoners have been freed or never taken in the first place because of the fear of world public opinion—a force which Amnesty helped to create? Who can say what a difference has been made, or might be made in the future, by the individuals whom Amnesty International has helped to release? Perhaps among them we can find a Martin Luther King, a U Thant, an Albert Einstein, or a Mother Teresa. How can we measure what impact even one of these people may have on our planet-sized problems?

In 1977 Amnesty International was awarded the Nobel Peace Prize. This award was not only a tribute to the work of the organization, and to the dedication of its leaders; it was a tribute to the hundreds of thousands of people around the world who had given their time and energy to promote a more just world. Amnesty International represents the power of (as one of their flyers states) "awakened world opinion." It is an example of what an aroused and concerned group of world citizens can do, in addition to, or in spite of, their own governments and their own world government, the United Nations.

## Other World Movements

The success of Amnesty International can be a source of inspiration to us all. But Amnesty International is also a failure, and this too can be a source of education and renewed commitment. It is a failure because for every freed prisoner there are hundreds who are not freed. For every country that relaxes its repression there may be one that becomes more repressive. For all that world opinion is clearly and unalterably opposed to torture, this practice is still widespread—so widespread that Amnesty International has termed it an epidemic.

What we can learn from this is that the need for citizen action is even greater than we might have imagined. The power of world opinion and of shameful publicity can go just so far in bringing global change. Many nations will feel perfectly free to ignore such bad publicity, especially if their rulers have everything to lose and nothing to gain by freeing their dissidents.

Consider another example. There is little doubt that world opinion is strongly, desperately, in favor of peace. Virtually no one favors wars and warfare, and even the professional warriors are frightened of a nuclear holocaust. The world faces its greatest danger from such weapons of massive destruction, yet these weapons are rapidly spreading to new countries. Most national leaders profess themselves to be in favor of disarmament and peace, and yet little seems to change, except to change for the worse.

It is apparent that the world's leaders will never bring peace, and peaceful disarmament, unless the world's people, acting together, force them to do so. The United Nations said this quite clearly at the end of its 1978 Special Session on Disarmament. After hearing for days that all the nations were officially for disarmament yet none of them seemed able to do anything about it, the Assembly appealed to "world public opinion" to get things moving.

What the United Nations was calling for was a worldwide citizen's movement for peace—one that could put pressure on national leaders to bring them to the negotiating table, and keep them there until they had given up their guns.

It appears that the delegates to the 1978 UN conference were telling us what advocates of representative democracy have always claimed: that an aroused, vigilant citizenry is a necessary component of a governing system. Just as our own country needs more than a once-every-four-years trip to the polling place for the maintenance of good government, so our globe requires an active and committed world citizenry. Not just to bring a better global system into existence, not just to press our leaders to address themselves to the things that need to be done (and undone!), but to make sure that our representatives follow through, that they stay true to their mandate, and that they do not engage us in some future foolish enterprise that may prove to be harmful to us all.

World-sized problems require world-sized citizenship. Humankind has evolved to the point where we are not only capable of communicating and functioning on a global scale, we are *required* to do so in order to preserve our species. Like it or not, we are being challenged by our own inventiveness to assume the responsibilities of global self-government, and that in turn demands of us that we begin to function as responsible world citizens, holding our own national government to its responsibilities to the rest of the world's people, and joining with others from many nations to challenge and monitor the world political and economic order as a whole.

## Our Responsibilities as U.S. Citizens

Those of us who are citizens of the United States have some special responsibilities, and some special opportunities, in the effort to promote a better world society.

On the positive side, we are fortunate to live in a society where civil and political rights are generally respected, and where communication with citizens in other countries is relatively simple and unhampered. We live in a nation that has enormous clout on the world scene, whether that be at the United Nations, in other international bodies, or in bilateral relationships. We have a valuable base of educated people and technological experience, as well as certain national resources like coal and our croplands, which could be used to benefit all the world's people.

Then there is the other side of the picture. Our nation is one of the two nuclear giants whose arsenals threaten global survival. We have the world's largest economy, and as a result we cause more pollution and consume more resources than any other nation. We are also the nation most responsible for the post World War II international economic system, a system that was deliberately designed to serve our interests.

Finally, we have been one of the world's major violators of human rights, not so much because of our domestic human rights record—which in recent years has been quite good—but because of our support of repressive regimes abroad. In the world order that our government constructed after 1945 the United States has propped up and helped create a string of human rights-violating regimes in many parts of the world. Our CIA helped to bring Chile's generals to power. It overthrew a progressive government in Guatemala and has supported repressive leaders in the Philippines, Argentina, Pakistan, and elsewhere. We have given military and economic aid to some of the most brutal dictatorships in the world and turned our backs on their jailed dissidents, their tortured peasant leaders, their murdered unionists.

We called General Park of South Korea and General Somoza of Nicaragua our friends and allies in a Free World bloc of nations, many of whose people were decidedly unfree. When pressed, our leaders would tell us that we needed to support such regimes because of the danger of communism, but in fact what we seemed to desire most of these elites was that they allow U.S. businesses to operate freely within their borders, or allow U.S. military bases on their lands, or lend us their vote on occasion at the United Nations.

Thus when Jimmy Carter took office in 1976 on a platform that promised United States respect for human rights, he perhaps did not realize that he had pledged his administration to a course that, if pursued honestly, would disrupt the system of alliances that we had formed, as well as subject the United States to a great deal of embarrassment for our past misdeeds.

The temptation for successive U.S. administrations to back away from an international policy of support for human rights will be very great—especially if this means that a new group of leaders arises in developing countries who are less disposed to grant favors to our businesses and our military. The nostalgic yearning for another leader like the Shah of Iran—who couldn't buy enough of our guns and missiles, whose family made arrangements of mutual profit with our corporations, and who generally backed our foreign policy—this yearning will exert great pressures on our leaders to unleash the CIA, to give military aid, to look the other way while people are being jailed and tortured.

Similarly there is now, and will continue to be, great pressure on our political leaders to continue the massive stockpiling of armaments, and to back projects which promise to develop even more esoteric and destructive weapons. There will be pressure to reduce our restrictions on pollution and there will be enormous pressure for our political leaders to keep up the high level of the U.S. lifestyle—despite the needs of people in other lands, despite the dangerous overconsumption of world resources, despite the burden on the environment.

World citizenship will not be easy, not because we in the United States need fear jail, torture, or exile, but because the challenges are so great and there are so many claims on our time and energy that we can easily become discouraged and feel overwhelmed. Besides that, the world's professional leadership will tell us that a group of amateurs can do nothing, that we should leave these problems to their good judgment and technical expertise. But just as the founders of Amnesty International did not allow such sentiments to deter them, neither should we.

## Citizens' Action Groups

One wishes that there were an Ecology International with the scope and sophistication of Amnesty International, or a Peace International, or an Economic Justice International.

Perhaps one day there will be citizens' organizations such as these, ones that command almost universal respect and that have a clear and effective role in influencing global institutions. Having researched the thousands of citizens' groups that are based in the United States and are open to general membership, I find that Amnesty International is the exception rather than the rule.

Yet there is clear movement in the global direction. The Audubon Society has recently established an International Division. Several women's organizations have been active in United Nations forums that bring together women's groups from all over the world. The anti-nuclear power movement is active in many countries, and its leaders are very global in their outlook.

The trend is clearly toward globally oriented citizens' groups with chapters in many countries. In the Resources section of this book, I have listed the most interesting and useful groups that I could find so that readers who want to become more involved can consider ones that they may want to join.

## Getting Involved

Often in the course of running workshops or making presentations on global themes I have met people who care very deeply about the world's ills, who feel that they would like to do something to promote global justice and world betterment, but who don't know where to begin. They feel responsible, and perhaps even guilty that their lifestyle or their government may be contributing to the world's problems, and yet they fear that they don't know enough about the complexities of planetary issues to contribute anything more than their own good intentions.

I always encourage such people to get involved in a group or a cause that touches them deeply. It may be peace, it may be hunger, it may be global institution-building. Only by taking our good intentions into the arena of social change can we learn more about what is possible, what is effective, and what is wise. Personally, I would rather have ten sincere and well-motivated people out there in the struggle for world betterment, than have ten supposed experts who have all the right technical training but no moral grounding for what they are doing.

It is only when we dare to risk involvement, and the inevitable mistakes and wrong turns that come with it, that we can hope to learn and to become more effective. As complex as the world may seem, its needs are graphically simple: people are hungry. . . people have no homes . . . some live in fear of others . . . our lakes are being poisoned . . . nuclear weapons threaten planetary life. These are simple realities, just as the impulse to make things better is a simple impulse.

Personally, I believe that God whispers in our ear, that God tugs at our hem, stirs our feelings, reminds us that we did not come into this world for self-satisfaction but for something higher—perhaps a chance for service, perhaps to spread a little love. I believe that right now, this very day, God is whispering to millions of people around the planet, whispering "it could be different . . . it could be better. . . there could be healing . . . and joy. . . and celebration. Unplug your ears, open your eyes, open your hearts. Come, follow Me."

## NOTES

1. Egon Larsen, *A Flame in Barbed Wire: The Story of Amnesty International* (New York: W.W. Norton and Company, 1979), p. 15. My special thanks to Mr. Larsen for taking the time to write this fine history of Amnesty International; his book provided the background for my description of the organization in these pages.

# RESOURCES

# Introduction to Resources

In order to make this introduction more interesting for the reader, I have chosen a question-and-answer format:

*Why should I bother to join a group? Can't I do just as much on my own?*
Joining a group is important for two reasons: first, because your lone voice can be multiplied a hundred- or a thousand-fold; second, because many groups possess a wealth of knowledge and experience that they can share with you, thus enabling you to deepen and enrich your understanding of the issues.

*Why have you developed such an elaborate listing of groups?*
Good question. One that I asked myself many times during the course of my research and compilation.

There are already several good guides to organizations, and they are readily available in your local library. These directories tend to make rather dry reading since they rarely evaluate the organizations, nor do they recommend particular groups. Often their write-ups on these groups are simply summaries of the information that the group itself has provided.

People have told me that such directories are not always helpful. They have asked me which groups I feel are really valuable. If you have read this book and like my point of view, then it is likely that you will find my suggestions of interest.

*What makes you an expert on judging the worth of a group?*
I don't consider myself to be an expert, nor would I claim that my resource listing is anything but subjective. I have, however, been actively involved in global issues for many years, and in the course of that involvement I have come into contact with and worked with a large number of activist organizations. In many cases, their leaders and staff are known to me, just as their work and reputation are known not only to me but to the broad community of peace and social activists.

Nevertheless, I have contacted hundreds of groups in the United States, and have spent many hours pouring over their literature and their record of accomplishments. In some cases I have learned of groups that previously were unknown to me, or have come to have a new respect for groups I already knew of but perhaps had underrated. One good example is the **United Nations Association** in the United States, a rather mainstream and establishment organization that has its hands full just trying to counter the myths and misunderstandings in the United States about the United Nations.

117

I also have learned about valuable new organizations which are worthy of note but which have not yet achieved widespread public recognition. A good example would be the **Solar Lobby** or **Freedom of Faith**.

*Do you endorse every group that you have listed in this resource section?*

Definitely not! Many of them are groups with which I have strong disagreements, but which I have listed as valuable sources of information and contrary opinion.

*Since you list a number of groups, how am I supposed to decide which one to join?*

I suggest you begin by writing to those groups that most attract your interest. A simple postcard will do, with your name and address and a request for information. Don't worry that writing to a group will lead to phone calls or personal recruitment efforts. I wrote to hundreds, and the worst thing that happened was that I ended up on a lot of mailing lists.

Once you have received their literature, sit back and see what you think. Do you find yourself in agreement with what they are saying? Do you share their vision? Can they point to concrete accomplishments and activities—recent ones, not things they did ten years ago? Are they set up to involve you in their activities, either through local chapters or other structures? (**Amnesty International**, for example, is excellent at involving individuals and groups, whereas some groups simply want you to send money.)

Finally, do they offer a chance for two-way communication with their supporters? That is, do they allow their vision and their priorities to be influenced by their supporters, or do they simply want you to buy in to their program? **New Directions**, for example, polls its members every year and sets its priorities accordingly. **Clergy and Laity Concerned** has local and regional gatherings (open to all members) to guide its efforts.

*I don't have time to be an active member of a group, but I would like to give money to something truly worthwhile. How do I decide?*

My first suggestion is that you consider giving your money to an advocacy group that is working on structural change—as opposed to a relief or development assistance organization. Why? Because for every ten dollars that goes to direct relief groups, the advocacy groups are lucky to get ten cents.

Recently I was at a meeting of a medium-sized aid and advocacy organization that had the experience of being flooded with funds for relief efforts in Kampuchea (Cambodia) but whose valuable peace and social justice programs were being closed one by one due to a lack of funds. "Why is it," one of the participants asked, "that you can get millions of dollars to bury the dead and bind up the wounded, but get almost nothing to stop the causes of war?"

People who are in a position to give large enough donations to make it important that the gifts be tax-deductible should think twice before passing over a group that does not have such status with the IRS. The **Coalition for a New Foreign and Military Policy** is such an organization— precisely because it is trying to do an effective job through lobbying the U.S. Congress. Sometimes it is worth writing to such a group to ask if they have a tax-deductible educational affiliate or fund. **Bread for the World** does, as do many other organizations that also conduct lobbying efforts.

If, however, you are determined to give money to an organization that provides emergency and relief aid, or that assists economic development—like UNICEF, CARE, World Vision, and so on—then consider giving to a group that has a program mix which combines: (1) relief, (2) assistance for self-help development, and (3) educational programs aimed at the U.S. audience which promote a deeper understanding of the *causes* of human suffering and misery. **Oxfam-America** and the **American Friends Service Committee** are good examples of such groups.

If you want to make sure that an aid organization is legitimate, you can write to the National Information Bureau (419 Park Ave. South, New York, NY 10016). NIB is an organization that evaluates charities to determine if they are honest in stating their purposes, keep their books properly, and are not practicing fraud. You can ask them about any organization that you are considering giving money to, and they will tell you whether that organization meets their standards. Note, however, that groups which do not meet one or more of their standards may still be quite above board and valuable—but should be investigated more closely.

*I know of a really good group that you didn't even mention. Does this mean you disapprove of this organization?*

No! I am sure that I have missed many hardworking and commendable groups. Please write to me in care of Orbis Books to let me know what I have missed, and I will investigate the group for inclusion in a future edition of this book.

*What other publications can guide me to additional organizations?*

### General

*The Encyclopedia of Organizations.* Too expensive to buy; in most libraries.

*NIB Wise Giving Guide.* The National Information Bureau, 419 Park Ave. South, New York, NY 10016. A list of several hundred major U.S. charitable organizations, and whether or not they meet NIB's standards. NIB also publishes detailed reports on individual organizations, and these reports can be obtained free for the asking.

### United Nations and International Organizations

*The Europa Yearbook.* Expensive; consult your library.

*The Statesman's Yearbook.* Held in most libraries.

### Human Rights

*Human Rights Directory.* Valuable, up-to-date, and not too costly ($5.00). Write to Human Rights Internet, 1502 Ogden St., NW, Washington, DC 20010.

### Development Assistance, Relief

*Food Production and Agriculture: Development Assistance Abroad.* A listing of U.S. non-profit organizations that try to combat world hunger through helping people to produce more food. Request from TAICH, 200 Park Ave. South, New York, NY 10003. Published in April 1981.

*U.S. Non-Profit Organizations in Development Assistance Abroad.* A comprehensive and yearly listing that will be in large libraries. Send $6.00 to TAICH, 200 Park Ave. South, New York, NY 10003.

*Who's Involved with Hunger.* Send $1.50 to WHES, 2000 P St., NW, Washington, DC 20036.

**Religious and Denominational Groups**

*The Yearbook of American and Canadian Churches.* Updated yearly and available in most libraries. For your own copy, send $11.00 to *Yearbook of Churches,* 475 Riverside Drive, New York, NY 10115.

**Domestically Oriented Groups**

There are thousands of advocacy groups in the United States that focus on domestic issues. Since I couldn't list all of them, you might want to consult:

*Citizens Energy Directory.* Lists over 500 activist energy-related groups in the United States. Send $7.50 to IEP, 1413 K St., NW, 8th Floor, Washington, DC 20005.

*Human Rights Organization and Periodicals Directory.* Lists major civil rights and economic rights groups. Send $6.00 to P.O. Box 673, Berkeley, CA 94701.

*Note: A bullet (•) in front of an entry in the following lists indicates that I highly recommend that particular book or organization.*

# Economic Justice

## FOR FURTHER READING

•Barnet, Richard J., and Ronald E. Müller. *Global Reach.* New York: Simon and Schuster, 1974.

A sweeping survey of the role of big business in the world economy. Focuses on all the major topics: labor, technology, transfer pricing, undermining of Third World economics, global resource use. The style is much more accessible than any economics book. If you want to know how the global corporations operate, and how they affect your life, this is the place to start.

•Lappé, Frances Moore and Joseph Collins. *Food First.* Boston: Houghton Mifflin Company, 1977.

Probably the best book on hunger and its real causes. Collins and Lappé point squarely to the national and international elites who carve up the land and its wealth for themselves while their own people hunger and perish. Every nation, they claim, can feed itself if it pays attention to human needs and stops reserving the best land for luxury export crops. The question-and-answer style of the book makes it difficult to read at length, but it does make possible selective reading. Thus, this is a good book to use with study groups.

•Nelson, Jack A. *Hunger for Justice.* Maryknoll, N.Y.: Orbis Books, 1980.

Nelson is active with Clergy and Laity Concerned (CALC), a peace and social justice group that gets high marks in my opinion. Grounding his arguments in biblical faith, the author argues that United States-sponsored militarism and military spending—and the grasping policies of multinational corporations—are at the base of world hunger. They not only exacerbate the problems, they operate to prevent solutions. His closing chapter ("Hunger and the Crisis of Faith") is *must* reading for anyone who thinks that being a Christian means ignoring such "worldly" problems as hunger and injustice.

Berger, Peter L. *Pyramids of Sacrifice.* New York: Basic Books, 1974.

"Rejection of *both* the Brazilian and Chinese models [of development] is the starting point for any morally acceptable development policy," says sociologist Peter Berger. In this book Berger sets out to debunk the myths of capitalist development and the myths of socialist development. He argues for intermediate structures that bridge the modern and non-modern world, and that are neither capitalist nor socialist.

Bergston, C. Fred, et al. *American Multinationals and American Interests.* Washington, D.C.: Brookings Institution, 1978.

An extensive exploration of the controversial role of multinational corporations in the global economy. There are chapters on job loss in the United States, raw materials, balance of payments, tax evasion, and the influence of MNCs on U.S. foreign policy. It also reviews and critiques the major works on MNCs, including *Global Reach* and *Sovereignty at Bay.*

Damadu, Ukandi G., et al. *Development Paths in Africa and China.* London: Macmillan Ltd., 1976.
A collection of essays that describes the development styles and choices of seven Third World countries. The seven are Kenya, Tanzania, Ghana, Sudan, Zambia, Nigeria, and China.

Discipleship Resources. *Dimensions of Hunger.* Available from P.O. Box 840, Nashville, TN 37202.
An excellent study/action guide that is designed to help get a congregational hunger task force or committee educated, motivated, and geared for action. Sections on the international setting, population, legislative lobbying, fasting, action ideas, and Bible studies.

Erb, Guy, and Valeriana Kallab, eds. *Beyond Dependency.* New York: Praeger, 1975.
A valuable collection of essays on Third World relations with the First World of capitalism. All of the contributors are experts drawn from Third World countries.

Galeano, Eduardo. *Open Veins of Latin America.* New York: Monthly Review Press, 1973.
The point of this well-argued book is that for five hundred years the European nations and now the United States have been pillaging and ruining Latin America. Makes you realize what our affluence is based upon.

Hanson, Roger D., et al. *The U.S. and World Development.* New York: Praeger, published annually.
An extremely useful tool for anyone who wants to keep abreast of U.S. policy on development. Annual issues give an overview of recent legislative developments and international initiatives and propose an agenda for action for the coming year. Plus, there are background essays on food, resources, etc. Prepared by the staff of the Overseas Development Council.

Lipton, Michael. *Why Poor People Stay Poor.* Cambridge, Mass.: Harvard University Press, 1977.
Lipton says that the rich-poor gap exists between nations but also between urban and rural sectors within nations. Gives plenty of evidence to support his case against urban bias and suggests new policies for developing countries.

Magdoff, Harry. *Imperialism: From the Colonial Age to the Present.* New York: Monthly Review, 1978.
Magdoff is one of the leading experts on colonial and post-colonial imperialism of the European and American variety, so much so that the prestigious *Encyclopaedia Britannica,* 15th ed., asked him to do their major essay on this period. This book

contains that essay, which takes the reader from 1763 to the present. Other essays are on post-World War II imperialism.

Mehmet, Ozay. *Economic Planning and Social Justice in Developing Countries.* New York: St. Martin's Press, 1978.
An extended argument for placing equitable development ahead of rapid growth. Dr. Mehmet says that agriculture and general rural development should be favored. Cites examples from Liberia, Pakistan, Brazil, and other Third World countries.

Mikdashi, Zuhayr. *The International Politics of Natural Resources.* Ithaca, N.Y.: Cornell University Press, 1976.
An exploration of the struggle between Third World raw materials producers and First World consumers. The author studies the oil producers association (OPEC) and asks whether similar bargaining tactics would work with sulfur, bauxite, copper, and a host of other raw materials.

Payer, Cheryl. *The Debt Trap: The International Monetary Fund and the Third World.* New York: Monthly Review Press, 1975.
All about how the Third World sinks ever deeper in debt, and how the IMF is used by its rich sponsors to control and "discipline" these countries.

Powelson, John P. *A Select Bibliography on Economic Development.* Boulder Colorado: Westview, 1979.
Over two thousand titles of recent books and articles on development issues.

Sauvant, Karl P., and Farid G. Lavipour, eds. *Controlling Multinational Corporations.* Boulder, Colorado: Westview, 1976.
A fine collection of essays on the nitty-gritty of regulating the power of international big business. The last third of the book is devoted to concrete proposals for national and international response to the MNCs.

Schachter, Oscar. *Sharing the World's Resources.* New York: Columbia University Press, 1977.
An interesting and readable review of the philosophical and moral debate about global resource-sharing. The author discusses just prices, sharing of technology, food security, the oceans, and the sovereignty questions that arise over mineral resources.

## ACTION AND INFORMATION GROUPS

There are hundreds of groups that focus on hunger and economic development. Most of them focus on direct relief aid, but do not deal with the larger institutional issues that I am most concerned with; thus I have listed only a few of the major relief organizations. My main focus in this listing is with action and educational groups. For directories to aid and relief organizations, see page 119.

•**Bread for the World,** 207 E. 16th St., New York, NY 10003. A very energetic and well-organized Christian citizens movement to combat world hunger. BFW has styled itself along the lines of Common Cause, focusing on the U.S. Congress and the Executive Department. Local chapters are established in congregations and communities, and these are linked together in district-wide and state-wide networks. BFW concentrates its energy on U.S. food and development policies—at home and abroad—and has already made itself felt in the halls of Congress. Staff members are available to help interested people form local chapters.

•**Institute for Food and Development Policy,** Box 40403, San Francisco, CA 94110. Founded by Frances Moore Lappé, co-author of *Food First* and author of *Diet for a Small Planet*, and Joseph Collins, co-author of *Food First*. The Institute supports continued research and advocacy in the hard-hitting style of *Food First*.

•**Institute for Policy Studies,** 1901 Que St., NW, Washington, DC 20009. A think tank on global issues and U.S. foreign policy. IPS focuses on the negative impact of big business on Third World development and on the shaping of U.S. policies. The Transnational Institute is a special program of the IPS at which exiles from the Third World do research on international economic issues. Richard Barnet, author of *Global Reach* is a leading figure in IPS.

•**New Directions,** 305 Massachusetts Ave., NE, Washington, DC 20002. A citizens lobby for world security, as they describe themselves. But security in this case does not mean bigger bombs and more bullets. Instead it means a safer, more just, and less dangerous world. For example, they have actively supported the SALT treaties and were a major force behind passage of the Panama Canal Treaty. One of their top priorities has been the reform of U.S. foreign aid, and they can be at least partially credited with a shift in U.S. aid to the poorest and neediest countries. In the long run, New Directions has the hope of being a globalist Common Cause.

**The Action Center,** 1028 Connecticut Ave., NW, Suite 302, Washington, DC 20036. A campus-based movement that is trying to mobilize young people "for Food, Justice, and Development." Begun by the National Student Association, the Center is now affiliated with the Institute for World Order. In addition to its support for campus work on hunger and justice issues, the Center regularly accepts interns who learn how to expand their justice advocacy work.

**The Africa Fund,** 305 E. 46th St., New York, NY 10017. The Fund gives development aid to the newly independent regimes of Mozambique, Angola, Cape Verde, and Guinea-Bissau. It also aids refugees from South Africa and Namibia and works to develop a better understanding in the United States of southern African issues. The Fund is affiliated with the American Committee on Africa.

**African-American Institute,** 833 United Nations Plaza, New York, NY 10017. A foundation-supported program that has helped thousands of Africans study in the United States. The Institute trains professionals and technicians for developmental posts in their own countries, arranges tours of Africa for American educators, develops curriculum resources for use in the United States, sponsors seminars and conferences, and gives special aid to refugees from the white-dominated regimes of southern Africa. Publishes *Africa Report* and *African Update*.

**African Bibliographic Center,** Box 13096, Washington, DC 20009. This is a resource and information center on African affairs and on U.S.-African relations. In addition to its up-to-date bibliographies, the Center provides a complete research service for interested individuals and organizations, and a daily news update that is available through a phone call to 202-659-2529.

**American Committee on Africa,** 305 E. 46th St., New York, NY 10017. Devoted to supporting the African people in their struggle for independence. To this end, the Committee brings Africans to the United States to publicize their cause, lobbies in Congress for a pro-African policy, distributes information about liberation struggles, and works actively against remaining colonial situations and against apartheid in South Africa. Founded in 1953, when most of black Africa was still under colonial domination, this Committee has seen remarkable changes in its lifetime.

**American Freedom From Hunger Foundation,** 1028 Connecticut Ave., NW, Suite 910, Washington, DC 20036. Originally begun as the informal U.S. liaison with the UN Food and Agricultural Organization, the AFFH has sponsored hunger walks on campuses and educational programs and seminars, and has played a key role in organizing U.S. support for and active participation in several world food gatherings. AFFH has recently joined forces with the U.S. Committee for Refugees.

**American Friends Service Committee,** 1501 Cherry St., Philadelphia, PA 19102. The AFSC sponsors development and relief programs in more than twenty countries around the world. It also supports programs in Washington and at the UN headquarters in New York, which work to promote broad changes in the international economic system. (See more extensive write-up in the Peace and Disarmament section.)

**The Asia Society,** 112 E. 64th St., New York, NY 10021. A foundation-funded program that seeks to develop a greater understanding in the United States of Asian art, culture, politics, and economics. In addition to sponsoring art exhibits, films, and performing arts tours, the Asia Society also hosts a series of conferences and seminars on Asian topics, exchange sessions between Asian leaders and their U.S. counterparts, and a curriculum development program for American educators.

**CARE,** 660 First Ave., New York, NY 10016. This well-known relief and development agency was begun in the aftermath of World War II. It now focuses on the Third World, providing self-help assistance, medical services and training, and a supplemental food program that feeds 20 million children on a daily basis. Constituent members of CARE include American Baptist Relief, the AFL-CIO, the Lions International, the National Council of Negro Women, and twenty-one other agencies.

**Church World Service,** 475 Riverside Drive, New York, NY 10115. An interdenominational Christian program that develops and funds programs to help poor and hungry people around the world. Programs include disaster aid, emergency food shipments, grass-roots development programs, health services, children's programs, and educational services.

**Co-ordinating Council for Hunger Concerns**, Rm. 838, 475 Riverside Drive, New York, NY 10115. Since so many religious groups sponsor hunger programs, development programs, and relief efforts, it makes sense that there be a central office that helps them keep in touch. This office is a part of the National Council of Churches and it relates primarily to the NCC's Protestant Christian constituency, but it is also in touch with hunger programs in other denominations and faiths.

**CROP**, Elkhart, IN 46515. A special project of the Church World Service that has a unique flavor. CROP does grass-roots fund raising and educational work through hunger walks, fasts, workshops, and marathons. Often it helps farmers send their donations of wheat or produce directly to needy people. Does excellent work with young people, and makes good use of local volunteers.

**Crossroads Africa**, 150 Fifth Ave., New York, NY 10011. Even before the Peace Corps was established, Crossroads Africa was sending Americans to live and work cooperatively in Africa. By 1979, over five thousand black, brown, and white Americans had experienced this intense eight-week immersion in African culture, and related programs have brought more than a thousand African students and leaders to this country. Special emphasis is placed on helping African-Americans share in this opportunity to explore their African roots. A smaller program links the United States and the West Indies.

**Cuernavaca Center for Intercultural Dialog on Development**, Apartado 580, Cuernavaca, Morelos, Mexico. A fascinating study center in Mexico that is available to Americans who want an experience in consciousness-raising about the realities of Latin America, including the oppressive structures, the imperialist role of the U.S. government, the struggles for liberation. Participants can live with Mexican families, study Spanish, talk with peasant leaders and exiles from other countries, wrestle with liberation theology, and more.

**EPICA—Ecumenical Program for Inter-American Communication and Action**, 1740 Irving St., NW, Washington, DC 20010. A research and information program designed to "inform, challenge, and mobilize religious bodies and church members on critical inter-American issues," especially issues of economic justice.

**Inter-Faith Center on Corporate Responsibility**, Rm. 566, 475 Riverside Drive, New York, NY 10115. Many churches and religious communities hold investment portfolios that include corporate stocks and bonds. Usually they have money in one or more banks. But are these banks and corporations using their money for unethical purposes? The ICCR was started in order to help churches invest morally and to use their financial clout to challenge outrageous practices. Recent concerns have been with corporate investment in South Africa, the Nestlé baby formula controversy, and the role of cash crops in Third World economies.

**International Voluntary Services, Inc.**, 1717 Massachusetts Ave., NW, Suite 605, Washington, DC 20036. IVS takes skilled volunteer professionals from the fields of agriculture, public health, co-op development, small business, and engineering, and places them in Third World countries where their skills are needed. By 1980, IVS had placed over a thousand volunteers in twenty-two countries.

**LADOC,**1312 Massachusetts Ave., NW, Washington, DC 20005. Acronym stands for "Latin American Documentation," a service of the International Justice and Peace Office of the U.S. Catholic Conference. Every other month, they compile an extremely useful packet of articles, many in translation, about the Latin American scene. Focus is on economic, social, and spiritual rights and practice. $6.00 per year.

**Meals for Millions,** 1800 Olympic Blvd., P.O. Box 680, Santa Monica, CA 90406. A program that began with simple relief work and which has now expanded to a self-help development focus. MFM supplies intermediate technology and training programs to villagers in India, Ecuador, Korea, and elsewhere.

**MERIP—Middle East Research and Information Project,** P.O. Box 3122, Columbia Heights Station, Washington, DC 20010. MERIP provides good political and economic background studies on the conflicts and general development of the Middle East area. Recent studies have included "Women Workers in Egypt," "Labor Migration in the Middle East," and "China and the Middle East."

**North American Congress on Latin America (NACLA),** Box 57, Cathedral Station, New York, NY 10025. The North American Congress on Latin America provides an excellent news and analysis magazine called *NACLA: Report on the Americas.* Strong especially on the relationship between U.S. companies and repressive regimes, NACLA has also published excellent studies on U.S. military involvement. Also publishes other periodic studies. The *Report* is $6.00 per year.

**Oxfam-America,** 302 Columbus Ave., P.O. Box 288, Back Bay Station, Boston, MA 02116. Oxfam got started in England as the Oxford Committee for Famine Relief in 1942 and over the years has established a reputation as a fine grass-roots development support agency. Oxfam depends on personal donations, and it channels these donations into development projects that have already sprung from local initiative. Thus Oxfam-America is supporting a pottery and cultural center in Peru, a land reclamation project in Ethiopia, and a development training center in Bangladesh. These are just a few examples of their excellent work.

**Partners of the Americas,** 2001 S St., NW, Washington, DC 20009. A program that seeks to link the Northern and Southern partners of the Western Hemisphere in joint programs of cultural exchange and self-help projects. Undertakes small-scale development programs that build schools, provide food, and offer disaster relief in needed areas.

**The Peace Corps,** 806 Connecticut Ave., NW, Washington, DC 20525. John F. Kennedy's legacy to youthful idealism and enthusiasm lives on in the Peace Corps. Americans, young and old, sign up for two-year stints in a host of Third World countries. Over the years, the Peace Corps has become more sophisticated in its development programs, and volunteers can expect to contribute to their assigned country as well as learn from it. The main disadvantage is that the Peace Corps is U.S. government sponsored and can never fully remove itself from U.S. foreign policy. An international Peace Corps, sponsored by the UN or chartered privately, is obviously a better proposition, but such a program is not generally available for the moderately skilled volunteer. In the meantime, the Peace Corps is definitely worth considering.

**Trade Union Committtee for International Co-operation and Development,** WDM Bedford Chambers, Covent Garden, London, WC2, England. A British-based movement that believes the existing international economic system needs to be replaced by one that is "based on social control and planning in the interests of all peoples and nations," i.e., a socialist system. While their focus is British unions, I mention them here as a resource because their newspaper, *Link International,* is a valuable source of news about labor struggles in all parts of the world.

**Third World Shops,** 428 E. Berry St., Fort Wayne, IN 46802. A fascinating idea that began in Europe and has now spread to the United States: a store that sells Third World products and remits the larger percentage of the profit to the originating country. But it is more: products from socially committed countries and co-ops are stressed, and there are periodicals and pamphlets available on economic issues. So shopping in these stores is a direct aid to self-help projects and an educational experience as well. Furthermore, Third World Shops often become centers of global justice activism in their communities. Why not start one in your town?

**U.S.-China Peoples Friendship Association,** 3500 Lancaster Ave., Philadelphia, PA 19104. This association has over one hundred affiliated chapters in the United States. Its purpose is to broaden U.S.-China understanding and exchange. Before the normalization of relations with China, this group was a real pioneer in opening lines of communication. Local chapters sponsor talks, seminars, and conferences on related topics, and the national chapter publishes *New China* magazine.

**Washington Office on Africa,** 110 Maryland Ave., NE, Washington, DC 20002. Sponsored by four Protestant denominations and the American Committee on Africa (see above), focuses on situations of neo-colonialism as well as goals listed for ACOA above.

**Washington Office on Latin America,** 110 Maryland Ave., NE, Washington, DC 20002. Established in 1974 by a coalition of religious and academic groups because of their concern for the economic, political, and social conditions in Latin America. Focuses on human rights questions, and on the impact of U.S. policy. Keeps its constituents informed so that they can lobby for change.

**Women in Development, Inc.,** 1302 18th St., NW, Suite 203, Washington, DC 20036. Aims to aid women in developing countries through direct aid and by linking women's groups from all over the world. Publishes a regular newsletter and does other media work.

**World Hunger Education Service,** 2000 P St., NW, Suite 205, Washington, DC 20036. A consultation and information center, the Service publishes a regular newsletter called *Hunger Notes* and sponsors two-week seminars in Washington for interested individuals who want to learn more about the issues involved in hunger advocacy.

**World Vision International,** Box O, Pasadena, CA 91109. An ecumenical Christian effort that raises money to be spent on development and hunger relief programs in many parts of the world. Has feeding programs, health centers, self-reliance projects. Also supports evangelization and Christian education programs.

**Worldwatch Institute,** 1776 Massachusetts Ave., NW, Washington, DC 20036. Founded by Lester Brown, this Institute has a group of top-notch writers and researchers who share a common concern for economic development and ecological safety. Their many publications on food, energy and pollution are all excellent, well-researched, and persuasive in their global vision.

# The Global Environment

## FOR FURTHER READING

•Brown, Lester R. *The Twenty-Ninth Day.* New York: W.W. Norton, 1978.

Probably the best book on world pollution and resource depletion. Brown brings fine scholarship and an easy reading style to his efforts. This book is a good example of the Worldwatch Institute's perspective—it is global, and grounded in a concern for basic human needs. Brown argues that the world's renewable resources (croplands, grasslands, ocean fisheries, and forests) are being rapidly overwhelmed by human use. What is needed is a "planetary bargain" between rich and poor societies to meet human needs in an ecological framework.

•Commoner, Barry. *The Closing Circle.* New York: Bantam, 1971.

Clear, precise, knowledgeable, Commoner shows that many of our most serious pollution problems come from careless technology rather than from overconsumption. As a trained biologist, he has much to say about the chain of life, the land, and water systems.

•Hayes, Dennis. *Rays of Hope.* New York: W.W. Norton, 1979.

An excellent book from the Worldwatch Institute. Hayes looks at how global society has been built on oil technology, and how we now have to move to a "post-petroleum" world. He explores the dangers of the nuclear option and recommends solar power instead. Hayes gives many examples of how alternative energies are already being skillfully used around the world.

Amory, Cleveland. *Man Kind?* New York: Harper & Row, 1974.

A well-written, humorous, sad look at what humans do to animals. Strongly exposes the hunting and trapping excesses that threaten a variety of species.

Berry, Adrian. *The Next Ten Thousand Years.* New York: E.P. Dutton, 1974.

A marvelously optimistic survey of all the wonderful, exciting things that await humankind once we break out into space. Berry thinks there are no limits to the potential for our technology and our wealth once we conquer the solar system—and beyond.

Berry, Leonard, and Robert W. Kates, eds. *Making the Most of the Least.* New York: Holmes & Meier, 1979.

A collection of the best presentations from an Alternative Development conference held in Racine, Wisconsin. The essays explore linkages between developed and developing countries and options for a new global network of small-is-beautiful societies.

Caldicott, Helen. *Nuclear Madness: What You Can Do!* New York: Random House, 1978.

Dr. Caldicott came to her anti-nuclear convictions through her research on its effects on children and adults. This book represents her own search and struggle with the deadly side effects of the "peaceful atom." It also is an argument against weapons proliferation. Widely used and cited in the anti-nuke movement.

Daly, Herman E. *Steady-State Economics.* San Francisco: W.H. Freeman and Co., 1977.

Daly's original proposal for a steady-state economy (i.e., consume only at a level that is sustainable over the long run) has provoked a heated debate about the future of the global economy. In this book, he develops his original idea and challenges his critics.

Eckholm, Erik. *Losing Ground.* New York: W.W. Norton, 1976.

Everywhere we look, humans are destroying the soil through destructive agriculture, urbanization, pollution, and deforestation. Eckholm surveys the global effects of all this and recommends policies for conservation. A Worldwatch Institute book.

***Environment Program Kit.***

An action packet prepared for use by people who want to grapple with ecology issues from a global perspective. Focus is on the UN and its programs. Write to UNA-USA, 300 E. 42nd St., New York, NY 10017. Cost: $2.50.

Hammond, Kenneth A., et al. *Sourcebook on the Environment: A Guide to the Literature.* Chicago: Univ. of Chicago Press, 1978.

A bibliography organized by topics, e.g., urbanization, resource recovery, etc. Also lists relevant periodicals and activist groups.

Kahn, Herman, and others. *World Economic Development: 1979 and Beyond.* New York: William Morrow, 1979.

The most recent update of Kahn's argument that we have plenty of growth still left. Kahn and his associates continue the theses of *The Next 200 Years,* asserting that global affluence is possible and warning that this bright future may be marred by wooly-minded, middle-class, ecological activists.

Lovins, Amory. *Soft Energy Paths.* Philadelphia: Ballinger, 1977.

Considered by many people to be the most pathbreaking, sensible book on energy options and their possible societal repercussions. Lovins has been dubbed the energy guru of the ecology movement, and he deserves the title in its most positive sense.

Lyons, Stephen, ed. *SUN!* Available from FOE, 124 Spear St., San Francisco, CA 94105.

Here it is: a comprehensive and readable guide to solar energy, solar society, and what we can do to make it happen. The official handbook for Sun Day, 1978.

Meadows, Donella H., et al. *The Limits to Growth.* New York: Signet, 1972.

This is the controversial study of world resources that helped start the whole debate for the 1970s. The authors explain how they used computers to study what growth would do to the global economy and environment. They show that we have to put a cap on growth of consumption/production or else we'll destroy the earth.

Mishan, E. J. *The Economic Growth Debate.* London: George Allen and Unwin, 1977.

Mishan is the economist who is generally credited with adding the greatest intellectual weight to the costs of growth debate. This book is divided into two parts: (1) a review and critique of the growth/no growth debate, (2) a reflection on what constitutes the good life, and how we might try to attain it.

Park, Charles F. *Earthbound.* San Francisco: Freeman, Cooper and Co., 1975.

A very fine introduction to the world's resources, how they are used, and the politics of trying to change our national and international patterns of consumption. Designed as a textbook, this volume has chapters on petroleum, mineral extraction, soils and water, and more. Well-written and easy to understand, but not simplistic.

Papanek, Victor. *Design for the Real World.* New York: Bantam, 1976.

Papanek is a creative industrial designer who shows how to build village pumps from discarded auto tires, to power a radio by a candle, and to build a mass distribution TV set for eight dollars per unit. He argues forcefully that we have enormous potential for designing new approaches to human problems, but that 90 percent of industrial design skills are currently wasted on military equipment or on useless face-lifts for old products. Draws heavily upon his work as a teacher and as a consultant for the United Nations.

Schumacher, E. F. *Small is Beautiful.* New York: Harper Torchbook, 1973.

E.F. Schumacher was an interesting character much influenced by Gandhi and Buddhism; he for many years ran the National Coal Industry in Great Britain. All of this combined to make a man who was skeptical about large plans and macro-technology, and who believed in the ability of small, local cooperation to achieve human ends. Schumacher was an early proponent of intermediate technology, and an early critic of western-dominated modes of developmental thought. A truly pathbreaking book.

Trzyna, Thaddeus C. *International Environmental Affairs: A Guide to the Literature.* Available from Center for California Public Affairs, P.O. Box 30, Claremont, CA 91711.

A detailed guide with special emphasis on the issues and activities of international groups.

Valaskakis, Kimon. *The Conservor Society.* New York: Harper & Row, 1979.

Canadians have been struggling with what a conservation-minded society might look like. This book summarizes a larger study by a team of experts that tried to project five scenarios for Canada's future, ranging from super-consumption to a society that does more with less, and one that does less with less. Quite relevant for the United States and Europe.

Warren, Betty. *The Energy and Environment Bibliography.* Available from FOE, 124 Spear St., San Francisco, CA 94105.
Lists magazines, books, films, and other sources.

*World Conservation Strategy.* Order from ICUN, 1196 Gland, Switzerland.
A joint publication of the United Nations Environment Program and two other action groups. Undoubtedly the best introduction and study guide on the global environment that has crossed my desk. Valuable because it outlines a broad world strategy for change.

*World Environment Report.* Order from WER, 300 E. 42nd St., New York, NY 10017.
A readable newsletter that contains news you won't see elsewhere, and from all around the world. Extremely useful for researchers and activists, but frightfully expensive ($179 a year).

World Future Society. *The Future: A Guide to Information Sources.* Available from WFS, 4916 St. Elmo Ave., Washington, DC 20014.
A huge and comprehensive guide to individuals, organizations, educational programs and courses, current research projects, periodicals, etc., on the future and futuristics. See also *The World Future Society Catalogue,* a buyer's guide to books, magazines, newsletters, learning materials, audio tapes, and films about the future, technology, and the environment.

## ACTION AND INFORMATION GROUPS

•**Friends of the Earth (FOE)**, 124 Spear St., San Francisco, CA 94105. One of the top environmental groups in the country. It got started by activists who felt that aggressive lobbying was needed to protect the environment—something that many environmental groups don't dare to do for fear of losing their tax-exempt status. So lobby it does, against the Alaska Pipeline, against killing whales, for a sane energy policy, etc. With a network of national offices and international affiliates, this is a fine group to consider joining.

•**The National Audubon Society**, 950 Third Ave., New York, NY 10022. Under the new leadership of Russell W. Peterson, the former Governor of Delaware, the Society is expanding its focus from wildlife to a host of environmental problems: radiation, population, energy, toxic chemicals. It is establishing an international division which will work with the UN Environment Program and other global efforts. In addition to maintaining seventy Audubon preserves in the United States and producing excellent wildlife films, the Society organizes its members into local clubs that act as watchdogs and as advocates. With 400,000 members and hopes for 800,000, this could be quite a force!

•**Worldwatch Institute**, 1776 Massachusetts Ave., NW, Washington, DC 20036. For my money, the best of the environmental think tanks. Their books and papers are written for the average reader and have solid scientific research behind them. Leading writers include Dennis Hayes, Lester Brown, and Erik Eckholm. Recent studies on energy, family planning, food, pollution, and the development of a post-petroleum society. The Institute is international in its perspective, with a deep concern for the Third World. A real leader in the field.

**Alternatives,** P.O. Box 429, 4741 Stagecoach Road, Ellenwood, GA 30049. A good place to write if you want to know more about alternative lifestyle issues. Alternatives is abreast of the movement, has an excellent book service, and publishes the *Alternative Celebrations Catalogue* as well as other consciousness-raising items.

**Center for the Biology of Natural Systems,** Washington University, St. Louis, MO 63130. A research institute headed by the justly renowned Dr. Barry Commoner, author of *The Closing Circle.* Dr. Commoner believes that most of our pollution problems have been caused by faulty use of destructive technology and his institute studies things like pesticides, chemical fertilizers, energy alternatives.

**Princeton Center for Alternative Futures,** 60 Hodge Rd., Princeton, NJ 08540. Not connected with the university. Once described by author Hazel Henderson as a "mom and pop think tank," this institute began with her and her husband; it now employs interns, researchers, etc. Has quite a good publications list on employment, energy, futuristics, and especially the interaction between environmentalism and economics.

**Rachel Carson Trust for the Living Environment,** 8940 Jones Mill Road, Washington, DC 20015. The Trust continues the work of Rachel Carson, author of *The Silent Spring.* Primarily educational in focus, it gives special emphasis to chemical poisons in the environment.

**Resources for the Future,** 1755 Massachusetts Ave., NW, Washington, DC 20036. A very fine research institute that gets top scientists and economists to do work on resource and environmental issues. Recent books and studies on regional development, the Soviet oil industry, metropolitan growth, resource problems in the Fourth World, and so on.

**Rodale Books,** 33 E. Minor St., Emmaus, PA 18049. The Rodale publishing complex involves two great magazines and a large model farm. Publishes many books on organic gardening, appropriate technology, alternative energy systems, etc., especially *Organic Gardening* and *Prevention.* The Rodale people have been talking good sense for years.

**The Sierra Club,** 530 Bush St., San Francisco, CA 94108. Has a strong program emphasis on wildlife protection and wilderness preservation. Especially good on public education, films, and publications. Maintains an international office near the UN in New York. This office publishes a regular "International Report" twenty times a year.

**Solar Lobby,** 1001 Connecticut Ave., NW, 5th Floor, Washington, DC 20036. A whopping 94 percent of the American people favor strong efforts to promote solar power. Why, then, are U.S. efforts so weak? Perhaps because we need a solar lobby that can lock horns with the nuclear and oil lobbies. At least this is what Robert

Redford, Dennis Hayes (of Worldwatch), William Winpisinger (Intl. Assn. of Machinists), and other sponsors of this group believe.

**TRANET, Transnational Network for Appropriate/Alternative Technologies,** P.O. Box 567, Rangeley, ME 04970. A truly transnational organization with a twenty-five member board drawn from all over the world. Tries to link appropriate technology ideas and people around the globe. Publishes a newsletter and a directory.

**Union of Concerned Scientists,** 1208 Massachusetts Ave., Cambridge, MA 02138. The UCS is in the forefront of the movement to halt the spread of nuclear power plants. As its name suggests, it began as an association of scientists who felt that the true facts about the dangers of nuclear power were being suppressed by the government. Uses petitions, publicity, lobbying, and legal initiatives to promote its program.

**United Nations Environment Programme,** P.O. Box 30552, Nairobi, Kenya, East Africa. A special program of the United Nations that is attempting to pull together the knowledge of governments and environmental experts from around the world. UNEP is not a regulatory agency; rather it tries to stimulate governmental and intergovernmental action on behalf of the world's environment. To this end it stimulates studies, joint research projects, conferences on issues like desertification, acid rains, industrial pollution, etc. Increasingly, UNEP will become the major global clearinghouse for environmental information. Publishes a regular newsletter called "Uniterra."

**World Wildlife Fund-U.S.,** 1601 Connecticut Ave., NW, Washington, DC 20009. A worldwide animal protection organization with twenty-seven national chapters. Works to protect wildlife by establishing special preserves, combatting predatory human practices, fighting to end pollution. Currently is engaged in a campaign called "The Seas Must Live," which is trying to protect marine life all over the globe.

# Peace and Disarmament

**FOR FURTHER READING**

•Barnet, Richard J. *The Giants.* New York: Simon and Schuster, 1977.

Barnet looks at the Soviet Union and the United States and finds that their two respective elites don't understand each other very well. A fun-to-read, witty, yet scholarly book which profits from the many direct interviews that the author has had with high U.S. and Soviet officials. His chapter on the Arms Race ("The Deadly Entanglement") is a tour de force.

•Lens, Sidney. *The Day Before Doomsday.* Boston: Beacon Press, 1977.

An excellent book on the arms race by one of my favorite writers. Lens is strong on history and research, and this makes his book all the more informative and persuasive. He shows that the U.S. government has never been very seriously interested in disarmament, that most of its public stands since World War II have been designed to placate the American public. He supports his charges with recently declassified documents.

•Sider, Ronald J., and Richard K. Taylor. *Christians in a Nuclear Age.* Downers Grove, Ill.: Intervarsity Press, due by September 1982 .

Richard Taylor has read to me several paragraphs from this forthcoming book, and shared the outline of the rest. I am convinced that this will be a milestone book for galvanizing Christians to work for peace and against nuclear weapons. Chapters will cover (1) the realities of nuclear war; (2) the imminent danger of nuclear war; (3) biblical and theological reflections on war and war-making; (4) what individuals, groups, and congregations can do to work for peace; (5) a challenging look at nonviolent methods for national defense. The title may change by the time it comes out, so use the authors' names to locate the book.

Aliano, Richard A. *The Crime of World Power.* New York: G. P. Putnam's Sons, 1978.

My nominee for most interesting essay on international affairs. Aliano loves comparisons, and in the process of a skilled and informed survey of how nations conduct themselves, he manages to compare U.S. foreign policy to the operations of the Mafia, Leninist organizations to the Jesuits, and so on. Good reading and plenty to think about.

*At the Turning Point.* A kit that has media ideas, essays, etc. Very helpful. Free from Institute for World Order, 1140 Avenue of the Americas, New York, NY 10036.

Barnet, Richard J. *Roots of War*. New York: Penguin Books, 1973.

Barnet believes that war is often caused by the desires or fears of elites who are in the upper echelon of decision-making. So this book explores how U.S. foreign policy is made, how the president and his advisors get information and make life-and-death decisions. Also considers the role of business and the military elite, and how public opinion can be molded by these elites. Barnet believes that we citizens can do something to change this, and his book is geared to peace advocacy and its potential.

Bidwell, R. G. S., ed. *World War III*. Englewood Cliffs, NJ: Prentice-Hall, 1978.

It is hard to imagine just how a World War III might start, how it would escalate, and where it would strike—though it is not too hard to imagine how it would end! This book looks at these questions, drawing upon the knowledge of a team of military and diplomatic experts.

Boston Study Group. *The Price of Defense: A New Strategy for Military Spending*. New York: Times Books, 1978.

A very thorough and impressive study by a group of researchers in Boston. Looks at what we are spending, the strategic or tactical reasons for it, and how we might: (a) do the same task with less or (b) drop the task. Most useful for peaceniks and others.

Boulding, Elise. *Bibliography on World Conflict and Peace*. Boulder, Colo.: Westview, 1979.

More than one thousand entries on peace and peacemaking.

*Disarmament Action Guide*. An excellent resource. Gives up-to-date information and current legislation. Regularly updated. Twenty-five cents from the Coalition for a New Foreign and Military Policy, 120 Maryland Ave., NE, Washington, DC 20002.

*Disarmament Kit*. Includes *World Military and Social Expenditures*, and a teacher's guide. Free from the Rockefeller Foundation, 1133 Avenue of the Americas, New York, NY 10036.

Epstein, William. *The Last Chance*. New York: Free Press, 1976.

Generally regarded as one of the best books on the arms race and the need for disarmament.

Liska, George. *Quest for Equilibrium: America and the Balance of Power on Land and Sea*. Baltimore, MD: Johns Hopkins University Press, 1977.

All about military power and how it has changed in the twentieth century. Liska explores how we first lined up against Britian, then the Soviet Union, then Germany and Japan, finally the Soviet Union again. Explores how power balances affect foreign policy and vice versa. Last four chapters trace our change from the world's preeminent power to one balanced with the USSR.

Melman, Seymour. *The Permanent War Economy*. New York: Simon and Schuster, 1974.

War and preparation for war are good business—at least for a powerful group of corporations that keeps the dollars flowing and our taxes high. Melman shows just how these corporations function, and why this is bad business for the American economy.

Myrdal, Alva. *The Game of Disarmament*. New York: Pantheon Books, 1976.

A superb guide to disarmament, what has been done, what could be done. Myrdal was a leader of the neutralist bloc in the United Nations in disarmament issues (she is a delegate from Sweden) and knows her subject inside and out. Each chapter takes up a different issue or sub-issue.

Nathan, James A., and James K. Oliver. *United States Foreign Policy and World Order*. Boston, MA: Little, Brown and Co., 1976.

A comprehensive survey of U.S. involvement in world affairs that begins with our intervention in the Russian revolution (1919–21) and brings us up to Nixon and Kissinger. If you want to know where we have been and what we did, this is a useful reference. With sections on Suez 1956, Cuba, Indochina, the Berlin Crisis, etc. Little is missed.

Rockman, Jane, ed. *Peace in Search of Makers*. Valley Forge, PA: Judson Press, 1979.

New York's Riverside Church has been the center of a new wave of peace organizing among U.S. church congregations. This book is a collection of presentations made at a historic convocation at Riverside in 1978. Contributors include the Rev. William Sloane Coffin, Jr., Richard J. Barnet, Cora Weiss, and others.

Spanier, John. *Games Nations Play*. New York: Holt, Rinehart and Winston, 3rd ed. 1978.

A book designed for the college-level reader on international politics. Clearly written, well-organized. The reader will have the makings of a good education by the end of the book. Chapters on how the world system is organized, how it works, how players (nations) navigate and compete, war, elites, bureaucrats, imperialism, and more.

Stockholm International Peace Research Institute. *Weapons of Mass Destruction and the Environment*. New York: Crane, Russak & Co., 1978.

We are now in an age when there seem to be a dozen horrible ways to destroy the world. This booklet looks at several weapons including chemical, biological, geophysical, nuclear, weather modification, and more. It then recommends ways of controlling these new mass weapons—and ones to come.

*World Disarmament Kit*. Topics for discussion, action suggestions. Contribution to World Without War Council, 175 Fifth Avenue, New York, NY 10010.

## ACTION AND INFORMATION GROUPS

•**American Friends Service Committee**, 1501 Cherry St., Philadelphia, PA 19102. Since beginning to work for the AFSC in 1979, I have come to a broad appreciation for this Quaker-inspired but widely supported peace and justice organization. Pacifist in its orientation, the AFSC has been promoting peace, equality, and human betterment since 1917; yet it retains a freshness and vitality that belie its age and worldwide reputation. The AFSC was in the forefront of the peace movement in the 1960s, and today continues actively to promote disarmament, challenge U.S. arms sales, and oppose the draft. With numerous regional offices throughout the country, each designing locally-relevant programs, the AFSC provides ample opportunity for grass-roots involvement by people of all faiths.

•**Coalition for a New Foreign and Military Policy,** 120 Maryland Ave., NE, Washington, DC 20002. A topnotch umbrella group that is geared up for grass-roots action on behalf of a more just (and sane) U.S. foreign policy. Particularly active in lobbying Congress against military spending, for limiting the arms trade, for new peace initiatives, against support of dictatorships, and so on. Actively involves its 8,000 grass-roots members in lobbying and public education. Publishes excellent action guides for use by local organizers on such topics as human rights, disarmament, spending priorities, the UN human rights covenants, and more. Before you join any peace or human rights group, consider joining and supporting the Coalition.

•**Mobilization for Survival,** 3601 Locust Walk, Philadelphia, PA 19104. A national coalition of peace groups and individuals who have united to press for four important goals: zero nuclear weapons, ban nuclear power, stop the arms race, and fund human needs. MFS is particularly interested in stimulating grass-roots efforts against war spending and nuclear power. MFS has been an active sponsor of hundreds of teach-ins, vigils, and demonstrations around the country.

•**New Directions,** 305 Massachusetts Ave., NE, Washington, DC 20002. A citizens' action group that hopes to build up a people's lobby for global justice. Active in promoting arms control with U.S. government, especially in the SALT debates. New Directions has some of the most sophisticated Congressional lobbyists in Washington.

**The American Peace Society,** Suite 504, 4000 Albermarle St., NW, Washington, DC 20016. This group, begun in 1828, is one of the oldest non-sectarian peace organizations in the world. Over its 150-plus year history, it has advocated peace and reconciliation, and raised a challenge to the Mexican-American War, the Civil War, the Spanish-American War, and so on. Its advocacy role is not being exercised; now its limited energies are concentrated on the publication of a scholarly quarterly, *World Affairs.*

**Another Mother for Peace,** 407 N. Maple Dr., Beverly Hills, CA 90210. A women's peace lobby that was begun during the years of the U.S. involvement in Vietnam.

**Arms Control Association,** 11 Dupont Circle, NW, Washington, DC 20036. A group that promotes a better understanding of arms control issues through its regular newsletter, *Arms Control Today,* and through regular conferences and seminars. Supported by arms control professionals like former Senator Joseph Clark, Herbert Scoville, Gloria Duffy, and William Kincade. Has ties to the State Department's arms control staff and other professionals.

**Center for Defense Information,** 122 Maryland Ave., NE, Washington, DC 20002. A research center that critiques U.S. military policies and spending. Draws upon the expertise of many former military people, and publishes their analyses for use by Congress and the general public.

**The Center for National Security Studies,** 122 Maryland Ave., NE, Washington, DC 20002. National security is a phrase that many U.S. administrations have used to justify spying on Americans, toppling foreign governments, hiding vital information from the public, and actively misleading the public. The NCSS is a joint project of the American Civil Liberties Association and the Fund for Peace. It does research on the government's covert activities, and advocates reform of the intelligence bureaucracy.

**The Center for War/Peace Studies,** 218 E. 18th St., New York, NY 10003. A research center on global issues whose motto is "applied research toward a world of peace with justice." Recent issues have included the law of the sea, arms control, UN reform, and the Middle East conflict. Publishes a regular magazine, *Global Report.*

**Church Women United,** Rm. 812, 475 Riverside Drive, New York, NY 10115. An ecumenical association of Christian women who meet and worship together in their local communities. It has a strong activist and globalist orientation, and involves its members in human rights advocacy, special support for the development of women, support for the United Nations, disarmament, racial justice, and justice in the United States.

**Clergy and Laity Concerned (CALC),** 198 Broadway, New York, NY 10038. A leader in the anti-war movement during the 1960s and 1970s, CALC involved Jewish and Christian people in local chapters throughout the United States. Current program emphasis is on challenging U.S. support of repressive regimes, especially in Indonesia, the Philippines, South Korea, and other countries that receive U.S. aid. Lobbies with Congress, sponsors demonstrations.

**Community for Creative Non-Violence,**1335 N St., NW, Washington, DC 20005. Radical Catholics and others who live in communal households in Washington, DC, and who are a constant thorn in the flesh of the Pentagon. Besides maintaining a soup kitchen and halfway house for the homeless poor in Washington, CCNV members are constantly being arrested for such things as chaining themselves to the White House fence, rubbing ashes on missiles, and pouring blood on the Pentagon steps. CCNV is linked with Jonah House (listed below) and a wide network of peace activists around the country.

**Council on Religion and International Affairs,** 170 E. 64th St., New York, NY 10021. Established in 1914 to give support to a just and peaceful U.S. foreign policy. Has an active seminar program that brings together business leaders and others. Publishes *Worldview* magazine. Develops programs on peace and global issues for use in a continuing education program for the clergy.

**Council for a Livable World,** 100 Maryland Ave., NE, Washington, DC 20002.    A Washington-based lobbying group that focuses its attention on the U.S. Senate. The CLW raises funds from its members and friends which are used in key Senate races or primaries where there is a clear-cut difference between the candidates on peace and disarmament issues. CLW has supported over thirty Senators over the past years, including Ted Kennedy, George McGovern, and Mark Hatfield. The CLW also prepares informational materials and seminars on defense issues for the use of Senators and their aides.

**The Disarm Education Fund**, 175 Fifth Ave., New York, NY 10010. Begun as a fund-raising group to support public education that will counter the well-financed efforts of groups like the American Security Council. Plans to develop films, brochures, radio spots, etc. Publishes a magazine called *Disarm News*.

**Federation of American Scientists**, 307 Massachusetts Ave., NE, Washington, DC 20002. A lobbying group that represents the opinions of thousands of progressive scientists. Began with the goal of ensuring civilian control over atomic power and armaments; now is active in supporting disarmament, challenging new Pentagon projects like the B-1 Bomber, and supporting the civil rights of scientists here and abroad.

**Fellowship of Reconciliation**, Box 271, Nyack, NY 10960. The FOR is an international peace group with chapters in twenty-eight countries. It began with the World War I conflict and has been working to build peace and world understanding ever since. In the United States, the FOR has been active in the civil rights and anti-Vietnam war movements, in environmental advocacy, and in attempts to promote peace in Northern Ireland and the Middle East. Draws its main membership from faith-centered individuals.

**The Fund for Peace**, 121 Constitution Ave., NE, Washington, DC 20002. Set up to counter the many right-wing programs that fill the airwaves. The Fund sponsors three research centers that do in-depth studies on the military and the U.S. intelligence network. They are the Center for Defense Information, the Center for National Security Studies, and the Center for International Policy. The Fund also sponsors the radio program "In the Public Interest," which is aired by over 300 stations around the United States.

**Institute for Policy Studies**, 1901 Q St., NW, Washington, DC 20009. A think tank that draws upon the writing and researching skills of Richard Barnet, Marcus Raskin, Michael Klare, Art Wascow, Eqbal Ahmed, and many others. Publishes useful studies on U.S. foreign and military policies, the role of multinational corporations, international economics, and world resource politics.

**International Peace Academy**, 777 UN Plaza, New York, NY 10017. While not an official UN agency, this private institute and study center seems to function like one. Its services are provided primarily to governments through training their diplomats and officials in peacekeeping and mediation techniques. The IPA studies all UN peacekeeping efforts and makes in-the-field inspections of their progress and problems. Has a transnational board of directors. A good publications program on UN peacekeeping.

**Jewish Peace Fellowship**, P.O. Box 271, Nyack, NY 10960. An association of Jewish clergy and lay persons that began in 1941. Has worked to establish the right of Jewish people to be conscientious objectors. Now focuses on reconciliation, nonviolent conflict resolution, and promoting social justice.

**Jonah House**, 1933 Park Ave., Baltimore, MD 21217. A small, yet powerful community that includes the Berrigans, Elizabeth McAllister, and others. Does direct action as described above (see CCNV), plus Jonah House sponsors training weekends for others who want to do likewise.

**NARMIC—National Action/Research on the Military-Industrial Complex**, 1501 Cherry St., Philadelphia, PA 19102. A fine research group that puts out good films, pamphlets, and leaflets on military-related topics. Recent offerings include "How to Research Your Local War Industry," "The Great American Bomb Machine," and a study on the U.S. role in the Philippines and ten other countries.

**National Peace Academy Campaign**, 1629 K St., NW, Washington, DC 20006. With West Point, Annapolis, and the Air Force Academy churning out people every year who are professionally trained to make war, wouldn't it be nice if we had a Peace Academy that trained people to make peace? George Washington thought so, and proposed the idea in 1782. Now there are people who are trying to get Congress to adopt the idea and who need political and financial support for their efforts.

**Operation Turning Point—End the Arms Race**, 1140 Avenue of the Americas, New York, NY 10036. A joint public education program sponsored by the United Nations Association, the Institute for World Order, and other groups. They want to reach the general public through creative use of media spots, special brochures, and a handy leadership kit designed for small group discussion.

**Peacemakers**, P.O. Box 627, Garberville, CA 95440. An association of people around the country who advocate not paying federal income tax in order to oppose war spending. Through *The Peacemaker*, their lively magazine, they stay in touch with anti-draft, anti-nuke issues in the country and support direct action movements.

**Peace Research Lab**, 438 N. Skinker St., St. Louis, MO 63130. A study and research center that is trying to promote a science of peace. Investigates the psychology of peace-making, asking how we can raise children who will be peacemakers. They research the techniques of non-violent direct action, asking if we can harness this truth force and apply it to promote peace. Publishes regular books and a magazine. Is linked with similar peace research centers in other parts of the world.

**Peace Science Society (International)**, c/o Peace Science Unit, University of Pennsylvania, 3718 Locust Walk, Philadelphia, PA 19104. An association of peace teachers and researchers from around the world. Many of its members teach "peace studies" programs in colleges, universities, and other institutions. Publishes *Papers* and the *Journal of Peace Science*. Holds annual conferences in the United States, Europe, and Japan.

**Promoting Enduring Peace**, P.O. Box 103, Woodmont, CT 06460. A research service that regularly reprints significant articles on peace and mails them out to members. Also sponsors seminars on peace issues, and trips to various parts of the world for students and others.

**SANE**, 318 Massachusetts Ave., NE, Washington, DC 20002. First begun to promote a ban on nuclear testing, SANE has played a leadership role in opposing such costly and dubious projects as the B-1 Bomber and the neutron bomb. It actively supports SALT and bold disarmament initiatives and works for a transfer of government spending from the military to needed domestic programs. SANE also sponsors a series of radio programs on public issues called "Consider the Alternative."

**Vietnam Veterans Against the War,** P.O. Box 20184, Chicago, IL 60620. Originally begun as a group to protest U.S. involvement in Vietnam and Indochina, the VVAW has continued to oppose other Vietnam-style involvements by the United States. It is active in advancing the interests of veterans and has joined in many other causes and marches against the "ruling class" of this country. In recent years, the VVAW has been much involved in left sectarian politics; it tends to be pro-Chinese and anti-Soviet.

**Women's International League for Peace and Freedom,** 1213 Race St., Philadelphia, PA 19107. Begun as a peace advocacy group in 1915. Continues to do good work in that area. WILPF also tries to unite women in various parts of the world around issues that oppress them and their societies. Has sponsored several international women's gatherings. Chapters around the world.

**Women's Strike for Peace,** 799 Broadway, New York, NY 10003. Begun in 1961 when 100,000 women in sixty cities marched to protest the nuclear arms race. WSP has been marching ever since. It continues to lobby for disarmament and against the dangers of domestic nuclear power plants.

**World Conference on Religion and Peace,** 777 UN Plaza, New York, NY 10017. A unique effort to bring together clergy and religious leaders from around the world in order for them to formulate common themes and goals for promoting peace. The keystone of the program is a regular world conference that brings together Buddhists, Christians, Jews, Moslems, Shintoists, Sikhs, and many others for face-to-face dialogue.

**World Peacemakers,** 2852 Ontario Road, NW, Washington, DC 20009. A Christian movement that grows out of the work of the remarkable Church of the Savior in Washington, DC. Convinced that the nuclear arms race is the overarching idolatry of our time, the World Peacemakers would like to stimulate the formation of local church-centered groups to pray, reflect, and ask for guidance for their opposition to the arms race. Each local chapter will decide its own path of resistance, but one initial suggestion is that people write to close friends and loved ones about these issues.

**World Without War Council,** 175 Fifth Ave., New York, NY 10010. A peace group that believes in non-violent action for building a sane world society. Supports the United Nations and measures to strengthen it. Currently has undertaken a major initiative to bring national peace and globalist groups together to identify common goals and needs. Has an annual intern program which helps train future activists. Extensive publications list.

# Social Justice

## FOR FURTHER READING

•Ashworth, Georgina, ed. *World Minorities*. London: Minority Rights Group, 1978.
   A world survey of thirty-three different minority situations. All are briefly related and accompanied by a short bibliography. A useful reference tool.

•Brown, Dee. *Bury My Heart at Wounded Knee.* New York: Bantam, 1971.
   Probably the most searing portrayal of what European settlers did to the Native American population.

•Freedman, James. *Untouchable: An Indian Life History.* Palo Alto, Calif.: Stanford University Press, 1979.
   A story of India's untouchables told through the words and story of one man whose life is an example of their history and present status.

•Newland, Kathleen. *The Sisterhood of Man*. New York: W. W. Norton, 1979.
   A book from the Worldwatch Institute. Newland looks at the situation of women all over the globe and focuses especially on health, employment, politics, education, legal status, and the family. The style is occasionally colorless, but the scope of the book makes it uniquely valuable.

•Woods, Donald. *Biko.* New York: Paddington Press, 1978.
   Stephen Biko was a black leader in South Africa who was "questioned to death" by the police. This book is an excellent and up-to-date guide to the problems of this racist bastion; contains a strong appeal for united international action to bring change before a civil war erupts.

Bertelsen, Judy S., ed. *Nonstate Nations in International Politics.* New York: Praeger, 1977.
   Non-states are a people who feel they are or want to be a state, but are not internationally recognized. Judy Bertelsen has collected nine essays on this problem and the topics range from the Kurds to the Navajos. One chapter is on the Zionist movement and how it finally got its own state. Another is on the Palestinian Arabs.

Boulding, Elise. *The Underside of History: A View of Women through Time*. Boulder, Colo.: Westview Press, 1976.
   For the reader who wants a deep understanding of the evolution of women's roles in

Western society. Boulding goes back to the Greeks and takes us on a lengthy but rich tour of history. While most of the book focuses on the West, there are several chapters on women in developing countries.

————. *Women: The Fifth World.* Foreign Policy Association Headline Series #248, New York: Foreign Policy Association, 1980.

A nice introduction to women's issues in a global context. Elise Boulding brings a background of scholarship, commitment, and personal activism to this 64-page booklet which is designed as a discussion starter for small groups. Chapters on history, alternative roles for women, the United Nations Decade for Women, and the future of the global women's movement. Followed by questions for discussion, and a bibliography.

Cross, Beatrice and Ronald, eds. *The Children's Rights Movement.* New York: Doubleday, 1977.

Over fifty essays and articles on children's rights. This book deals primarily with the abuse and oppression of children in the United States. However, much of what is said can be applied to most countries in the world. Five sections discuss oppression, the movement for children's rights, a Bill of Rights for children, and self-help activities of young people. Also a brief essay on the Rights of Children in World Perspective, and a reproduction of the UN Declaration on the Rights of the Child.

Dunn, L. C. et al. *Race, Science and Society.* London: George Allen and Unwin, Ltd., 1975.

Excellent series of essays from world experts on the theories and practice of racial discrimination. Essays cover racism, tribalism, caste, and ethnic Chinese in Southeast Asia. First commissioned by UNESCO.

Giele, Janet Zollinger, and Audrey Chapman Smock, eds. *Women: Roles and Status in Eight Countries.* New York: John Wiley & Sons, 1977.

A result of a Ford Foundation project that brought women together to study how women's rights could be promoted in different societies. Each chapter focuses on a country and gives an historical background as well as a current assessment of women's status. The countries are Egypt, Bangladesh, Mexico, Ghana, Japan, France, the United States, and Poland.

Hunt, Chester L., et al. *Ethnic Dynamics.* Homewood, Ill.: Dorsey Press, 1974.

Very useful selection of chapters on such diverse subjects as minorities in the USSR, disputes within Belgium and Northern Ireland, minorities in Islamic states, Nigeria, and much more. Extensive bibliography.

Kohr, Leopold. *Development Without Aid: The Translucent Society.* New York: Schocken Books, 1979.

A society is translucent when it is small enough to be readily seen and understood by its people. Small states are more likely to solve their problems than big ones, the author argues. This fits in with his argument in other writings that big states should be broken up.

Rubin, Leslie, and Brian Weinstein. *Introduction to African Politics*. New York: Praeger, 1974.

A very helpful, well-written, and thorough discussion of the problems and practice of nation-building in Africa. Discusses inter-ethnic conflicts, coups, the problems of westernized elites, and *apartheid*.

Sidorsky, David, ed. *Human Rights: Contemporary Issues and Jewish Perspectives*. Philadelphia: Jewish Publication Society, 1978.

Good collection of essays on the situation of Jews in the USSR and Iraq. Many articles on the history of persecution of Jews, and on the tradition of Jewish concern for human rights. Includes a review of minority treatment in Israel.

## ACTION AND INFORMATION GROUPS

•**Amnesty International**, 304 W. 58th St., New York, NY 10019. The Nobel prize-winning human rights organization that has chapters all over the world. Amnesty opposes torture, capital punishment, and tries to free "prisoners of conscience." In the latter category are people who work for social justice causes, religious activists, advocates of national rights. See my extensive write-up in the Human Rights section.

•**Amnesty International: Inter-Religious Urgent Action Network**, 3618 Sacramento St., San Francisco, CA 94118. A special program of A.I. that links religious congregations together in support of prisoners of conscience around the world. Focuses often on cases of religious persecution. Open to individual or chapter membership.

•**Minority Rights Group**, Benjamin Franklin House, 36 Craven St., London WC2N 5NG, England. Far and away the best group in the field of minority oppression. One wishes that there were a full-scale chapter in the United States. Concerns itself with the same variety of issues that I have described in the social justice chapter: women, religious minorities, ethnic minorities. As of 1979, the MRG had commissioned thirty-seven different studies of minority group oppression, all of which are regularly updated. Works primarily through publicizing these situations, getting the word to the press and to activists.

•**Women's International Network**, 187 Grant St., Lexington, MA 02173. Formed to link women's groups around the world and to let Americans know what is going on elsewhere. Publishes an excellent and information-filled magazine called *WIN News*. Has begun to initiate actions: one to call attention to the genital mutilation of women; another to have the U.S. Congress hold hearings on the human rights of women.

*General Groups*

**The Anti-Slavery Society for the Protection of Human Rights,** 60 Weymouth St., London, W1N 4DX, England. Petitions governments and international agencies on behalf of oppressed peoples. Concerned with indigenous minorities, children, women, debt slavery. Publishes occasional studies and reports.

**B'nai B'rith**, 1640 Rhode Island Ave., NW, Washington, DC 20036. An ecumenical Jewish organization that actively works on human rights and social justice issues. In addition to its support of Jews in the USSR, Syria, and Iran, the B'nai B'rith has also tried to help the Kurds in Iraq and Iran, and the Christian minority in Lebanon.

**Church Women United**, Rm. 812, 475 Riverside Drive, New York, NY 10115. An ecumenical association of Christian women who meet and worship together in their local communities. It has a strong activist and globalist orientation and involves its members in human rights advocacy, special support for the development of women, support for the United Nations, disarmament, racial justice, and justice within the United States.

**Cultural Survival**, 11 Divinity Ave., Cambridge, MA 02138. Has a special concern for helping small indigenous groups of people survive their impact with industrial culture. As we know, many of these groups have been physically or culturally destroyed by such contacts. Cultural Survival works with national governments and international agencies to protect the rights of these people. The closest thing we Americans have to Britain's Minority Rights Group, listed above.

**National Council of Churches of Christ—Commission on Justice, Liberation and Human Fulfillment**, 475 Riverside Drive, New York, NY 10115. A special unit of the NCC that is directly concerned with Third World people inside and outside the United States. This unit is largely staffed and run by U.S. minority people and is an advocate for Native Americans, Blacks, and Hispanic Americans. It also is much involved in advocating self-determination for Taiwan and South Africa, supporting political prisoners in Puerto Rico, Korea, and Uruguay. Promotes dialogue with North Korea and Cuba.

*Children*

Children are subject to brutality and gross deprivation of their rights in many societies, including ours. Several groups pay attention to the special needs of children. Among them:

**The Anti-Slavery Society for the Protection of Human Rights,** 60 Weymouth St., London W1N 4DX, England.

**The Association for Childhood Education International,** 3615 Wisconsin Ave., NW, Washington, DC 20016.

**The Coalition for Children and Youth,** 815 15th St., NW, Washington, DC 20005.

**End Violence Against the Next Generation,** 977 Keeler Ave., Berkeley, CA 94708.

**International Union for Child Welfare,** Rue de Varembe, 1, CH-1211, Geneva, 20, Switzerland.

**United Nations Children's Fund (UNICEF)—U.S. Committee,** 331 E. 38th St., New York, NY 10016.

**Women's International Network,** 187 Grant St., Lexington, MA 02173. Concerned about genital mutilation of girls.

*Native Americans*

Few of us are aware that Native American (Indian) communities in the United States are in many ways legally separate nations within U.S. boundries. Thus our relations with these people is an international problem.

**American Indian Movement,** 1209 4th St., SE, Minneapolis, MN 55414; International Program: 777 UN Plaza, Room 10-F, New York, NY 10017. Struggles for the honoring of treaty rights between the U.S. government and Native American peoples. AIM was the organization involved in the Wounded Knee confrontation. Uses international publicity to promote its aims.

**Indian Law Resource Center,** 1101 Vermont Ave., NW, Washington, DC 20005. Provides legal support to Indians in the Western Hemisphere. Also does research.

**Indian Rights Association,** 1505 Race St., Philadelphia, PA 19102. Works to protect treaty rights of Native Americans.

**International Indian Treaty Council,** 777 United Nations Plaza, Room 10-F, New York, NY 10017. In 1974 delegates from ninety-seven Indian nations gathered to share their common concerns. They developed this Council, whose purpose is to bring the situation of the Western Hemisphere's Indians to world attention. Has focused on the UN as a place to publicize their aims.

**Interreligious Foundation for Community Organization, Inc.,** Rm. 572, 475 Riverside Drive, New York, NY 10115. A project of the National Council of Churches, IFCO funds and supports grass-roots efforts by U.S. minorities to build communities and counter oppression. It has given considerable attention to the cause of Native Americans.

**National Congress of American Indians,** Suite 700, 1430 K St., NW, Washington, DC 20005. A coalition of many Indian leaders from around the country, united in common interest and self-preservation. Becomes involved with land, water and fishing rights, civil rights, and so on. This is the main group through which one can become aware of the thinking and plans of the tribal councils.

**Native American Rights Fund,**1506 Broadway, Boulder, CO 80302. Established in 1971 with a grant from the Ford Foundation, the Fund provides legal assistance to individuals and tribes in cases involving lands, tribal rights, human rights, and conflicts with the U.S. government. The Steering Committee is made up of Native Americans, and most of the lawyers are also Indians.

**North American Indian Women's Association,** Box 314, Isleta, NM 87022. An association of Native American women that works for inter-tribal communication and the betterment of family and economic life.

**United Effort Trust,** 1430 K St., Suite 700, NW, Washington, DC 20005. Established by Native Americans to protect their land and legal rights. Works through state and federal channels.

### Palestinians

**American Near East Refugee Aid (ANERA),** 900 Woodward Bldg., 733 Fifteenth St., NW, Washington, DC 20005. Aids Palestinian refugees in the Middle East. Supplies educational and humanitarian assistance as well as publicity for cases of human rights violations.

**Committee on the Exercise of the Inalienable Rights of the Palestinian People,** c/o United Nations, New York, NY 10017. A special United Nations program that tries to promote the rights of the Palestinians through public information and special studies.

**Palestine Arab Delegation,** 441 Lexington Ave., New York, NY 10017. Advocates U.S. even-handedness in the Middle East, specifically that the United States not ship arms or give aid either to Israel or to the Arab states. Feels the Palestinian people have been robbed of their homeland by the Zionist movement.

**Palestine Human Rights Campaign,** 1322 18th St., NW, Washington, DC 20036. An American group with ties to the Arab-American community in the United States. It is concerned with human rights violations by the Israeli government.

### Religious Freedom

**American Jewish Congress,** 15 E. 48th St., New York, NY 10028. Concerned with general human rights questions but especially with the situation of Jewish people in the Soviet Union, Israel, and other parts of the world.

**Appeal of Conscience Foundation,** 119 W. 57th St., New York, NY 10019. Concerned with violations of religious rights. Has an ecumenical membership. Makes fact-finding visits to various countries, and publicizes its results.

**Center for Russian and East European Jewry and Student Struggle for Soviet Jewry,** 200 W. 72nd St., New York, NY 10023. Concerned both with Jews who want to be free to emigrate and with the rights of those who stay. Tries to provide assistance to families of prisoners.

**Freedom of Faith,** 170 E. 64th St., New York, NY 10021. A new organization, FOF wants to establish church-based action groups to work for religious rights for all faiths in all parts of the globe. They intend to use letter-writing campaigns, publicity, conferences, and prisoner adoption to further their aims.

**Medical Mobilization for Soviet Jewry,** 680 Main St., Suite 303, Waltham, MA 02154. Concerned with imprisonment and harassment of Jews in the Soviet Union. Publicizes cases where psychiatry and medicine are misused to control people. Organizes protests of medical professionals against Soviet repression.

**National Conference on Soviet Jewry,** 2025 Eye St., NW, Washington, DC 20006. This is a major nationwide coordinating agency for American activity on behalf of Soviet Jews. It has thirty-eight national member agencies and over two hundered local affiliates. The Conference has two goals: to help Jews emigrate from the Soviet Union and to help those Jews who want to stay to have the freedom to practice their religion and way of life.

**National Interreligious Task Force on Soviet Jewry,** 1307 S. Wabash Ave., Chicago, IL 60605. With virtually the same goals as the Conference (above), this group seems to have a special base in the Christian community and in the attempts in the United States at Christian-Jewish dialogue.

**Research Center for Religion and Human Rights in Closed Societies,** 475 Riverside Drive, Suite 448, New York, NY 10115. Focus is on communist countries. Primarily works through its publications and press releases. Publishes *RCDA (Religion in Communist Dominated Areas).*

**Society for the Study of Religion and Communism,** P.O. Box 171, Wheaton, IL 60187. Has an extensive publications list of books and pamphlets on religious practice in Eastern Europe and Russia. Also publishes *Religion in Communist Lands.*

*Southern Africa-South Africa*

The number of American-based groups working on the South African situation is enormous; I have listed just a few. For more information, see the excellent study-action guide on southern Africa put out by the AFSC, 1501 Cherry St., Philadelphia, PA 19102 ($1.00).

**Ad Hoc Monitoring Group on South Africa,** c/o Representative Andrew McGuire, 1112 Longworth House Office Bldg., Washington, DC 20515. A congregational lobbying group on U.S.-South African policy.

**Association of Concerned African Scholars,** P.O. Box 791, E. Lansing, MI 48823. Composed of academicians in the field of African studies. Concerned primarily with influencing U.S. policy on southern Africa.

**Center Against Apartheid,** c/o United Nations, New York, NY 10017. A United Nations program. Publicizes the abuses of the *apartheid* system in South Africa. Provides information, documents cases, tries to rally aid for prisoners and for liberation movements.

**Congressional Black Caucus,** 306 House Annex One, Washington, DC 20515. Made up of the black members of Congress. Has paid particular attention to U.S. policy in southern Africa.

**February 1 Movement,** P.O. Box 2413, Washington, DC 20013. A black activist student organization, concerned with racism in Africa. Chapters throughout the United States.

**Interfaith Center on Corporate Responsibility,** 475 Riverside Drive, Rm. 566, New York, NY 10115. Tries to help churches and religious institutions invest their money responsibly. Has given a particular emphasis to using investments to pressure companies to stop loans or other support of the South African government.

**International Defense and Aid Fund for Southern Africa,** 1430 Massachusetts Ave., Rm. 201, Cambridge, MA 02138. Works especially on political prisoner issues. Provides legal defense and family support within southern Africa (currently Namibia and South Africa).

**Southern Africa Committee,** 156 Fifth Ave., New York, NY 10010. Works for the liberation of southern Africa through public forums and publicity.

*Women*

I have listed a considerable number of women's clubs and organizations whose primary focus is on national and local matters. I have done so because these groups are often linked with international federations of similar clubs, and because they participate in UN and other international gatherings.

For more information on national and international women's organizations, see *Women's Organizations and Leaders Directory—International Edition*, available from Women Today, Today News Service, National Press Building, Washington, DC 20045.

**American Association of University Women,** 2401 Virginia Ave., NW, Washington, DC 20037. An association of college-educated women throughout the United States. Often concerned with women's issues that transcend national boundaries; supportive of the United Nations. Affiliated with the International Federation of University Women.

**American Home Economics Association,** 2010 Massachusetts Ave., NW, Washington, DC 20036. Concerned with the role of women in all societies, their freedom, health, and the health of the family. Linked with similar groups in other countries.

**Committee to Organize Women's World Banking,** P.O. Box 1691, Grand Central Station, New York, NY 10017. Formed out of a subgroup at the 1975 international women's gathering in Mexico. Wants to help integrate women in developing countries into the monetary economy.

**Country Women's Council U.S.A.,** 307 North Fulton St., Keota, IA 52248. Has over 3 million members in local chapters around the country. Affiliated with the Associated Country Women of the World. Tries to promote a better standard of living for rural women and to develop greater international understanding among women.

**Federation of Organizations for Professional Women,** 2000 P St., NW, Suite 403, Washington, DC 20036. A coalition of over one hundred women's organizations in the United States, including many academic societies and caucuses. Primarily a communications network, and a presence in the nation's capital. Has sponsored the International Center for Research on Women, which focuses on research and information sharing on the role of women in development around the world.

**Feminist Alliance Against Rape**, P.O. Box 21033, Washington, DC 20009. A national association of women who are concerned about violence against women. Along with several other similar organizations, they publish *Aegis*, a magazine on rape and violence issues.

**International Feminist Network**, c/o ISIS, PO Box 301, 1227 Carouge, Geneva, Switzerland. This network has been formed "to give support and solidarity to women everywhere in combatting injustices against women." It has affiliates around the world. U.S. affiliate: *Off Our Backs*, 1724 20th St., NW, Washington, DC 20009.

**International Labour Organization: Office for Women Workers' Questions**, CH-1211, Geneva 22, Switzerland.

**International Women's Year Tribune**, Rm. 815, 345 E. 46th St., New York, NY 10017. A regular newsletter that attempts to follow up on the momentum of the International Women's gathering that was sponsored by the United Nations in 1975. Carries reports on activities by women around the world.

**League of Women Voters**, 1730 M St., NW, Washington, DC 20036. An active association that is dedicated to informing women and the general public about local, national, and international issues. Does excellent work in sharing information about the UN and U.S. foreign policy. Their Overseas Education Fund has paid special attention to women in the economic development process.

**National Association of Colored Women's Clubs, Inc.**, 1601 R St., NW, Washington, DC 20009. An association of black Americans. Promotes racial understanding, and the moral, intellectual, and spiritual welfare of women.

**National Council of Negro Women**, 1346 Connecticut Ave., NW, Washington, DC 20036. Has over four million members and affiliates. Stresses community service and the development of women's leadership in national and international organizations.

**National Council of Women in the United States**, 345 E. 46th St., New York, NY 10017. Claims over four million affiliated members in the United States. A communications center for issues of concern to women.

**National Federation of Business and Professional Women**, 2012 Massachusetts Ave., NW, Washington, DC 20036. Affiliated with over fifty other national chapters in the International Federation of Business and Professional Women. The International Federation stands for women's right to work, equal pay for equal work, increased opportunities for advancement and removal of discrimination against employment of married or older women. Members have also campaigned actively to place more women in public office and policy-making positions. Local chapters sponsor literacy programs, urge progressive legislation. The National Federation is active through the United Nations.

**National Organization of Women (NOW),** 425 13th St., NW, Washington, DC 20004. This activist women's organization maintains a lively interest in international issues, and is the group most likely to be sympathetic to the views of radical Third World women.

*Family Planning*

Many people feel that family planning and the ability to regulate the size of the family is an important issue for women—especially in societies where women are limited to a reproductive and housewife role. The following organizations are involved in these issues:

**The Pathfinder Fund,** 1330 Boylston St., Boston, MA 02167.

**Planned Parenthood—World Population,** 810 7th Ave., New York, NY 10019.

**The Population Council,** One Dag Hammarskjold Plaza, New York, NY 10017.

**Population Institute,** 110 Maryland Ave., NE, Washington, DC 20002.

**Zero Population Growth,** 50 E. 40th St., New York, NY 10008.

# Global Institution-Building

## FOR FURTHER READING

•Falk, Richard A. *A Study of Future Worlds*. New York: Free Press, 1975.
   In this book Falk describes how one might go about organizing a world polity that supports ecology, political justice, peace, and human betterment. Begins with an interesting survey of how the world is and might be organized, using schematic drawings to illustrate his point, then goes on to outline how one form of centralized world government would work.

•Keys, Donald. *The United Nations and Planetary Consciousness*. Order from Planetary Citizens, 777 UN Plaza, New York, NY 10017. Cost: $3.50.
   Donald Keys is considered to be a leader in world federalism, as well as a leading thinker on the spiritual evolution of planetary structures. His perspective is unique and enthralling, reflecting a patience that comes from years of working with and around the United Nations.

•Luard, Evan. *Socialism Without the State*. New York: St. Martin's Press, 1979.
   An expert on international structures and peacekeeping, Luard is also a member of the British Parliament. In this book he argues that the state is crushing human diversity and freedom; he recommends a change in global structures which would strengthen world institutions, yet strengthen local institutions as well.

Angell, Robert C. *The Quest for World Order*. Ann Arbor: University of Michigan Press, 1979.
   This book argues that slow but sure progress is being made in building a new world order—primarily through cooperative efforts in the environment and in technical and scientific areas. Also supports the idea that we are learning new ways of planetary dialogue and negotiation.

Brown, Seyom, et al. *Regimes for the Ocean, Outer Space, and Weather*. Washington, DC.: Brookings Institution, 1978.
   How, exactly, can we organize global structures for controlling the use of "common" properties, keeping them from destruction, and providing maximum good to humankind? This book, a fine example of Brookings' policy research, tries to answer the question.

Finger, Seymour Maxwell and Joseph R. Harbert, eds. *U.S. Policy in International Institutions*. Boulder, Colo.: Westview Press, 1978.
   A collection of thirty-five essays from as many authors. Focus is on U.S. role in

world institutions. Experts take a look at monetary issues, disarmament, the UN, global resources, etc. A gold mine of comment and analysis.

Lazlo, Ervin. *A Strategy for the Future*. New York: Geo. Braziller, 1974.
A systems approach to world government and environmental maintenance. Focuses on a proposal for a world governmental system that includes a World Treasury, World System for Ecological Balance, World Economic System, World Security Forces, and so on.

Lentz, Theo. F., ed. *Humantroitism*. Available from 6251 San Bonita Ave., St. Louis, MO 63105.
An interesting series of essays that are united by a central theme: humans need to be loyal to humanity as a whole and to our planet. One essayist calls this "global altruism." Essays focus on ways to understand and develop this new form of identity.

Luard, Evan. *The International Regulation of Civil Wars*. New York: New York University, 1972.
A series of essays on modern civil wars and what the international community has or has not done to stop them. Begins with a survey of pre-United Nations efforts. Chapters on Laos, the Congo, the Spanish Civil War, Yemen, Cyprus. Each chapter is arranged by history, goals, resources, components, etc. to make comparisons possible.

―――. *The International Regulation of Frontier Disputes*. London: Thames and Hudson, 1970.
Nothing can start a war as fast as a good old-fashioned border dispute. Eight major essays explore how the League of Nations and the United Nations have tried to deal with this problem. Other essays on regional organizations, mediation, arbitration, and judicial settlement.

Mazrui, Ali, A. *A World Federation of Cultures*. New York: Free Press, 1976.
A discussion of the cultural dimension of global interaction, that is, how Western white culture has affected other cultures and produced a kind of cultural imperialism that parallels economic domination. Author argues for a greater interpenetration of Western and Third World cultural perspectives and for a world government based on language-cultural constituencies. A truly innovative contribution from a Third World (African) view.

Mendlovitz, Saul H. *On the Creation of a Just World Order*. New York: Free Press, 1975.
Eight authors from around the world contribute unique and thought-provoking essays on various aspects of global institution-building. This book is a kind of sampler of the good ideas coming out of the Institute for World Order, of which Mendlovitz is the Director.

President of the United States. *U.S. Participation in the U.N. A Report*. Department of State (Washington, D.C., annual).
Every year, the president tells Congress what we have done in the United Nations

system. This covers votes, speeches, work with the various UN agencies, etc. Boring reading, but a good reference tool.

Rikhey, Indar Jit, et al. *The Thin Blue Line*. New Haven: Yale University Press, 1974.
   The UN peacekeeping forces—who wear blue uniforms—are indeed often a thin line between warring armies. Here is a history of how the UN has fared, with case studies of Cyprus, the Middle East, and the Congo. Plus a discussion of what the UN has not done. A final section on the future discusses how the peacekeeping machinery can be strengthened.

Tinbergen, Jan, Anthony J. Dolman and Jan van Ettinger. *Reshaping the International Order*. New York: E. P. Dutton & Co., 1976.
   Want to know what a group of international experts thinks can be done to make a better world? Here it is: specific answers in the area of food, energy, environment, arms reduction, ocean management, etc. Plus background pieces on the current situations in each of these areas. This study was commissioned by the Club of Rome.

*United Nations: List of Publications*.
   A regular guide to the many studies and publications that are produced by the United Nations. For a copy, write to UN Publications, Room A-3315, New York, NY 10017.


## ACTION AND INFORMATION GROUPS

•**Institute for World Order**, 1140 Avenue of the Americas, New York, NY 10036. A top-notch think tank that wants to "stimulate a worldwide social movement dedicated to the transformation of the present international system of competing sovereign states to a just world order which has the capacity to provide peace, social justice, economic well-being, and ecological balance throughout the globe." Most of its work so far has been in drawing together scholars from around the world who formulate position papers, write books, and talk to each other about global issues. Their work is often the best in the field. Their efforts have stimulated world order teaching programs in hundreds of colleges and universities throughout the United States.
   Their long-range goal is to stimulate a worldwide movement of people who press for a more sane and just world order. The only concrete program that moves toward advocacy is the Action Center, which tries to organize young people around food, development, and other issues.

•**United Nations Association of the United States (UNA-USA)**, 300 E. 42nd St., New York, NY 10017. A citizens' support group for the work of the United Nations. Has a large national membership, an excellent publications program, and a network of local chapters that sponsor UN days, Model UN Conferences, and other educational activities. UNA–USA has a prestigious board of sponsors drawn from unions, business, academia, and government. In other words, the UNA–USA tries to mobilize mainstream support for the United Nations. I have developed a real respect for its work.

**American Movement for World Government**, 777 U.N. Plaza, 11th Floor, New York, NY 10017. Sponsors seminars and educational programs on UN and world government issues. Also publishes *World Peace News*.

**Campaign for U.N. Reform**, 600 Valley Rd., Wayne, NJ 07470. The former World Federalists-USA has subdivided into a number of new bodies. *New Directions* is one manifestation of this devolution, as is the Campaign for U.N. Reform. The Campaign advocates a stronger UN through changes to improve the World Court, the peacekeeping function, the financial base, and so on.

**Campaign for World Government, Inc.**, 331 Park Ave., Glencoe, IL 60022. An organization that was pushing for a democratically elected and federal world government back in 1945 when the UN was born. It is still pushing for the idea now. Testifies before Congress, has an active publications program, works with other federalist groups on a variety of global issues.

**The Center for War/Peace Studies**, 218 E. 18th St., New York, NY 10003. A research center on global issues whose motto is "applied research toward a world of peace with justice." Recent research issues have included the law of the sea, arms control, UN reform, and the Middle East conflict. Publishes a regular magazine called *Global Report*.

**Commission to Study the Organization of Peace**, 866 UN Plaza, Rm. 405, New York, NY 10017. A globalist think tank that concentrates on UN issues. It was formed in 1939 and some of its proposals for global reform were adopted by the UN Charter. Since then it has issued key studies on a host of issues ranging from disarmament and human rights to the U.S. role in the United Nations.

**The Council of Youth**, c/o Taize, 71250 Taize-Community, France; or 2150 Almaden Rd. 114, San Jose, CA 95125. A non-denominational Christian movement that has brought together thousands of young and not-so-young people from around the world in an attempt to form a "people of the beatitudes" who are poor, committed to global justice, and to a renewed church at work in the world. I include it here because of its international membership and globalist commitment.

**The Council on Foreign Relations**, 58 E. 68th St., New York, NY 10021. A high-powered, foundation-funded research and study association that regularly brings together top leaders from the business, financial, political, academic, humanitarian, and journalist communities for exchanges of ideas. Council programs routinely tap highly placed domestic and foreign leaders who come to talk knowing that they are speaking to a powerful elite in American decision-making. Membership in the Council is by invitation only; only 1,878 people were members in 1978. Members include David Rockefeller, Henry Kissinger, Barbara Walters, David Brinkley, Alexander Haig, Vernon Jordan, and other such luminaries. The Council sponsors special study groups which produce "objective studies" on such topics as U.S.-China policy, disarmament, world resources, the North-South debate, the United Nations, etc. It sponsors the highly influential magazine *Foreign Affairs*.

**Federal Union, Inc.**, 1875 Connecticut Ave., NW, Washington, DC 20009. Federal Union promotes the idea of building a strong world government through establishing a federal "democracy of democracies." Advocates of this idea consider the United States, Canada, Western Europe, and Australia/New Zealand as the natural countries to form the initial framework. They suggest that we could begin by establishing a common citizenship, common currency, common defense and trade policies and building on top of these a new world federal unit. Federal Union promotes these ideas through publications, conferences, and grass-roots educational campaigns.

**Fellowship of World Citizens**, 166 Second Ave., New York, NY 10003. A kind of grass-roots non-organization that doesn't collect dues or sponsor projects. Instead it tries to encourage people to recognize their world citizenship and act upon that realization with others of like mind from their locality.

**Global Perspectives in Education, Inc.**, 218 E. 18th St., New York, NY 10003. An association of U.S. educators who want to develop good materials and lesson plans for teachers in grades K–12 who want to teach about global issues. Excellent resource packets are available on the environment, women and men, "planet-knowing and planet-caring," and much more. Publishes a regular magazine called *Intercom.*

**International Association for a Union of Democracies**, 414 W. 20th St., New York, NY 10011. An effort to promote the federal union of the Atlantic democracies (basically the NATO countries) as a first step toward a democratic world government. Has based its efforts among the legislatures of the NATO countries, and has recruited a number of former prime ministers, cabinet officials, and members of parliament to its cause. Now is trying to develop national chapters with grass-roots support.

**Members of Congress for Peace Through Law**, Rm. 3538, House Annex II, U.S. House of Representatives, Washington, DC 20515. A coalition of U.S. senators and representatives who are internationalist in their perspective. The members support global justice issues like disarmament, human rights, and the strengthening of international institutions. In 1979 the MCPL had 174 members from both Houses. Naturally, the group concentrates primarily on legislative issues.

**Ocean Education Project**, 245 2nd St., NE, Washington, DC 20002. A citizens' effort to lobby for a progressive U.S. position on the Law of the Seas Treaty Conference. A key issue in these negotiations is whether some or all of the world's oceans will be seen as common property of humankind and whether profits from ocean mineral extraction can be used for a world development fund.

**Quaker United Nations Program**, 777 UN Plaza, New York, NY 10017. The Quakers may be a small denomination, but they have one of the largest programs related to the UN, with offices in New York and Geneva. This program focuses on supporting disarmament, human rights, and economic justice efforts at the UN. It also sponsors valuable off-the-record seminars for UN delegates on a variety of controversial topics. Because of its broad advocacy work, the program receives wide backing from the general public. Publishes *In and Around the UN.*

**U.S. Committee for UNICEF**, 331 E. 38th St., New York, NY 10016. The U.S. Committee raises money for the laudable work of UNICEF (the United Nations Children's Fund), work that includes health and feeding programs for the most needy people in the world, especially children and their mothers.

**World Constitution and Parliament Association**, 1480 Hoyt St., Suite 31, Lakewood, CO 80215. A global association of people who have a bold idea: to form a strong world government from the ground up. They have drafted a remarkable World Constitution that provides for a world executive, world court, and world parliament. They are organizing a global grass-roots campaign to have the Constitution adopted by governments and by popular referendums. Part of the process of their campaign is electing a Shadow World Cabinet and later a Provisional World Parliament to press for a new system.

**World Council for Curriculum and Instruction,** Box 171, Teacher's College, Columbia University, New York, NY 10027. This is an association of secondary and college educators, and others, who are concerned with developing teaching programs that promote the ideals of peace and human rights. Its membership is international, including people from socialist and Communist countries. The Council hopes to stimulate new research and ideas through the cross-fertilization of getting its members together.

**World Federalists Association,** 1011 Arlington Blvd., Suite W-219, Arlington, VA 22209. One of the key globalist groups of the 1950s and 1960s, the WFA recently subdivided into a number of organizations and committees. The parent organization is still active in promoting a strong world government through conferences, study groups, and publications.

**World Peace Through Law Center,** Suite 800, 1000 Connecticut Ave., NW, Washington, DC 20036. An impressive global association of professionals who are concerned with building global legal structures. Affiliated organizations include the World Association of Judges, the World Association of Lawyers, the World Association of Law Professors, and the World Association of Law Students. Publications are numerous and include the *World Law Review, World Jurist*, and the *World Legal Directory.* Sponsors numerous conferences on trends and developments in world law. Aids efforts to promote ratification of international treaties.

**World Without War Council,** 175 Fifth Ave., New York, NY 10010. A peace group that believes in nonviolent action for building a sane world society. Supports the United Nations and measures to strengthen it. Currently has undertaken a major initiative to bring national peace and globalist groups together to identify common goals and needs. Has an annual intern program which helps train future activists. Extensive publications list.

## UN AGENCIES AND PROGRAMS

The United Nations has programs which are under the direct control of the organization, like the High Commissioner for Refugees, and programs which are independently chartered, but are considered to be affiliated in the UN network, like the International Labour Organization. I have listed UN system agencies as follows:

The Secretariat
The General Assembly
The Economic and Social Council
Affiliated Agencies and Programs

General information about the UN and its activities can be obtained from the UN Information Centre, Suite 714, 1028 Connecticut Ave., NW, Washington, DC 20036.

*The Secretariat*

This is the administrative office of the United Nations, under the control of the Secretary General. While many of the programs listed below have their home offices in various parts of the world, information on most of them can be obtained from their offices at UN Headquarters, New York, NY 10017.

**United Nations Children's Fund (UNICEF).** Supports development, health, education, and food programs, with a special emphasis on children and mothers or mothers-to-be.

**United Nations Conference on Trade and Development (UNCTAD).** A program that focuses on trade issues and has a strong Third World emphasis. UNCTAD was the chief agency behind the Declaration on a New International Economic Order.

**United Nations Development Program (UNDP).** The aid and development program of the United Nations. Chronically underfunded and subject to heavy influence by the United States (a principal donor), the UNDP nevertheless struggles along doing the best it can.

**United Nations Environment Program.** Begun in the mid-1970s, the Environment program is still at the stage of making studies and inviting cooperation. It is an important start and much progress is expected.

**United Nations High Commissioner for Refugees (UNHCR).** A valuable advocacy and aid program for the millions of refugees around the world.

**United Nations Industrial Development Organization.** A special program that is trying to bring more rapid industrialization to underdeveloped countries.

*The General Assembly*

The full membership body of the UN, the General Assembly, is dominated by Third World votes and often likes to keep new programs directly under its control. Some of its major programs are:

**Committee on the Peaceful Uses of Outer Space.**

**Conference of the Committee on Disarmament.** Made up of most of the principal atomic powers. This is the committee that has endless discussions on disarmament, but one day may actually be used for substantial changes.

**International Law Commission.** A hard-working commission that hammers out proposals for new treaties and other reforms of international law.

**Peace Observation Commission.** Can send observers to report firsthand on conflict areas.

**Special Committee on Apartheid**

**Special Committee on the Ending of Colonialism**

**Special Committee on Peace-Keeping Operations**

**U.N. Commission on International Trade Law**

**U.N. Scientific Advisory Committee.** Advises the General Assembly on questions related to the peaceful use of atomic power.

**U.N. Scientific Committee on the Effects of Atomic Radiation**

*The Economic and Social Council*

This Council is made up of a rotating membership of fifty-four countries; it oversees a number of significant UN programs:

**Advisory Committee on the Application of Science and Technology to Development.**

**Committee for Development Planning**

**Committee on Natural Resources**

**Committee on Science and Technology for Development**

**Commission on Human Rights**

**Commission for Social Development**

**Commission on the Status of Women**

**Economic Commission for Africa**

**Economic and Social Commission for Asia and the Pacific**

**Economic Commission for Latin America**

**Economic Commission for Western Asia**

*Affiliated Agencies and Programs*

**International Court of Justice,** UN Information Centre, Suite 714, 1028 Connecticut Ave., NW, Washington, DC 20036; or ICJ, Peace Palace, The Hague 2012, Netherlands. All UN members are automatically part of the ICJ, or World Court, as are Switzerland, Liechtenstein, and San Marino. The Court can advise the UN and can judge cases were the concerned states have agreed, or in cases where treaties provide for ICJ judgment (almost 700 treaties have such provisions).

**Food and Agriculture Organization (FAO),** Via delle Terme di Caracalla, 00100 Rome, Italy. The FAO has been a leader in promoting agricultural development and the preservation of forests and fisheries. It was a major force behind the convening of the World Food Conference in 1974.

**General Agreement on Tariffs and Trade (GATT),** Villa le Bocage, Palais des Nations, Geneva, Switzerland. The major international body that develops world trade policy, GATT has over one hundred members and affiliates. Significantly absent are many of the communist countries. Common tariff and quota policies are developed in GATT's major trade conferences, the most recent of which concluded after six years of hard negotiations.

**International Atomic Energy Agency (IAEA),** Kaerntnerring 11, 1010 Vienna, Austria. The IAEA was set up with three goals: (1) to promote the peaceful use of atomic energy, (2) to establish safety and other standards for the transferral, storage, and use of fissionable material, (3) to try and keep nations from using such materials for military purposes. While the IAEA is credited with doing a good job with those nations that have agreed to its regulation, these nations tend to be the ones that do not want to develop atomic bombs anyway.

**International Bank for Reconstruction and Development (World Bank),** 1818 H St., NW, Washington, DC 20433. Member countries of the International Monetary Fund are also members of the World Bank, and may apply to it for loans to finance development projects. The World Bank makes "hard" loans at commercial interest rates and "soft" loans at much lower rates. Recent emphasis has been on the poorest twenty-five countries in the world. Significantly, most communist countries are not a part of either the IMF or the World Bank, both of which tend to be strongly influenced by the United States and its allies.

**International Labour Organization (ILO),** 1211 Geneva 20, Switzerland. The ILO was begun in 1919 and has the task of trying to harmonize the divergent interests of labor, business, and government. To accomplish this a country's delegation to the ILO is composed of representatives from all three sectors. The ILO has a broad mandate to promote labor rights and better living and working standards, and is generally credited with having the best record on human rights issues of all the UN bodies. Unfortunately, this isn't saying much, since the ILO, like the UN, is hampered by divisions between communist and non-communist countries, and between rich and poor nations. The ILO has a good research and information program. It has played an active role in trying to end forced labor conditions in many parts of the world.

**International Monetary Fund (IMF),** 19th & H Streets, NW, Washington, DC 20431. Created in 1945 to give "stability" to world currency exchanges, the IMF often plays a significant role in disciplining members who are having balance-of-payments problems. Many Third World countries belong to the IMF, but are critical of a voting system that gives the richer members more power.

**United Nations Educational, Scientific and Cultural Organization (UNESCO),** 7 Place de Fontenoy, 75700 Paris, France. UNESCO's main task is to promote international understanding through intellectual and cultural exchange and cooperation.

UNESCO sponsors many scientific and academic conferences each year, engages in programs that challenge discrimination on the basis of race, sex and ethnicity. It also aids developing countries in literacy, communications, and teacher training programs. All in all, UNESCO is doing a valuable job and it stands as one of the best examples of international cooperation.

**World Food Programme (WFP)**, Via delle Terme di Caracalla, 00100 Rome, Italy. A joint venture of the UN and the FAO, the World Food Programme solicits food donations from countries with surpluses and then uses the food for emergency relief and self-help projects.

**World Health Organization (WHO)**, Avenue Appia, 1211 Geneva 27, Switzerland. Another excellent example of international cooperation. The WHO has almost universal membership. Since 1948 WHO has engaged in global programs to eliminate or reduce the incidence of smallpox, malaria, and numerous other diseases which recognize no national borders. The WHO helps developed countries through promotion of health information sharing, and through a global disease warning system. Most of its energies are devoted to the health needs of developing countries. This is accomplished through training, supplying medical equipment and drugs, research, and direct health services.

# Human Rights

**FOR FURTHER READING**

•Ajami, Fouad. *Human Rights and World Order Politics.* Available from the Institute for World Order, 1140 Avenue of the Americas, New York, NY 10036; $3.50; 33 pages.

A concise and well-argued pamphlet that explores the debate between advocates of political rights versus advocates of economic rights. The author, a Third World scholar currently at Princeton, supports a dual approach.

•Amnesty International. *Amnesty International Annual Report.* Available from AI-USA, 2112 Broadway, New York, NY 10023; most recent cost, $3.95; 352 pages.

A yearly review of human rights developments around the globe, with reports on over one hundred countries.

•———.*Report on Torture.* Available from AI-USA, 2112 Broadway, New York, NY 10023; hardback, $8.95; paperback, $3.95; 285 pages.

A chilling book that finds the practice of torture in the world "has reached epidemic proportions." Surveys over sixty countries where torture is alleged. Opening essays on the methods and definition of torture and on international efforts to halt these practices.

Buergenthal, Thomas, and Judith V. Torney. *International Human Rights and International Education.* U.S. National Committee for UNESCO (1976).

An excellent guide in the field of international human rights education. Contains resources, background essays, and the texts of UN covenants. Available from the U.S. Government Printing Office, Washington, DC 20402; $4.00; 211 pages.

Chalidze, Valery. *To Defend These Rights.* New York: Random House, 1974.

Everything you ever wanted to know about the operation of Soviet law and how it is used against dissidents. Also how minorities fare, how the human rights movement is doing, etc. Chalidze was a leading human rights advocate in the USSR and is now living in New York City.

Glaser, Kurt, and Stefan T. Possony. *Victims of Politics: Human Rights, Discrimination, and Oppression in the World Today.* New York: Columbia University Press, 1978.

A vast (584 pages) and expensive ($30) survey of examples of oppression from all over the globe and in all its forms. Goes on to draw generalizations from this survey and to make policy recommendations.

Herman, Edward S., and Noam Chomsky. *The Political Economy of Human Rights.* South End Press (Box 68, Astor Station, Boston, MA 02123), 1979.

Reviewers seem to agree that "devastating" is the proper adjective to apply to this powerful two-volume study of U.S. foreign policy. Herman and Chomsky have the virtue of bringing massive and detailed research to their intellectual labors, and this study is a fine example. Volume I, *The Washington Connection and Third World Fascism*, explores how the United States set up a network of repressive dictatorships among our non-European allies in the "Free World." Volume II, *After the Cataclysm*, focuses specifically on our involvement in Southeast Asia and its aftermath. One special contribution of this study is the many examples of how the media apologizes for and justifies U.S. foreign policy.

Joes, Anthony James. *Fascism in the Contemporary World.* Boulder, Colo.: Westview Press, 1978.

A most intriguing book. Joes argues that most modern dictatorships of the left or right have more in common with fascism of the Italian variety (1922–1943) than with any other system. The common elements are a one-party system, militarism, a chronic underdevelopment that is attacked by mass mobilization, appeals to national spirit. Takes brief looks at examples and variations ranging from Franco's Spain to Communist China.

Lens, Sidney. *The Forging of the American Empire.* New York: Thomas Y. Crowell, 1974.

A brilliant and challenging look at the realities of America's expansion from 1776 to the present. Discusses our conquest of the native population, the war with Mexico, our seizure of the Philippines, our domination of the Caribbean nations—the works.

Luard, Evan. *Socialism Without the State.* New York: St. Martin's, 1979.

An expert on international peace-keeping, Luard is also a member of the British Parliament. In this book he argues that the state is crushing human diversity and freedom, and he recommends a change in global structures which would strengthen world institutions, yet strengthen local institutions as well.

Moody, Peter R. *Opposition and Dissent in Contemporary China.* Stanford, Calif.: Hoover Institution Press, 1977.

The complete guide to opposition movements inside and outside China. Very thorough.

Pollis, Adamantia, and Peter Schwab, eds. *Human Rights: Cultural and Ideological Perspectives.* New York: Praeger, 1979.

These essays help us realize that the Western notion of human rights is not the only view of the subject. Explores human rights from other perspectives: Islam, Socialism, Africa, Latin America.

Robertson, A. H. *Human Rights in Europe.* Manchester University Press (1977); in the U. S., Humanities Press (Atlantic Highlands, N.J.).

A complete review of the origins and workings of the European Commission and European Court of Human Rights—which happen to be the most highly evolved human rights organizations in existence. Dr. Robertson is the former Director of Human Rights for the Council of Europe.

## ACTION GUIDE

*Human Rights Action Guide*
A regularly-updated guide to the issues, legislation, and strategies involved in human rights advocacy for Americans. Focuses especially on U. S. foreign policy, legislation, and foreign and military aid. Suggests action priorities for the coming year. Available from the Coalition for a New Foreign and Military Policy, 120 Maryland Ave., N.E., Washington, DC 20002. (The most recent *Guide* cost 25 cents and was sixteen pages.)

## ACTION AND INFORMATION GROUPS

Special thanks to Laurie S. Wiseberg and Harry M. Scoble of the Human Rights Internet, who painstakingly gathered the information on human rights groups from which some of these descriptions are summarized. Their latest compilation is the *Human Rights Directory*, available from Human Rights Internet, 1502 Ogden St., N.W., Washington, DC 20010.

•**Amnesty International.** 304 W. 58th St., New York, NY 10019, or 3618 Sacramento St., San Francisco, CA 94118. Unquestionably the leader of the human rights movement, Amnesty began in 1961 with a determination to work on behalf of "prisoners of conscience" in all parts of the world. Amnesty at last count had over 100,000 dues-paying members in more than eighty countries, and many if not most of those members are taking time each month to work on the release of a specially "adopted" prisoner.

Amnesty International's office in London is well-known for the detailed thoroughness of its research into particular human rights cases and into allegations of torture. AI teams often receive permission to investigate alleged violations in the country involved. Their publications on specific countries or on broad surveys like the one on torture are all excellent. Of the 15,000 prisoners adopted from 1977 to 1979, over half were released. Thus it came as no surprise that Amnesty was awarded the Nobel Peace Prize in 1977.

Two further points about Amnesty should be mentioned. First, its potential caseload of prisoners numbers in the hundreds of thousands, and thus there is always a need for further members and adoption groups. Second, Amnesty focuses on the specifics of individual cases and on patterns of abuse, but does not involve itself in "political" questions. For example, Amnesty might discuss Czechoslovakia's governmental repression of its citizens, but would not be expected to discuss the role of the Soviet Union in sustaining this repressive regime; similarly, Amnesty would cite cases of violations by the government of the Shah of Iran, but would not devote great attention to the U. S. role in setting up that regime and in training its secret police.

•**Coalition for a New Foreign and Military Policy—Human Rights Working Group.** 120 Maryland Ave., N.E., Washington, DC 20007. Who says the peace movement is dead? The Coalition is a direct outgrowth of the energies and experiences that were galvanized during the years of our military involvement in Vietnam. Its membership includes over thirty-five organizations, ranging from the International Longshoremen's Union to Women's Strike for Peace.

The Human Rights Working Group is a sub-committee of the Coalition yet casts its own net and includes another forty to fifty human rights groups within its ranks. The Coalition's main focus is lobbying, at the grassroots and national levels, for a U. S. foreign policy that is "peaceful, non-interventionist, humanitarian, and open." To this end, the HRWG has focused on the issue of US military and economic aid to repressive dictatorships. Working with friends in the Congress, the HRWG has helped to put restrictions on this aid, whether through national or multinational channels (e.g., the World Bank).

The HRWG is also developing a campaign to press for ratification of the UN human rights covenants now before the Senate.

For my money, anyone interested in human rights activism ought to consider joining and supporting the Coalition.

•**Human Rights Internet**, 1502 Ogden St., N.W., Washington, DC 20010. Publishes an extremely valuable newsletter for international human rights activists and researchers. Focus is on U.S. based groups, what they are doing, what they have published, what conferences and symposia are upcoming, and what's new on the legislative front. Most recent issue was forty-eight pages, crammed with information. Comes out nine-twelve times per year; $20.00 for individuals, $30.00 for institutions, from HRI.

**American Association for the Advancement of Science—Clearinghouse on Persecuted Scientists**, 1515 Massachusetts Ave., N.W., Washington, DC 20005. The AAAS Clearinghouse serves as a conduit for information about and advocacy on behalf of the scientific community in foreign countries whose human rights and/or scientific freedom have been violated. It has thirty-three participating organizations, ranging from the American Anthropological Association to the Society for Industrial and Applied Mathematics.

**American Christians for the Abolition of Torture**, 300 W. Apsley St., Philadelphia, PA 19144. An ecumenical movement to end torture, promote human rights, and work for the release of prisoners of conscience. ACAT began in France, where it now has over 10,000 members. Affiliated organizations are located in Switzerland and Belgium. The U. S. affiliate uses non-violent direct action to awaken people's awareness of the gravity of this situation, in addition to prayer, lobbying, and letter-writing.

**The American Federation of Labor—Congress of Industrial Organizations (AFL-CIO)**, 815 16th St., N.W., Washington, DC 20006. The powerful umbrella group that draws most of the nation's unions together for joint efforts. The AFL-CIO has a strong International Division that has concerned itself with "democratic" union rights and other human rights issues. It has been strongly criticized, however, for being primarily concerned with combatting Communism and becoming a willing arm of U. S. Cold War foreign policy. Recently member unions have pushed the AFL-CIO to speak out on human rights violations in Chile and Nicaragua (under Samoza).

One program of the AFL-CIO focuses on labor and human rights in Latin America. It is called the **American Institute for Free Labor Development** and suffers from the shortcomings noted above. Its address is 1015 20th St., N.W., Washington, DC 20036. There is also an **Asian American Free Labor Institute** at 815 16th St., N.W., Rm. 406, Washington, DC 20006. Also **African American Labor Center**, 345 E. 46th St., New York, NY 10017.

**AFL-CIO Member Unions**. Many member unions of the AFL-CIO co-operate in its international programs. Most also have their own international divisions and concern themselves with labor rights in their field. Several have taken independent initiatives to promote human rights and are real leaders. Especially noteworthy are the **American Federation of Teachers (AFT)**, 11 Dupont Circle, Washington, DC 20036; **International Longshoremen's and Warehousemen's Union (ILWU)**, 1188 Franklin St., San Francisco, CA 94109; and **United Auto Workers**, 1125 15th St., N.W., Washington, DC 20005.

**American Jewish Committee and the Jacob Blaustein Institute for the Advancement of Human Rights**, 165 E. 56th St., New York, NY 10022. Works to promote human rights through research, publicity, and conferences on relevant issues. Publishes *Commentary* magazine.

**B'nai B'rith International**, 1640 Rhode Island Ave., N.W., Washington, DC 20036. A very active organization that has a special concern for the rights of Jewish people in all parts of the world. Publicizes violations, aids in the release of prisoners, helps refugees get resettled. Also is active in general human rights work, especially in working to have the U.S. ratify the various international covenants on human rights.

**Center for International Policy**, 120 Maryland Ave., N.E., Washington, DC 20002. Publishes periodic reports on key aspects of U. S. foreign policy legislation, especially economic and military aid, with a focus on human rights violators. Studies are designed for lobbyists and Congresspeople and are extremely thorough and detailed. Recent studies focused on Argentina, Uruguay, Brazil, the Philippines, Indonesia, and others.

**Center for National Security Studies**, 122 Maryland Ave., N.E., Washington, DC 20002. Does basic research on the CIA and other U. S. intelligence agencies, focusing on covert and illegal activities that violate human rights.

**Clergy and Laity Concerned (CALC)**. See the description in the Peace and Disarmament section.

**Commission on Security and Co-operation in Europe**, c/o Congressman Dante Fascell, Chairman, CSCE, U.S. House of Representatives, Washington, DC 20515. A U. S. governmental body, made up of representatives from both houses and from the executive. Monitors compliance in Europe with the Helsinki accords. In its few years since 1975, the Commission has published enormously detailed reports on human rights in both East and West European countries—but especially in the communist countries.

**Democratic Socialist Organizing Committee**, 853 Broadway, Rm. 617, New York, NY 10003. A very fine political action group that represents the best aspects of the International Socialist movement as seen in Sweden or with the New Democratic Party in Canada. The DSOC takes the word "Democratic" very seriously, and its human rights sub-committee has been involved in protesting the situations in the USSR, Argentina, Chile, etc. Much of DSOC's strength comes from the progressive unions.

**Fellowship of Reconciliation (FOR)**, P.O. Box 271, Nyack, NY 10960. The FOR is a long-standing peace group that was begun in the midst of World War I. It and its international affiliates work for peaceful resolution of conflict between people and nations. Recent human rights concerns have been with Nicaragua, Northern Ireland, and Vietnam. Publishes *Fellowship Magazine.*

**Freedom House**, 20 W. 40th St., New York, NY 10018. Publishes *Freedom-at-Issue* magazine and a yearly assessment of civil and political liberties for every country in the world.

**International Commission of Jurists,** American Association for the ICJ, 777 UN Plaza, New York, NY 10017. The ICJ is an international organization that draws its support from judges, law teachers, practitioners of law, and other members of the legal community and their associations.

National sections of the ICJ have been established in over fifty countries. They supply the International Secretariat (in Geneva) with materials on legal developments in their respective countries, and in a number of countries they have initiated reforms of the law.

The ICJ makes private interventions on behalf of political prisoners and sends missions to different parts of the world to observe important political trials and to report on the climate of human rights respect (a recent mission was to Iran). The headquarters in Geneva acts as an international center for information on the international protection of human rights.

**The International League for Human Rights**, 777 UN Plaza, New York, NY 10017. The League has been on the human rights scene for a long time and has probably had significant impact on the international environment for human rights. It has tended to be relatively dormant in the past few years, but is currently undergoing a renaissance.

The League prepares special reports on human rights violations, makes presentations to governments and international bodies, organizes investigative teams to visit violating countries, publicizes cases of repression, sends observers to trials, and proposes new legislation. Most recently, the League has also undertaken an effort to develop and train a corps of legal specialists in human rights law, and is promoting legal aid to individuals and groups who suffer from repression.

Recently, the League has been involved with situations in Iran, Yugoslavia, and Paraguay, and it has criticized the U.S. in its policy toward Micronesia.

**The Lawyers Committee for International Human Rights**, 236 E. 46th St., New York, NY 10017. At present, the Committee is concentrating on five principal areas: representation of individual clients (such as those seeking exit visas, people seeking family reunification, or political refugees seeking asylum in the U.S.); preparation and filing of complaints to international organizations detailing human rights violations in particular countries; intervention in domestic laws to help promote human rights in foreign countries; and representation of human rights organizations at various special conferences and sessions of the United Nations (since they happen to be just around the corner).

The Committee also sponsors a series of training sessions and workshops conducted by international legal scholars and practitioners, intended primarily to assist the volunteer attorneys in handling international human rights cases.

**Members of Congress for Peace Through Law**, 201 Massachusetts Ave., N.E., Suite 201, Washington, DC 20002. A coalition of U. S. representatives and senators who have what might be called an "internationalist" perspective and who tend to support international institution-building, the UN, and a more humanitarian U.S. foreign policy. Its membership includes Republicans and Democrats. Of its eight committees, one is focused on human rights and has had quite an impact on legislation.

Though you cannot join this group—unless you happen to get elected to the Congress—I thought you might like to know that it exists. Naturally, it would be happy to accept donations for its educational work. And it is a good source of information on Congressional activities in international areas.

**Minority Rights Group**, 36 Craven St., London WC2, England. Specializes in the problems of oppressed ethnic, religious, linguistic minorities. Recent studies on migrant workers in Western Europe, Native Americans, Jehovah's Witnesses in Central Africa, Armenians.

**National Council of Churches—Human Rights Office**, 475 Riverside Drive, New York, NY 10015. Co-ordinates the role of the NCC in promoting human rights. Focus is on linking with member churches in other countries, influencing U. S. policy. Work has involved countries around the world.

**New Directions**, 305 Massachusetts Ave., N.E., Washington, DC 20002. Begun with the hope of becoming the "Common Cause" of global activism. Tries to involve members in lobbying Washington for a progressive foreign policy. In human rights, New Directions has worked for the ratification of the human rights covenants and the Genocide Treaty. Wants human rights to be a legislated priority in foreign aid.

**P.E.N. American Center**, 156 Fifth Ave., New York, NY 10010. An international association of writers that tries to help other writers who get into trouble with their government, as many writers do. The letters, PEN, stand for poets, playwrights, essayists, editors, and novelists.

**United States Committee for Refugees**, 1625 Eye St., N.W., Suite 719, Washington, DC 20006. Concerns itself with the plight of refugees around the world. The Committee's main focus is on education and information sharing, but it also testifies before Congress and works with specialized United Nations agencies.

The importance of this Committee, and other groups working on refugee issues, is that often people are forced to flee their country and have nowhere to go. Settlement—and for political refugees, asylum—is of great importance to their survival. The United States has a record of openness to refugees from left-wing governments (e.g. Cuban exiles, Russian exiles, etc.) but not with refugees from right-wing governments (Chile, for example). An important goal for human rights activists is to provide asylum for oppressed dissidents regardless of their political persuasion.

**United States House of Representatives—Committee on International Relations**, Washington, DC 20515. This committee has conducted over forty hearings on human rights, primarily through its Subcommittee on International Organizations. These hearings usually draw upon experts for testimony and often contain outlines of administration action and thinking from top policy-makers in the department of state.

Extremely valuable material, and usually free. Recent hearings have included East Timor, Cambodia, Vietnam, Argentina, Uruguay, Paraguay, El Salvador, and much more. (A hint: when writing for a specific document, it helps to write to your particular Congressperson and ask her/him to get it. That way it's always free.)

**United States Senate—Committee on Foreign Relations**, Washington, DC 20510. Unfortunately, the Senate has not been as zealous on human rights as the House (this was due primarily to the leadership of Congressman Don Fraser, who was a leader in the House on human rights). Recent hearings have been few, but very useful. Write to ask for a list.

**United States State Department—Bureau of Human Rights and Humanitarian Affairs**, Room 7802, Department of State, Washington, DC 20520. This special bureau was established under President Carter; its task is to monitor the human rights situations in countries around the globe and to suggest appropriate U. S. policy responses. As this new office has been meshed into the bureaucracy, its members have been placed on some very crucial policy committees, such as those deciding on U. S. arms sales, where often the Human Rights person can advocate shifts in policy.

The Bureau also handles requests for information about particular political prisoners and often will have our embassy raise questions in the country involved. It also tries to maintain good contacts with non-governmental human rights groups around the country.

Under President Carter, the Human Rights Bureau was led by an activist with a civil rights background. Whether the Bureau will continue to play an aggressive role in the future depends upon the wishes of the president and perhaps also on the degree to which human rights activists insist that it play its mandated role.

# Denominational and Sectarian Religious Organizations

The listing below is provided for people who would like to contact their denomination in order to find out what it is doing in the global justice field. Interfaith and ecumenical religious organizations have already been listed in the appropriate resource sections.

Special thanks to the *Yearbook of American and Canadian Churches* (Abingdon Press, Nashville, Tenn.) from which most of these addresses are taken. For more detailed information, please consult the latest edition of the *Yearbook* in your local library.

**ASSEMBLIES OF GOD**, Division of Foreign Missions, International Headquarters, 1445 Boonville Ave., Springfield, MO 65802.

**BAPTISTS**
**American Baptist Churches, USA,** c/o Headquarters, Valley Forge, PA 19481. Board of National Ministries (especially for Native Americans); Board of International Ministries.

**Baptist Joint Committee on Public Affairs,** 200 Maryland Ave., NE, Washington, DC 20002. A lobbying presence of eight national Baptist bodies. Pays attention to international policy issues, supports human rights and other global justice causes.

**Baptist World Alliance,** 1628 16th St., NW, Washington, DC 20009.

**General Association of Regular Baptist Churches,** 1300 N. Meacham Rd., Schaumburg, IL 60185.

**Foreign Mission Board,** 3806 Monument Ave., Richmond, VA 23230.

**The Christian and Missionary Alliance,** 350 N. Highland Ave., Nyack, NY 10960.

**CHRISTIAN CHURCH** (Disciples of Christ), Box 1986, Indianapolis, IN 46204. Disciples Peace Fellowship; Division of Overseas Ministry; International Human Rights Program.

**CHRISTIAN REFORMED CHURCH IN AMERICA,** 2850 Kalamazoo Ave., SE, Grand Rapids, MI 49508. Board for Christian Reformed World Ministries; Christian Reformed World Relief Committee.

**CHURCH OF CHRIST, SCIENTIST,** Christian Science Church Center, Boston, MA 02115.

**CHURCH OF GOD**, Foreign Missionary Board, Box 2498, Anderson, IN 46011.

**CHURCH OF GOD**, World Missions, Keith St. at 25th St., NW, Cleveland, TN 37311.

**CHURCH OF THE NAZARENE**, Department of World Mission, 6401 The Paseo, Kansas City, MO 64131.

### EPISCOPALIANS
**The Episcopal Church**, 815 Second Ave., New York, NY 10017. Office of Church in Society; Office of Venture in Mission.
**Episcopal Churchmen for South Africa**, 853 Broadway, Room 1005, New York, NY 10003.

### SOCIETY OF FRIENDS (QUAKERS)
**American Friends Service Committee**, 1501 Cherry St., Philadelphia, PA 19102. (See my description in the Peace and Economic Justice sections.)
**Evangelical Friends Mission**, Box 671, Arvada, CO 80001.
**Friends Committee on National Legislation**, 25 Second St., NE, Washington, DC 20002. A leader in peace and justice lobbying in Washington.
**Friends World Committee**, Section of the Americas, 1506 Race St., Philadelphia, PA 19102. Coordinates the activities of Friends groups in the Western Hemisphere. Sponsors a Right Sharing of World Resources Program, and International Quaker Aid.
**Friends General Conference**, 1520-B Race St., Philadelphia, PA 19102.
**Friends United Meeting**, 101 Quaker Hill Drive, Richmond, IN 47374.
**Quaker United Nations Program**, 777 UN Plaza, New York, NY 10017. (See my description in the section on Global Institution Building.)

**GREEK ORTHODOX ARCHDIOCESE OF NORTH AND SOUTH AMERICA**, 8-10 E. 79th St., New York, NY 10021. Office of Foreign Missions; Office of Public Affairs.

**JEHOVAH'S WITNESSES**, 124 Columbia Heights, Brooklyn, NY 11201.

### JUDAISM
*Conservative Judaism*
**United Synagogue of America**, 3080 Broadway, New York, NY 10027.
**The Rabbinical Assembly**, 3080 Broadway, New York, NY 10027.

*Orthodox Judaism*
**Agodath Israel of America**, 5 Beekman St., New York, NY 10038.
**Rabbinical Alliance of America**, 156 Fifth Ave., New York, NY 10011.
**Rabbinical Council of America, Inc.**, 220 Park Ave. South, New York, NY 10003.
**Union of Orthodox Congregations of America**, 116 E. 27th St., New York, NY 10016.
**Union of Orthodox Rabbis of the United States and Canada**, 235 E. Broadway, New York, NY 10002.

*Reform Judaism*
    **Central Conference of American Rabbis**, 790 Madison Ave., New York, NY 10021.
    **Union of American Hebrew Congregations**, 838 Fifth Ave., New York, NY 10021.


## LUTHERANS

    **American Lutheran Church**, Board for World Mission and Inter-Church Co-operation, 422 S. 5th St., Minneapolis, MN 55415.
    **Lutheran Church in America**, 231 Madison Ave., New York, NY 10016. Divison for World Mission and Ecumenism; Office of Social Concerns, Church and Society.
    **Lutheran Council in the USA**, Office for Governmental Affairs, Suite 2720, 475 L'Enfant Plaza, SW, Washington, DC 20024.
    **Lutheran Church—Missouri Synod**, Board of Social Ministry and World Relief, 500 N. Broadway, St. Louis, MO 63102.
    **Lutheran Peace Fellowship**, 168 W. 100th St., New York, NY 10025.
    **Wisconsin Evangelical Lutheran Synod**, General Board for World Missions, 12367 Lomica Dr., San Diego, CA 92128.


## MENNONITES

    **Mennonite Board of Congregational Ministries**, Box 1245, Elkhart, IN 46515.
    **Mennonite Central Committee**, 21 S. 12th Street, Akron, PA 17501.


## METHODISTS

    **African Methodist Episcopal Church**, Board of Missions, 475 Riverside Drive, Rm. 1926, New York, NY 10115.
    **African Methodist Episcopal Zion Church**, Department of Overseas Missions, 475 Riverside Drive, Suite 1910, New York, NY 10115.
    **Christian Methodist Episcopal Church**, Board of Missions, 2780 Collier Drive, NW, Atlanta, GA 30018.
    **United Methodist Church**, 475 Riverside Drive, New York, NY 10115. Board of Church and Society; Board of Global Ministries; UN Office, 777 UN Plaza, New York, NY 10017.


## MORMONS

    **Church of Jesus Christ of the Latter Day Saints**, The Relief Society, 50 East North Temple St., Salt Lake City, UT 84111.
    **Reorganized Church of Jesus Christ of the Latter Day Saints**, World Headquarters, Box 1059, Independence, MO 64051.


## PRESBYTERIANS

    **Presbyterian Church in the United States**, 341 Ponce de Leon Ave., NE, Atlanta, GA 30308. Division of International Mission; Division of Corporate and Social Mission.
    **United Presbyterian Church**, 475 Riverside Drive, New York, NY 10115. Office of Peace and International Affairs; Ministry of Health, Education and Social Justice.
    **United Presbyterian Peace Fellowship**, Box 271, Nyack, NY 10960.

## REFORMED CHURCH IN AMERICA
**American Indian Council**, Box 49, Mescalero, MN 88340.
**General Program Council**, 34 Bel Air, NE, Grand Rapids, MI 49503.
**National Office**, 475 Riverside Drive, New York, NY 10115.

## ROMAN CATHOLICS
**Conference of Major Religious Superiors of Men**, 1330 Massachusetts Ave., NW, Washington, DC 20005.

**Catholic Near East Welfare Association and The Pontifical Mission for Palestine**, 1011 First Ave., New York, NY 10022. Does educational, refugee, and relief work in eighteen countries, ranging from Afghanistan to the Balkans.

**Catholic Peace Fellowship**, Box 271, Nyack, NY 10960.

**Center of Concern**, 3700 13th St., NE, Washington, DC 20017. A radical Catholic think tank that prepares excellent and thought-provoking studies on justice issues.

**Jesuit Office of Social Ministries**, 1717 Massachusetts Ave., NW, Rm. 402, Washington, DC 20036.

**LADOC**, 1312 Massachusetts Ave., NW, Washington, DC 20005. An information service on events and issues in Latin America, supported by the United States Catholic Conference.

**Leadership Conference of Women Religious of the USA**, 1302 18th St., Suite 701, Washington, DC 20036.

**Maryknoll Fathers, Brothers, and Sisters**, Maryknoll, NY 10545. Among Catholics the Maryknoll overseas mission program is a true pioneer. Their more than one thousand representatives overseas perform direct human services, but also place emphasis on human rights, and on organizing for social justice. Maryknoll men and women do a good job of educating their U.S. supporters about the larger issues behind the daily realities of human suffering.

**National Convergence of Justice & Peace Centers**, 2747 Rutger St., St. Louis, MO 63104. A loose association of many justice groups around the country. Almost all of them are grounded in Catholic social teaching and inspired by the vision of a church that identifies with the poor and oppressed. Many of these centers are semi-officially tied in to a diocese.

**Network** (A Catholic women's political action group), 1029 Vermont Ave., NW, Washington, DC 20005.

**St. Joan's International Alliance**, 435 W. 119th St., New York, NY 10027. An international association of Catholic women that has worked to promote women's rights in many parts of the world.

**United States Catholic Conference**, The Office of Social Development and World Peace, 1312 Massachusetts Ave., NW, Washington, DC 20005.

**THE SALVATION ARMY**, 120 W. 14th St., New York, NY 10011. International and development work is coordinated from the International Headquarters, Queen Victoria St., London, EC4P 4EP, England.

**SEVENTH-DAY ADVENTISTS**, Public Affairs Department, 6840 Eastern Ave., NW, Washington, DC 20012.

**UNITED CHURCH OF CHRIST**, 475 Riverside Drive, New York, NY 10115. Board for World Ministries; Division of World Mission; Division of World Service.

See also: Council for American Indian Ministry, 122 W. Franklin Ave., Rm. 300, Minneapolis, MN 55404; Office for Church in Society, 297 Park Ave. S., New York, NY 10010.

**UNITED PENTECOSTAL CHURCH INTERNATIONAL,** 8855 Dunn Rd., Hazelwood, MO 63042.

# Audio-Visual Resources

## ORGANIZATIONS

**Anti-Defamation League: Human Relations Materials for the School, Church and Community**, 315 Lexington Ave., New York, NY 10016. This catalogue contains a listing of films on racism and prejudice. Most are U.S.-oriented, but the lessons apply to many situations: Christian-Jewish, black-white, etc.

**California Newsreel**, 630 Natoma St., San Francisco, CA 94103. A source for rentals of films on national and international issues. Recent releases include a hard-hitting ABC documentary on torture, and a strong film on multinational corporations called "Controlling Interest." Also has a special collection on Southern Africa.

**Center for Defense Information**, 122 Maryland Ave., NE, Washington, DC 20002. The Center has produced a powerful film on the arms race, called "War Without Winners."

**Centre for World Development Education**, Parnell House, 25 Wilton Road, London SW1, England. The CWDE has a broad selection of resources on the Third World and development issues, including slide kits on "Shanty Towns," "A Family in Jamaica," and more. Write for their catalogue.

**Church World Service: Interpretation and Promotion Program**, 475 Riverside Drive, Rm. 656, New York, NY 10115. CWS has available a group of films about world hunger. Most are designed for a Christian audience and are meant to promote the "One Great Hour of Sharing" program.

**National Action/Research on the Military-Industrial Complex (NARMIC)**, 1501 Cherry St., Philadelphia, PA 19102. NARMIC is mainly a source of written materials on the military and U.S./Third World relations. However, they have produced a slide-tape study of the multinational corporations and the need for a New International Economic Order that is outstanding. Write to them for rental information.

**Tricontinental Film Center**, 330 Avenue of the Americas, New York, NY 10014. The best source for films made by Third World producers, and other non-U.S. sources. A broad and excellent selection is available for rental. Also films on Native Americans, racism, and domestic economics.

**United Nations Association**, 300 E. 42nd St., New York, NY 10017. Has a list of recommended films on the UN and issues related to UN activities. Cost: 25 cents.

## BOOKS

Cyr, Helen W. *A Filmography of the Third World*. Metuchen, NJ: Scarecrow Press, 1976.

Three cheers for the hard work that Helen Cyr put in to assemble an annotated list of hundreds of films about the Third World. Films are grouped by region and then by country. Everything from travelogues to radical critiques. Tells you where to rent or buy each film. Indexed.

Dougall, Lucy. *The War/Peace Film Guide*. Available from World Without War Publications, 67 E. Madison St., Chicago, IL 60603; $1.50.

A comprehensive guide to films on war, conflict, mediation, weapons, and peacemaking.

Martin, Marie. *Films on the Future*. Available from World Future Society, 4916 St. Elmo St., Washington, DC 20014; $6.00.

A broad listing of films on technology, planning, and the future. Tells where to get each film and how to order. Regularly updated.